The
Gerry Hitchens
Story

The
Gerry Hitchens Story

—— From Mine to Milan ——

Simon Goodyear

Foreword by Jimmy Greaves

First published in Great Britain in 2009 by The Breedon Books Publishing Company Limited, Breedon House, 3 The Parker Centre, Derby, DE21 4SZ

Reprinted in 2010 by The Derby Books Publishing Company Limited, 3 The Parker Centre, Derby, DE21 4SZ

ISBN 978-1-85983-844-0

Printed and bound by Cromwell Press Group, Trowbridge, Wiltshire

Contents

Dedicated to the everlasting memory of a great footballer,
Gerald ('Gerry') Archibald Hitchens, 1934–1983,
and to my father,
David William Goodyear, 1938–2008.

In Memory of Meriel Ruth Hitchens, 1938 - 2009,
who passed away soon after the publication of this book,
reunited with her beloved Gerald.

Acknowledgements

I wish to record my eternal appreciation to the Hitchens family, with special mention going to Meriel Hitchens (Gerry's widow) for giving me permission to write the book and for allowing me to share some of her special and very personal memories of her famous husband. I am also particularly grateful to Marcus Hitchens (Gerry's eldest son), who has shared his huge passion and enthusiasm with his father's life in preparing this very special book, and to Nicola Hitchens for her assistance with the Italian input. It has been a real team effort, and without their approval and help it would not have been possible to produce this biography of their immortal hero.

It is fair to mention that this book was the original inspiration of my late father, David Goodyear, an author of 13 books, including three about his beloved Aston Villa. As a lifelong Aston Villa fan, he was a great admirer of Gerry Hitchens and followed his progress throughout his career and will no doubt be leading the immortal 'Gerry Hitchens Appreciation Society' in the sky.

Thanks also go to Terry Baker of 'A1 Sporting Speakers' who was kind enough to pass on my request for Jimmy Greaves to write a (very touching) foreword for this book – thank you Jimmy and Terry. I would also like to thank Neil Rioch, founder and chairman of the Aston Villa Former Players' Association for his help and support, Mr John Lerwill, Aston Villa club historian, for his contribution, and Mr John Miles (FCoL).

I must also thank the following ex-teammates and friends of Gerry's for sharing their memories: Sir Bobby Charlton, Jimmy Armfield (OBE), Peter McParland (MBE), Bobby Thomson, Ron Wylie, Jimmy MacEwan, Luis Suárez, 'Gigi' Riva, Mario Corso, Giancarlo Cella and, lastly, Mr Ifor Roberts and Mr Phil Lloyd-Jones for their input.

Finally, I must also acknowledge the world-renowned journalist and author Brian Glanville for his contribution.

Simon Goodyear

Foreword by Jimmy Greaves

England Striker (1959–1967)

Jimmy Greaves is a true football icon and phenomenal striker, scoring 366 goals in 530 domestic League matches for Chelsea, AC Milan, Tottenham Hotspur and West Ham United (plus 54 Cup goals), as well as a remarkable 44 England goals in 57 capped appearances. Jimmy also holds the record for most hat-tricks for England – six in all.

It gives me real pleasure to introduce this long overdue book about a man who was not only one of my favourite footballers but also one of the nicest blokes to cross my path. Gerry was a gentleman both on and off the pitch, and 'cool' before the word had been invented.

The standout picture of Gerry for me is of him always immaculate in his appearance, even managing to look neat and tidy in the heat of battle when the rest of us were sweaty and unkempt. We were good pals when we were supposed to be sworn enemies in the days when he was playing for Internazionale and I was with rivals AC Milan.

It really was similar to slave labour for footballers in those days, when in England there was a maximum wage of £20 a week. We had obviously gone to Italy for the money (as much as £80 a week), but were made to earn every penny.

They treated players like prisoners, locking us away in training camps miles away from the temptations of real life. Players from rival clubs even thinking of having any contact with each other away from the pitch was close to a hanging offence. On the old hush-hush, Gerry and I used to meet up in a bar at Milan mainline railway station, where it was so busy that nobody would notice us tucked in a corner having a natter over a couple of pints.

I 'jacked' in the Italian life after a few months because I was sick to death of being treated like a kid. Gerry, a few years older and more mature than me, stuck it out and became an idol out there.

Like I say, he was 'Mr Cool' and very particular about the way he dressed. I still laugh at the memory of him arriving to join the 1962 World Cup squad for the Finals in Chile. He had a huge trunk with him containing, wait for it, **19** beautifully tailored Italian suits. There were also handmade silk shirts and natty ties. When we got to Chile we found ourselves plonked 100 miles from any civilisation in a mining centre, and we rarely got out of tracksuits and shorts. Gerry did not get the chance to wear one of his suits.

One of the games we played together for England is a particularly pleasant memory. We were a goal down to a magnificent Italian team in Rome's huge Olympic Stadium in 1961 when Gerry and I popped up with a goal each late in the game. Suddenly, the ground was so quiet you could have heard spaghetti landing on the terraces.

I hope this book serves as a reminder of just what an exceptional player Gerry was. Like the great John Charles, he spent so long playing in Italy that he is overlooked when people start talking about the outstanding British players of the 1960s. Aston Villa supporters of a certain age will tell you that he was a magnificent striker.

He was taken from us too early, and I am delighted that Simon and Marcus are producing this tribute to the memory of a lovely bloke. Gerry was a real class act, on and off the pitch.

Jimmy Greaves

A Note from the Author

It seems amazing that a biography of one of the greatest strikers of his generation has never been written before now. There were at least two firm offers of a book put to Gerry and Meriel Hitchens in the past, but Gerry, being a very modest man, thought that there was not enough of a story to write about. Meriel, however, thought otherwise. Contrary to his theory, there is very much of a story – a fascinating and compelling one – and therefore I am delighted to be able to tell his story at long last.

Even more than 25 years after his death at the age of 48 the name of Gerry Hitchens still brings debate and stirs up much interest and fascination among the football purists in England, Wales and Italy of a certain generation who were brought up to appreciate the work rate and enthusiasm of a truly great football player.

As a lifelong Aston Villa fan, my late father watched with interest from the Holte End terraces as this 'raw' but strong and powerful talent soon became a Villa 'idol' to the thousands of Villa fans by scoring goals by the hatful during the late 1950s and early 1960s. Gerry always had a 'soft spot' for Villa as a youngster and later made his name there and was truly proud to be associated with such a great club.

As an author himself, my father always contemplated writing a book on this footballing 'great', his hero, Gerry Hitchens. He thought it would make a good read, but unfortunately time prevailed, and sadly he did not undertake the project.

In the 1980s, however, just after Gerry's death, my father, while working as the historian and archivist at Aston Villa FC, was contacted by Marcus Hitchens, Gerry's eldest son. During the years that followed my father put together some scrapbooks for Marcus, consisting of numerous press cuttings and photographs about his famous father. Marcus and my father kept in touch for some time after, but they lost contact in recent years. With his passing in 2008, I felt inspired to fulfil the idea left by him to write a biography of this quiet man and great footballer, whom my father always talked about with great affection. What started as a somewhat 'romantic' idea ended up being quite something else; a trip down memory lane for the Hitchens family and a fully engrossing but joyful experience for me. The compiling of the book became somewhat of an obsession for Marcus and I, and the interest that has been shown by the numerous legendary players that have agreed to contribute from both the English game and from Italy has been extraordinary. It just goes to show that the name Gerry Hitchens is still widely known and talked about with such affection, and such is the legacy which Gerry himself has left that so many people have made the effort to talk about their friend.

This book is an inspirational story of a genuine, working-class boy 'come good', typical of the *Roy of the Rovers* storybook, and a player who became a 'pin-up' and 'idol' to thousands of fans in England and Italy. Hopefully the book will be an inspiration to anyone reading it, young and old alike. The message is that hard work, passion and commitment can achieve as much as individual talent and flair, whether it is as a footballer or anything else in life, and Gerry had these in abundance.

With the help of Meriel, Marcus, the Hitchens family and friends, and my own extensive research, I have tried to put together, not only an honest, detailed and accurate biographical account of the story of Gerald Archibald Hitchens – player, husband and father – but also a brief historical insight into the football world in Britain and Italy during the 1950s and 1960s. I am honoured to undertake this biography for the proud family of their hero and my father's favourite footballer, Gerry Hitchens.

For all of those who get goosebumps every time you grab a beer and discuss the 'good old days', this book is dedicated to you. I hope you enjoy the story as much as I did writing it.

Simon Goodyear

Prologue

This is a story about a proud Englishman, with a Welsh accent, who spoke fluent Italian. Enjoy!

The idea of a young English lad being plucked from a mineshaft to find himself playing football in the Italian League (Serie A) and in the World Cup only a few years later is something that dreams are made of. But, this is exactly what happened to one such talented, working-class lad from a small Shropshire mining village in the late 1950s.

This is a story of a boy who rose from 'rags to riches' and is an inspiration to any young person who has a bit of talent and a desire to become a footballer. It is a story with many twists and turns, starting when he turned professional in 1953 and peaking when he saw the light at the end of the Wembley tunnel a few years later as he played his first game for England. Gerry Hitchens was born to play football!

Football has had its share of working-class heroes in the past, although they tend to be dated further back in time, with images of them being either strapping centre-halves or centre-forwards, while the romantic notion has the hero emerging from a coalface in the North East of England carrying his pick in one hand and his boots in the other.

The 1950s saw the mining industry spawn one such hero, but one from an area less renowned for its capacity to produce heroes, or footballers for that matter. Perhaps that helps explain why the story of this particular local boy made good was so different from all the rest.

Gerald ('Gerry') Archibald Hitchens was an uncomplicated footballer, with obvious natural talents and virtues. He was quick, strong and brave and was known for never giving up the chase. He had natural ability and passion, along with the will to learn and improve; however, Gerry had a bit extra to offer – the instinct to sniff out half-chances and to score goals from anywhere, with either foot or his head. He was considered an 'all-round striker' – good in the air without being an old-fashioned English target man, and a dangerous predator without being an out-and-out goalscorer. In today's game, he would be compared to Fernando Torres with his long, flowing blond hair and ability to turn players and score goals.

Gerry was initially offered a trial with West Bromwich Albion, but back then he was a somewhat unassuming figure and was happy enough to take the smaller step to join non-League Kidderminster Harriers in 1953. With the Harriers, he quickly showed he would make the grade, and it would only be a year later that he would make that step closer to 'the big time'. Welsh club, Cardiff City, made a positive move for Gerry in January 1955 and signed him for a bargain £1,500. Gerry was no 'big-time Charlie' but certainly this move furthered his reputation, and he continued his footballing apprenticeship with Cardiff City. He later became the first City player in 30 years to score over 20 League goals.

In 1955 he met the love of his life: a beautiful 17-year-old Welsh girl called Meriel Jones from Pontypridd in South Wales, and from that day on his life would change forever.

In 1957 Gerry moved to Aston Villa, and at the end of the 1960–61 season he had scored an amazing 42 goals in 56 appearances and contributed no fewer than 11 goals as Villa went all the way to the first-ever Football League Cup Final. He earned several awards for his performance that season and was also recognised by the England selectors as he made his full England debut against Mexico at Wembley in 1961.

In typical style, it only took Gerry one minute to net his first goal for England in a crushing 8–0 victory. This was followed by a call-up to England's European summer tour of 1961. It was against a strong Italian side that earned Gerry his second full cap, and the eyes of Europe were focused on this quiet, working-class boy from Shropshire.

At the start of the 1960s, Italian clubs were beginning to invest in foreign players in a big way for the first time in their history, and British players made a massive impact. From virtually nowhere, Gerry Hitchens was the name on everyone's lips and a wanted man in Europe after his two goals against Italy.

With such great British household names as Jimmy Greaves, Denis Law and Joe Baker all heading in the same direction at around the same time, Gerry might well have been the player most people expected to fail, but as it turned out he was the only one of the four to make a decent go on the continent. All of a sudden, the Italian paparazzi were following Gerry and the beautiful Meriel everywhere, and the spotlight was certainly on them in Milan.

Gerry remained in Italy for eight seasons and played for four clubs, including Internazionale, Torino, Atalanta and Cagliari, before returning home to play for Worcester City and finally ending his career at Merthyr Tydfil in Wales.

Given his background, Gerry brought a sense of perspective to his footballing career, and while he was always a fierce competitor he remained a shining example of sportsmanship and good humour throughout. Some people say that the great John Charles was a model by which all foreign players – especially British players – have been measured: an exemplary figure on and off the field, who played the game fair, but with bravery and naïve, physical power. The same can be said of Gerry Hitchens.

He had a wonderful career, which took him from a village team in Shropshire to the San Siro Stadium in Milan and beyond. He played with some legendary footballers – Jimmy Greaves, Bobby Moore, Bobby Charlton, Trevor Ford, Peter McParland, Luis Suárez, Luigi ('Gigi') Riva and played against the likes of Matthews, Finney, Di Stefano, Puskas, Lofthouse, Charles, Edwards, Pelé and Yashin to name but a few.

These values continued to make him well liked and admired after his football career ended. He continued to play in charity games, and it was a great sadness when he died prematurely in April 1983, playing the game he loved most. It is a pity I did not have the opportunity to meet such a lovely bloke and a great footballing role model. Gerry's memory will live on in this book forever.

Born to Play Football

'...the only trouble was telling him that there was another 10 players in the team.'

Coal-mining as a fully-fledged industry began in Staffordshire with small private mines at the end of the 18th century. The presence of coal and clay meant the Industrial Revolution arrived quickly to the area. In the Cannock area of South Staffordshire there were several deep mines, and for Violet and Frank Turner coal-mining was their life; however, a mining accident forced Violet to nurse her husband Frank for some time until, sadly, he died from his injuries. Violet and Frank had a son, Hubert, and two daughters, Ida and Beryl. Hubert also worked for many years at the pit and was married to Daisy. Ida's husband George was also a miner and Beryl, who lived with her husband in Lichfield, had a delightful singing voice, it was said.

Violet now had to go to work in order to bring her children up, and one of the jobs she took up was as a cleaner at the colliery where Frank had worked. This was where she later met Archibald Hitchens, who worked the same shifts as her. Archie had a cheeky streak about him and used to whistle at Violet, and she replied in kind, and things developed from there. Violet and Archie were later married, and Archie continued to work at the colliery, but the couple later opened their own fish and chip shop in the local village of Rawnsley, near Cannock.

On 8 October 1934, five years before the outbreak of World War Two, Gerald Archibald Hitchens was born, a son with stars in his eyes. Several months after he was born, a gypsy took one look at baby Hitchens and said that 'he would travel the world'. What fortune-teller could have possibly fortold that Gerald Archibald Hitchens would one day grace the football fields of Great Britain, Europe and further afield and be paid handsomely to play the game he loved?

In 1937, the couple decided to move their family from Cannock to another typical mining village in Highley, Shropshire. They moved into an end of terraced house, number 4/16 Beech Street, a fairly ordinary street where they eventually spent most of their lives. The house was cold and sparsely equipped, having an outside toilet where Archie hung up his old miner's lamp, but the living room was heated by a roaring coal fire – of course, the coal was 'free' as Archie was a miner. Bathing was done in a big tin bath, and there was no central heating. The walls were thin, and Gerald's children recall being woken rather often by Archie's snoring.

Archie's typical day consisted of a very early start, ready for a long, hard shift down the local Alveley pit. It would be down the pub for a pre-lunch pint, and then he would then have a 'nap' after lunch. Meanwhile, Violet found work at the local primary school as a cook. It was a hard life, but the family were happy.

Both Archie and Violet took part in most local events which took place in the twin pit villages of Highley and Alveley, especially when it came to Carnival Day, which was a big event in the villages. As most families had someone working at the pit everyone seemed to take part. Archie loved his garden, and every year he grew prize chrysanthemums, especially for Carnival Day and for other shows; he also grew flowers for his local pub, the Malt Shovel in Highley.

For Gerald, growing up in a small mining area in the 1940s and 1950s brought a sense of remoteness, but it was a close community where everyone knew each other. Gerry went to the Highley County School, where his favourite subjects were geography and woodwork, while he hated poetry, but his love of football began.

A major influence on the boys at Highley County School was headmaster Major F.C. Smith. He knew Gerry would be destined to be a footballer from an early age, and he stuck out in Major Smith's mind, 'I knew Gerry especially would do well, but the only trouble was telling him that there was another 10 players in the team as well. He wanted to do all the work himself. I had a hard time telling him. He worked very hard at football and wanted to take the whole opposition on himself.' According to Major Smith, Gerry started to take a real interest in football at the age of 10, which is late compared to children of today, who start getting involved with clubs at a much earlier age. The first competition he played in was the Windsor Clive Cup, and he was overjoyed about his participation, even though his team lost 10–0. Violet remembered Gerry playing football every night after school, 'We couldn't hold him. Gerald used to be out every night. He was born with football in his veins, and he said he would not stop until he got to Wembley.' Gerry had kicked a football ever since he learned to walk, and all through his childhood all his parents ever heard was football, football and more football. 'Every weekend, the boiler used to go on. He used to play in the dirt until it was coming out of his ears,' Violet once recalled.

From an early age, however, it was clear that Gerry wanted to be a footballer and nothing else. He once thought about becoming a motor engineer, but football was his first love. It was the after-school activities that proved he would be a useful footballer, as the school did not have a regular football team. Gerry was also far too small to play for the village team, so most of the football he played was for the scout's team, and he was a centre-forward even then.

When Gerry was 14, he started to keep a diary for a while, starting on Sunday 8 February 1948:

Sunday	Went shooting in morning.
	Went to church.
	Played football on Rec.
Monday	Played football on Rec.
	Went to pictures.
	Had suit too small, sent it back.
Tuesday (Shrove)	Played football.
	Went out to fish shop, had pancakes.
Wednesday	Played football on Rec.
Thursday	Went to pictures with EH.
	Played football.
	Played football on Rec.
Friday	Took meat out.
	Broke up from school.
	Played football on Rec.
Saturday	Saw football match.
	Went to pictures.

Every week the diary entries were almost identical – played football, played football, played football, day after day after day, but one day – and one day only – on the 5 March Gerry played rugby. Nobody knows why!

Gerry was very fond of going to the pictures and went there twice a week. He must have either cycled or caught the bus to Bridgnorth, where the nearest cinema was located. After school and in the summer months he always worked, whether it be picking crops at a local farm or working as a delivery boy at the village butchers for a Mr Davies, taking the meat round a couple of times during the week. He was very industrious and always kept busy, and this was the work ethic he instilled into his own children later in life. Young Gerry also appeared to like his fish and chips from the local fish shop by all accounts; however, Gerry soon got bored of the diary, but funnily enough carried on playing football.

One day, Gerry opened the shop early before Mr Davies arrived and switched all the machinery on in readiness for the day's trade. When Mr Davies arrived, however, his face dropped as he realised he had left the previous day's takings in the mincing machine, which had already been switched on by Gerry. Some of the money was saved, but most of the notes had been through the mincer. Mr Davies was not happy, although it was his own fault.

At the age of 15, Gerry left school and instead of dedicating his life to becoming a footballer, he settled into the life dictated by the situation and his talents and became a miner like his father. In between work he played football in the village for Highley Miners reserve team, but was quickly promoted to the first team. 'It was then, that we realised Gerald had some talent. We could see that he was going to go places,' Violet once said.

Once he had made the first team, he started practicing relentlessly, every night turning out on a patch of wasteland in the village called 'The Orchard'. Gerry would be seen in the village with half a dozen or so young lads kicking a football around on that patch of wasteland at Garden Village, Highley, also known as 'The Rec'. Rounded stones marked the corners, and players shed their extra clothing for goalposts for these impromptu games of soccer. This really was the 'jumpers for goalposts' era and was a very common sight, but for some of these lads the future lay in professional football and not as a bank clerk, butcher, builder or miner.

For such a small village such as Highley, tucked away in the Shropshire countryside, you would not really expect to find an up-and-coming footballer and one that would in later years be so famous and play at the very highest level. Locally, however, Beech Street was later known as the 'street of stars' or 'Soccer Road' because there were not one but a whole host of footballers that were groomed in or around Beech Street. What was the reason why Highley had produced more than its fair share of footballers? Was it because it was the lowest parish above sea level in Shropshire, and the air denser than anywhere else in the county?

There was Stan Jones, who started off playing shoulder to shoulder with Gerry at 'The Orchard' and later went on to play for West Bromwich Albion. Another one of those 'jumpers for goalposts' youngsters was John Bannister, who went on to represent England as an amateur and played for the county. Ted Hemsley was another who lived in Beech Street, just down the road from the Hitchens household, and he went on to play for Sheffield United. Aubrey Haycox, a friend of Gerry's who worked at the same mine, was a member of the 'group'; he lived just round the corner and the 'magic' of 'Soccer Road' rubbed off on him as well. He went on to become a professional and later became club captain at Kidderminster Harriers and played in the same team as Gerry. 'We all grew up at a time when television wasn't as popular as it is today, and there was nothing much else to do. The village was split into three parts, and we used to hold matches between ourselves. Each part had a "team", and we used to have some exciting games. Highley has always had a good football team. Our parents played before us, and the village has always had one of the strongest teams in Shropshire,' Aubrey once commented. He added that as Highley was a mining community, with strong men working in the pits, they needed a pastime and so took up football and retained it even after things like television grew in popularity. It was thought that the generation prior to this crop of footballers were no mean players themselves, and the 'bug' was passed down a generation.

It was not long before Gerry's bustling style of play and goalscoring exploits for Highley Miners Welfare FC attracted attention from elsewhere. One year he scored an amazing 90 goals in a season. Several scouts took notice of this big, strong centre-forward, but still the 'big boys' were slow on the uptake for his services.

It was left to non-League Kidderminster Harriers to show real interest in Gerry, and they were just quicker than any other club in securing his signature. He was initially offered a trial with West Bromwich Albion, but Gerry was a somewhat unassuming figure and was happy enough to take the smaller step to join Kidderminster. He most likely thought he was not good enough to play for a top-flight club at that stage of his life. In any case, Gerry had agreed verbally to sign for Kidderminster Harriers and in that, he kept his word. Any regrets about not joining the bigger club were tempered by doubts as to whether he would have made the grade at Division One level, while financially he may have been better off staying down the pit and picking up part-time money as well with Kidderminster.

Gerry's father, Archie, always saw something extra special in his son's ability to become a top-class footballer, something that other people failed to see at the time. He was the one who always knew his son would be a big star one day, and the move to Kidderminster was a step in that direction. He was nearly 19 years old and he was somewhat 'old' to have been signed up for the first move of his career, but it was a move which would mould Gerry's life forever.

Harriers' First Superstar

'The Harriers treated me well, and it was while playing for them that I was spotted by Cardiff.'

Kidderminster Harriers
September 1953–January 1955

The summer of 1953 was an important time for several experienced players who were to become popular local heroes in the eyes of the Kidderminster townsfolk. The club had brought in some new talent from clubs like Walsall, Aldershot and Stirling Albion, while there was some raw talent waiting to emerge from the reserves, like Jimmy Kerr, Gilbert Heron and Ray Hardiman. There was a blond-haired lad called Gerald Hitchens, however, who was playing for a miners' team in nearby Highley and who could run for ever, attracting interest from Southern League side, Kidderminster Harriers.

Kidderminster Harriers were the pioneers of floodlit football in the Midlands. In 1951–52 the revolutionary use of floodlights by the club gave Harriers the distinction of staging the first floodlit game in the history of the FA Cup, Southern League, Birmingham League, Worcestershire Senior Cup and Birmingham Senior Cup at their home ground at Aggborough.

Eighteen-year-old Gerald Hitchens was recommended to Ted Gamson, former Football League referee and then secretary of Harriers. Gerry was apparently watched by Bolton Wanderers scouts while playing for Highley, and Wellington Town were also reportedly interested in him, even before Kidderminster came in for him.

Harriers became even more keen on Gerry after he had played for Highley Miners in the Harriers Junior Cup Final at Aggborough at the end of the 1952–53 season, and he scored a couple of goals. He must have impressed Ted Gamson because the Southern League club immediately offered him amateur papers to sign. Gerry's friend, Aubrey Haycox, who played for Harriers and was a miner at the same pit as Gerry, encouraged him to sign for Harriers, and the rise to semi-professional status was made a little bit easier seeing a familiar face at the club. From then on, Aubrey would drive him and several of the other lads to the games, as he was the only one who had a car in those days and Kidderminster was not easy to get to from Highley without transport.

His first appearance in the reserve side was on 20 August 1953, and he scored seven goals in his first five appearances, which prompted Kidderminster to quickly promote him to the first team. His full debut was on 8 September 1953 in the Worcestershire Senior Cup at Aggborough against Cradley Heath. It ended in a resounding 5–0 victory for Harriers and saw Hitchens score from a header for the fifth, his very first senior goal; it also continued his excellent record of scoring in every game he played since signing for the Harriers. Young Gerry made a good impression with everyone in that first outing, with his confidence on the ball, boundless energy and will to do well. It was noticeable that he was still a 'raw' talent, but he soon showed his manager, former Aston Villa and England outside-right Leslie Smith, he would be a useful addition to the team and one for the future.

Gerry was brought down to earth in his next game as he was back in the reserves against Bloxwich, but he made everyone take note as he scored a hat-trick in a 4–1 win, and he threatened the goal every time he got the ball. He was now being talked about in the local press and by the fans. His first headline in the *Kidderminster Shuttle* was:

Goalscoring Gerald Routed Bloxwich

Harriers moved quickly to prevent bigger clubs from snapping up the bright young striker as they offered Hitchens a £2 per week full-time contract before the home game with Llanelly on 12 September 1953. The young striker did not waste any time, as he scored again in a 3–2 win in his first Southern League game. After a defeat at Yeovil in the next game and scoring in the defeat at Weymouth in the League, Hitchens got his first taste of the FA Cup in a qualifier against Bilston and again found the net from a rebound in a 2–0 win.

Gerry showed promise from the start and carried on the incredible skill of scoring he had at Highley by scoring four first-team goals in the opening five games for Harriers and was also leading scorer in the reserves. It was a great way to celebrate signing his first contract.

Even though he had only been on the books of Harriers for a short time, Gerry was now creating a lot of interest in the local paper, but they could not get his name right. They referred to him as 'Hitchen', 'Hitchin', 'Hitchins', but rarely as his proper surname of 'Hitchens', and they often also used his full name of 'Gerald' and not 'Gerry'.

It was a matter of nearly five months before Gerry appeared in the first team again, having been kept out by Jamaican-born striker Gilbert Heron. While he was out of the first team, Hitchens continued to score goals for the reserves and was still leading goalscorer.

Hitchens only scored two more goals in the Southern League in that first season, both of which came in a game at home against Hereford in the Southern League Cup in February 1954. The season ended with Gerry making 14 appearances in the first team, scoring six goals, but he was top scorer in the reserves. Both the first team and the reserve team finished a respectable fifth in their Leagues that season.

At the end of the season a number of players were released due to the low budget that Southern League teams had to keep, with the possible exception of Worcester City, who were seen as the big spenders of the League; however, Gerry had obviously made a good enough impression in his 14 appearances and was retained by the club and offered another contract. They must have seen the future potential in this young, blond striker. Gerry accepted the terms of the contract, which included a small increase in his wages, as the Harriers employed a new youth policy of developing the youngsters from the reserves and slowly introducing them into the first team when they were ready.

The start of the 1954–55 season saw him back in the reserve team and the Birmingham League, which at that time included clubs like Aston Villa. He and his strike partner, Ray Hardiman, were given the nickname of 'the tearaway twins' by the local newspapers because they could not stop scoring goals. By mid-September, Hitchens had scored six of the 12 Birmingham League goals for Harriers and was in line for a call-up for an FA Cup game against Hednesford after he had impressed in a first-team outing by scoring two goals in the previous game at home to Hereford. The headline in the *Kidderminster Shuttle* read:

Hitchin to lead Cup Attack?

In the Cup tie away at Hednesford, Hitchens opened the scoring, but it was not enough to see Harriers through to the next round. Gerry then had a run of seven League games in which he scored six goals and was now more of a first-team regular than a reserve. Like in the previous season, scouts had been alerted to the goalscoring exploits of the miner from Highley, and the Crystal Palace chairman and chief scout attended the home game against Weymouth on 23 October to see Gerry. The game saw him rise to the occasion and score two goals, but his efforts could not stop another Harriers defeat.

With Gerry now a consistent first-team player and scoring a few goals as well, more scouts were again out in force, this time from the 'bigger' clubs like Tottenham and Bolton, not only to keep tabs on Hitchens but also to watch the Harriers inside-forward, Peter Cocum, in the away game against Guildford City. Once again, there was no further talk of any transfer. Just before his premature death in 1955, George Summerbee and his son, Mike, went to watch Kidderminster Harriers at Aggborough one Saturday afternoon. George, who was on a scouting mission for Bristol City, noticed this big, blond striker playing for the home side, and he obviously thought this Gerry Hitchens was a bit useful but Mike thought otherwise and replied to his father, 'Dad, he's a donkey!' How wrong he was! George never took Mike to another game after that.

By signing the improved contract at the start of the season, Harriers obviously knew they had a significant star in the making by retaining Hitchens and that he would attract the attention of the 'big boys' sooner rather than later. With the club in a difficult financial situation, it was keen to promote its best talent, and Hitchens was their number one 'ace' in the pack.

The Southern League matches against Barry Town and Bedford Town were watched by more scouts from West Bromwich Albion, Aston Villa and Cardiff City. When Hitchens scored the opening goal in a 6–3 victory against Bedford Town on 22 January 1954, little did he know that not only would it be his last game for Harriers but it would also be the game that signalled the start of a glittering football career.

Kidderminster Harriers had a history of selling their best talent for the highest possible price during that period in their history, with the sale of Jack Edwards to Notts County for £1,000, Jock Mulraney to Aston Villa for £850 and Bob Raine to Aldershot for £650. Southern League sides could not survive on gate receipts alone, so they had to find other ways of supplementing their income, and these were significant sums of money for the club.

Some of the problem was down to 'too many armchair sportsmen' as reported in the local press, who at the time insisted that the emergence and increased popularity of a relatively new invention called 'television' was having a dramatic effect on attendances at Southern League grounds. Kidderminster's average attendance was less than 3,000 and dropping.

On 25 January 1955 Gerry Hitchens was signed by Cardiff City for a fee of around £1,500, which was the largest transfer fee ever received by Kidderminster Harriers for a player. In just over 18 months with Harriers he had made 40 first-team appearances and scored 20 goals, which was a good strike rate for such a young player, or any player for that matter.

'The Harriers treated me well, and it was while playing for them that I was spotted by Cardiff,' Gerry commented after his transfer was agreed.

Since arriving from Highley Miners Welfare Club at the age of 19 as a 'raw' but adaptable talent, Hitchens had added considerable skill to his previous assets of unbounded enthusiasm and stamina at Kidderminster Harriers. His meteoric rise in the football world over two seasons had seen him join a club where he would become understudy to the legendary Welsh international centre-forward, Trevor Ford.

'Bluebird' of Happiness

'The boy has that rare soccer ingredient known as 'it''

Cardiff City
January 1955–December 1957

The 1954–55 season started badly for Cardiff City as they lost 1–0 to Burnley in the opening match of their Division One campaign. It progressed in a similar manner in the next three games as the 'Bluebirds' conceded 14 goals in their first four games, including two heavy defeats by Preston (5–2 and 7–1). This caused shockwaves among the City supporters, but an unbeaten run of seven games restored City's pride and confidence as the legendary Trevor Ford started knocking in the goals.

Three new players were given their debuts during the opening matches. Inside-forward Ron Stockin was signed from Wolves for £12,000, along with Islwyn Jones and Cecil Dixon. The team chopped and changed during the opening fixtures in order for new manager, Trevor Morris, to find the best combination and pattern of play. After victories over Tottenham, Portsmouth and Aston Villa, where Trevor Ford scored twice against his former club, things were looking up for the Bluebirds. New boy Stockin started to repay his fee by scoring seven goals in 10 games.

A week before Christmas 1954, winger Gordon Nutt was signed for £12,000 from Coventry City, and he was followed by 20-year-old Gerry a few weeks later. A string of inconsistent results followed until the end of the season. The 'Bluebirds' had been dragged into a relegation battle for the final few matches of the season and when they were due to play Wolves, who were neck and neck with Chelsea in the race for the title, in the penultimate match of the season at Ninian Park, City were desperate for a victory in order to save themselves from relegation to Division Two.

Hitchens had been signed by City on 25 January 1955 for £1,500 on a part-time professional contract but did not start a game for the first team for a few weeks as the manager thought he was not ready for the big League. He had no regrets at leaving Kidderminster, however, and thought it was the right time to join a bigger club and make the step up into the League. He was tested in several second-team games before his debut and unsurprisingly scored a few goals, but

Gerry was still a 'raw'-boned miner, working part-time in the Nantgarw pit near Pontypridd, South Wales, while playing football for City. His talent shone through this tough period, and he soon decided to become a full-time professional and left the mines.

'He's still the same old Gerald. It hasn't changed him,' said his parents, who were keen to stress that their son, even though he had been signed by a professional club, still held his head above the water.

The 30 April 1955 was a monumental day in the life of Gerry Hitchens. It was his League debut as a full-time professional footballer, although he had played in the Welsh Cup semi-final earlier in the month. It was the last home game of the season for the Bluebirds, and Cardiff were playing Wolverhampton Wanderers in a relegation battle which was more like a baptism of fire than a smooth entry into 'big-time' football for Gerry. In a game that may have saved Cardiff's season, he rose to the occasion by scoring one of the three goals in a thrilling 3–2 victory in front of 32,000, with Trevor Ford netting twice. Gerry gave the Welsh legend the support up front he had lacked all season and had the satisfaction of scoring his first goal in top-class football within three minutes. Gerry also started the last game of the season against Huddersfield Town at Leeds Road in the number-nine shirt, replacing Ford. City finished the season in 20th spot and just missed out on relegation, helped by that goal from Hitchens against Wolves.

The next season, City manager Trevor Morris made some more signings to bolster his squad. Harry Kirtley, Howard Sheppeard and Johnny McSeveney were all bought from Sunderland for a combined fee of £9,000; however, there was controversy when star striker Trevor Ford refused to sign a new contract. Directors finally gave in to his demands, but Ford's career with City became stormy after that period of dissatisfaction.

Gerrys' first League goal in the 1956–57 season came in the 3–2 win over Sheffield United at Ninian Park in only their second win in nine outings. City were 2–1 down at the half-time interval but Trevor Ford, returning from injury, secured an equaliser just after the re-start. City were in the lead for the first time in the game in the 58th minute when a corner was swung in from Dixon on to the head of Hitchens, who hit the back of the net with a bullet header to win the game.

In late September, City sank to their lowest depths and saw themselves at the foot of the League table. They accepted an offer of Brian Walsh plus £20,000 from Arsenal in exchange for Mike Tiddy and Gordon Nutt, who City signed only the previous season. Nutt had failed to live up to expectations following his move from Coventry City.

City's form at the start of the season was dreadful, with heavy defeats away to Arsenal (3–1), at home to Wolves (9–1) and away at Bolton (4–1). Following on from some dismal away defeats, and leaking 13 goals in the previous two games, Hitchens was a doubt for the game at Manchester City but was selected only a quarter of an hour before kick-off, replacing Ford at number nine. Gerry produced a brilliant display, despite the 3–1 defeat, and was denied at least one goal by some fine saves by City's legendary goalkeeper, Bert Trautmann.

After the game, Gerry was the most talked about player after a fine performance deputising for Trevor Ford, who watched from the touchline with a swollen ankle injury. It was being said that he would be difficult to drop from the team after that performance.

City's first away win of the season was against Preston on 8 October, Gerry's 21st birthday, and was followed by home wins against Everton and Birmingham City. The Everton game saw the absence of Trevor Ford once again, and this gave Gerry another chance to shine, and he took it with both hands. He showed everyone what he was made of, with his willingness to run after every ball and his gritty determination, and he was an inspiration to his teammates. Gerry was desperately unlucky not to score in that game, and he ran the Everton centre-half, Tom Jones, ragged for 90 minutes.

The game against Birmingham saw Trevor Ford refuse to play at inside-left, causing confusion in the City dressing room before the game, and Hitchens replaced the Welsh legend just before the kick-off. The Cardiff manager commented on the incident, 'It is refusal to play.' Ford's take on the matter was slightly different, as he stated that he had agreed to play inside-left, 'If that is what Mr Morris says, I have no comment to make.'

Gerry was given a 'roving' role, and it paid off as he caused chaos in the Birmingham penalty area with his enthusiasm and ability in a 2–1 victory at Ninian Park. City were still just above the relegation zone, and there were problems teetering within the club. Trevor Ford was suspended by the club for two weeks for the incident against Birmingham and then placed on the transfer list. He had signed for Cardiff City in December 1953 for £29,500, a club record fee at the time, and was regarded as a legend at the club. Ford was demoted to the second team for a spell after his suspension, and after being recalled into the first team City had a reverse in fortunes and lost only once in the next 14 matches. It was during this period that young Gerry found his scoring boots, and it seemed he had finally settled into top-flight football as he scored 10 goals during this mid-season spell for City.

Off the field, Gerry was enjoying his life as a full-time footballer, and he was beginning to attract the attentions of the opposite sex, and one lady especially caught his eye. Meriel Jones was an attractive local 17-year-old girl from Pontypridd and was studying chemistry and physics at the local college in Cardiff in order to become a physiotherapist. It was November 1955, and after another day at college, Meriel, along with some of her friends, went to the Kardomah Café, a usual ritual among Cardiff students. On one particular day, a Canadian friend of Gerry's approached Meriel and asked her if she knew who 'that chap was', pointing across towards Gerry. Meriel replied, 'I haven't got a clue.'

Gerry's friend was surprised she didn't recognise the up-and-coming City star: 'That's Gerry Hitchens.'

'Who's that?' Meriel asked, not knowing any footballers at the time as she was more of a rugby fan.

'Well, he really likes you anyway.'

Meriel seemed pleasantly surprised and responded, 'Oh, okay, fine.' She did not think much of it, but she thought he was not bad looking either. After a few minutes, Gerry's friend approached Meriel again as Gerry was too shy to do it himself and said that Gerry would like to go out with her. Meriel, being a typical old-fashioned Welsh girl, replied, 'Well, if he wants to take me out he'll have to come and ask me himself.'

So, Gerry's Canadian friend and Meriel's friend both got up and approached the counter at the same time, which left Gerry and Meriel alone on their respective tables. It was an obvious set-up. Gerry eventually plucked up enough courage to ask Meriel to come and sit next to him. Meriel was coy and said she was 'very busy studying' when Gerry asked her if she would like to go out. He then asked her if she was free at the weekend, and that also hit the brick wall as Meriel said she 'usually did her homework at the weekends'. This went on for some minutes, but eventually Meriel gave in and they arranged to go out to the 'pictures'.

On that first date, a smitten Gerry took Meriel to see a new film called *Love Me or Leave Me*, which starred James Cagney and Doris Day. It was *Love Me* forever after that for Meriel and Gerry.

The couple had several dates over the next few weeks and were getting on pretty well, and it seemed that Meriel and Gerry were 'officially' an item. With Christmas approaching, Meriel's parents invited Gerry to spend the festive period with them, which would have made a pleasant change from the 'digs' he was staying at in Cardiff at the time, as his landlady, Mrs Wilson, chain-smoked and the awful smell of cigarettes always lingered on his clothes.

Mr Wilson was employed by City, and the couple had a few other City players staying with them at the same time as Gerry. The lads found out that Mrs Wilson had never been to watch a match before, and so the players invited her to Ninian Park to watch them play. While she was standing on the terraces, near the goalposts, watching the team in their pre-match warm-up, she was struck in the stomach by a wayward ball, kicked into the stand by one of the players. Stunned by the fierceness and pace of the hard leather ball, Mrs Wilson fell to the ground and had to leave for emergency treatment. She never got to see 'her boys' play and probably never went to another match again!

One day, Meriel and her mother went to pick Gerry up from in his digs and were invited in by Mrs Wilson. Meriel's mother took one breath and said, 'He can't possibly live here any longer.' So in no time at all, Gerry was whisked out of his digs and invited to live with Meriel and her parents. Meriel's father, Harold, was delighted to have 'his son' living with them, while Meriel's mother equally adored him and was beginning to take Gerry's side whenever there was an argument between the couple.

Meriel came from a stable, middle-class background where both of her parents had their own businesses. Mrs Jones owned a china shop in Pontypridd and Harold ran a builders' merchants and later owned a steel fabrication business in the area. The Jones's had a lovely housekeeper at the time called Mrs Edwards. She was always referred to as 'Mrs Edwards', never by her forename, and she always called her employers Mr and Mrs Jones but was considered to be 'one of the family' (she remained their housekeeper for more than 20 years afterwards until they moved to North Wales in 1979).

Meriel was worried that her father would drive Gerry mad as he did not like soccer at all, being a true Welshman and a rugby fan. Although there was a lot of ribbing from Meriel's friends, who said things like 'soccer's played with the wrong shaped ball', Meriel's mother said from the very first time her daughter started talking about Gerry and the way she spoke about him that she knew 'he was the one'. Gerry was polite and 'had something about him' she used to say.

Something that Gerry was not used to was playing football at Christmas. This had always been a traditional time for games to be played over the festive period, on either Christmas Eve or Boxing Day, or even Christmas Day. On Christmas Eve 1955, the time of year was all but forgotten as Gerry was given the best present ever as he grabbed a late winner for City in front of a crowd of 22,000 at Ninian Park and his first goal since September. He was the only player to receive any sort of ovation from the crowd in what was a dreadful match.

One of the Bluebirds' finest performances came against Wolves when they beat the Midlands team by 2–0, with goals from Hitchens and Ford in front of 37,000 stunned fans on New Year's Eve. City, who had experienced an embarrassing 9–1 home defeat by Wolves early on in the season, got their 'revenge' and ended Wolves's two-year unbeaten home run. This was the great Wolves side which included England skipper, Billy Wright.

The great win was marred by the repeated booing of Trevor Ford because of a heavy tackle on Wolves legend Billy Wright, which the home fans did not approve of. Hitchens replaced Neil O'Halloran at centre-forward, and his luck was out as he saw several chances go wide until just after half-time, when he eluded Wright and dribbled the ball to complete a spectacular move with a low shot into the back of the net, giving the Wolves 'keeper, Sims, no chance. Trevor Ford doubled the lead in the 70th minute when he accepted a long ball wide on the left and, all on his own, passed a square ball to Gerry who returned the ball with a neat pass to Ford, and he beat Sims with a lovely left-footer from eight yards.

Ford was in trouble again just after another incident with Wright when, with the crowd booing as he took a throw-in, the referee took his name. As the game drew to a close, there were more incidents between Ford and Wright, but he remained on the pitch and the score stayed at 2–0 to City.

The New Year saw a good away victory for Cardiff at Leeds United in the FA Cup, with Hitchens once again getting on the score sheet and ending another long unbeaten home record.

In the first League game of the New Year, Cardiff entertained a Manchester City side containing the legendary goalkeeper, Bert Trautmann. He was quoted in the newspapers as saying that he believed Gerry would be a player with a great future after giving the City centre-half, Charlie Wayman, the runaround and dominating the middle of the park like a veteran striker. He found out how good Hitchens and Ford were during Cardiff's 4–1 home win, with the pair working at full thrust and Hitchens scoring another two goals in Cardiff's highest score of the season. Trautmann also predicted that the young Cardiff star would be in the England set-up very soon.

The Welsh Cup came as a relief to City during a season of mixed fortunes in the League. It was a competition that Cardiff had previously won in 1938 so it was about time the South Wales side had a good run. Starting in the fifth round in early February and proceeding nicely into round six by beating Pembroke Borough in a replay, with Hitchens netting four goals in the two games. Next up was a home tie against Wrexham, and he scored a hat-trick, following the one scored in the previous round. At 5–1 and cruising at half-time, City tried to make an exhibition of it after the break, but it turned out to be the wrong ploy as Wrexham made them fight all the way and pulled two goals back to give City a big shock, but they withstood the onslaught to win 5–3.

Back in the League, the Hitchens–Ford partnership was producing the goals for City. In February, Hitchens had scored four in four and Ford three in four, including one against a Championship-chasing Blackpool side containing the great Stanley Matthews, who, at 41, was playing in his first League game at Ninian Park; however, the great Matthews did not make an impact in the game against a strong City side.

The following week saw another football legend turn out at Ninian Park, when a strong Preston side, which contained Gerry's footballing hero, England legend Tom Finney, were out-classed by Cardiff. Again, the token legendary player was nowhere to be seen in a match which saw the Hitchens–Ford combination score two of the three goals.

Long before the days of Alf Ramsey and his cynical policy of not picking players who did not play in England, the English Football Association picked Gerry Hitchens for the summer tour of South Africa in 1956, despite the fact he was playing in Wales. There were those cynics in Wales at the time, who insisted that non-Welsh British players who played for Welsh clubs would have no chance of gaining a place in their respective international teams. The selection of Hitchens, and of Danny Malloy, who was selected to represent the Scottish B team, disproved the rule and the FA secretary, Sir Stanley Rous, insisted that the Cardiff players were not being restricted and would be considered for selection for the English national team.

With the news of his selection for the FA tour of South Africa still fresh in his mind, Gerry was on target twice for City against a good Burnley side on a cold and icy February day in Lancashire. The City forwards were somewhat bashful up to the 40th minute when the young Hitchens changed the game and held on to a corner from Walsh, did a neat shimmy to bring the ball down to his feet and calmly punted it into the net from two yards. That goal, scored just before the break, took the sting out of Burnley, but they continued to attack in the snow. After the break, Hitchens doubled the lead completely against the run of play. The ball was picked up by him out of nowhere, and he steered it clear of the Burnley 'keeper, who fell flat on his face in the snow.

A visit to top of the table Manchester United proved to some that Cardiff City were a great side in the making as the Bluebirds almost took the unbeaten home record of the famous 'Busby Babes'. City proved to be hard to beat against a United side who were six points clear at the top, as Gerry once again salvaged a point for City with a gift of a goal from an erroneous back pass.

By mid-March, City were back to Welsh Cup action and faced a tie against Oswestry Town at Wrexham's Racecourse Ground. The crowd of 10,000 saw a feast of goals by the two strikers, who had been scoring for fun. By half-time the game was all but over at 5–0, with Gerry grabbing another hat-trick and Trevor Ford chipping in with two goals. The scoring was not finished in the second half either, as Hitchens scored another two to see City race their way into the Final. In a one-horse race of a game, he stole the limelight with his five goals, and if luck had been on his side Ford would have grabbed five as well.

After three back-to-back defeats in the League at the start of April – although Hitchens continued to find the back of the net – City were back on track with a 2–0 win against Luton Town, including an early goal by Hitchens which changed City's luck after those bad defeats. With the season drawing to a close, City had fought off relegation fears with two goalless draws before they met Arsenal at Ninian Park in the final League game of the season. It was almost three draws in a row when Gerry equalised after an early 'Gunners' goal to send the teams in level at half-time. On the hour, the Londoners were ahead through Tapscott and held out to claim the double over City in a typical end-of-season game. The season ended with City in 17th spot in Division One, and Hitchens was City's top League scorer with 15 goals, two goals more than Ford, in his first full season as a professional footballer.

In the Welsh Cup, fortunes were much better for the Cardiff club. On their way to the Final the Bluebirds scored 23 goals in the four games, including nine in the fifth-round replay and seven in the semi-final against Oswestry. In those two games Hitchens had clocked up eight goals and Ford five. Even though the two games were against non-League opposition, the goals still had to be scored.

It seemed like it was an easy passage into the Final, where they met their bitter rivals, Swansea, in front of a crowd of 37,000 at Ninian Park. The game started with tragedy as City inside-forward Harry Kirtley was stretchered off with a broken leg. City did not need 11 men to beat Swansea, and two goals from Brian Walsh plus one from McSevenney put the Bluebirds 3–0 ahead. Swansea staged a brave comeback, however, and pulled two goals back to make it a grandstand finish, but City hung on to their lead to win the Welsh Cup for the first time since 1930. Victory in the Cup was Gerry's first taste of winning silverware. In the five games during the winning campaign he netted 12 goals, while Ford's contribution was eight.

The year of 1956 was proving to be very special for Gerry Hitchens. Not only was he top goalscorer in his first full professional season with 28 goals in all competitions, but he was also slowly getting a reputation in the game as an up-and-coming talent. He had won his first Cup medal with City and had been called up by the FA for an official tour of South Africa. Twelve months ago he had been playing non-League football with Kidderminster Harriers in the Southern League. Was all this a dream come true?

A day after the FA Cup Final between Manchester City and Birmingham City on 5 May 1956, the squad of 18, including Gerry, flew out to tour South Africa and play 18 games, including Tests in Johannesburg, Durban, Cape Town and Salisbury. The tour was a great success, and Gerry finished as top goalscorer with 17 goals in 12 matches. Shortly after the tour, a Cardiff City XI visited his old club, Kidderminster Harriers, for a pre-season benefit match under the floodlights at Aggborough. Gerry came up against his old friend and Harriers captain, Aubrey Haycox, who came from the same mining village as Gerry and had introduced him to the Harriers. 'I have much to thank Aubrey for,' he said.

During the close season of 1956–57 veteran full-back and club captain Alf Sherwood moved to Newport County after he had spent 15 years with Cardiff. He had seen the club move from Division Three South to Division One and win the Welsh Cup in his last season. He was capped 39 times by Wales and made 354 appearances. Only one new player arrived, in the form of Lovell Athletic's Brayley Reynolds for £2,500. City manager, Trevor Morris, relied on virtually the same squad who had battled so well in the previous campaign to start the new season. Morris had made Trevor Ford captain following the departure of the City legend Sherwood and volunteered to play out of his normal position of centre-forward. This was a complete reversal from the previous season when he had refused to play out of position.

The season started with an opening day trip to Highbury to face Arsenal in front of 51,000 but both sets of fans went home empty-handed as the game petered out into a goalless draw, with missed chances for both sides. An emphatic 5–2 victory over Newcastle in the first home game of the season in front of a crowd of 42,000 was followed by a 3–3 draw against Burnley and Gerry's first goal of the season. Two defeats followed, and it appeared that even this early into the season City were heading for a long, hard slog.

When Cardiff City's scouts poached Hitchens from Kidderminster Harriers they reported that he had the ability to do everything except head the ball. However, the game against Sheffield Wednesday at Ninian Park proved them wrong as he scored with an eighth-minute header from a pin-point Danny Malloy cross. The Wednesday defenders man-marked Hitchens from every corner but were so pre-occupied with the blond centre-forward that they failed to spot Johnny McSeveney, who was 'gifted' the winner as he stood unmarked, and he met a corner-kick with his head for a perfect winning goal.

Gerry then went on a barren run and saw his side only pick up two points from the following five games. During that spell, Gerry's strike partner, Trevor

Ford was quoted as saying, 'I'll play anywhere you ask me for Cardiff – even in the reserves.' The 'Welsh wizard' was then back at centre-forward against Leeds United a couple of games later, and helped the Bluebirds to a 4–1 win by scoring, with Hitchens grabbing two goals.

Following his successful scoring record on the South African tour in the summer, Hitchens was then selected to lead the attack for his first England Under-23 match against Denmark in Copenhagen in September 1956. The news left Wolves manager, Stan Cullis, and other Division One managers, wondering how this wonderkid had slipped from their grasp nearly two years earlier. He was said to be worth 10 times the £1,500 that City had paid for him and on the verge of an inevitable full England cap. Cullis led a list of plaudits praising the young and rugged Cardiff striker by saying that he was surely near to a first senior England call-up. Cullis paid the ultimate accolade to Gerry in the press, 'The boy has that rare soccer ingredient known as "it" – the touch of natural genius and zeal which makes the difference between a good player and a potentially great one. Only one in a thousand has "it". You only hope and pray that every youngster you sign is "the one".' He went on, 'Cardiff have misfired up here in the past, but they took a chance with Hitchens and, though he still has a few things to learn, he has turned out to have "it" in plenty.'

On the 3 November 1956, Cardiff City supporters saw the last of Trevor Ford in a blue shirt in the home match against Manchester City as yet another controversy followed when extracts of his (then) unpublished book, *I Lead the Attack,* were printed in a Sunday newspaper, which reportedly earned the player £5,000 in serial rights. The story dealt with him being involved in illegal payments made to players while playing for Sunderland. These stories led to him being banned by the Football League.

Another story appeared in the press before the game against Charlton on 10 November, saying that Ford wanted to quit British football and had walked out on Cardiff to play in Los Angeles. Hours after telling City boss Trevor Morris he was 'retiring' he revealed that he hoped to discuss the move to the US club. He told Morris, 'I have slept on things and decided to hang up my boots. I will not be playing in the reserves…' Ford, dropped by Wales and now dropped by his club, continued, 'I'm not going to be messed about anymore.' Morris knew nothing of the American club's offer, however, although Ford was told to 'expect contact' from them. The American side subsequently declared that the story was not true.

Although some people thought that Ford had retired, he was officially banned *sine die* (indefinitely) on the 30 January 1957, aged 33. The ban was cut to three years on appeal in March 1958. Three weeks later he was back playing football, this time in Holland for PSV Eindhoven.

Life went on without Ford, but City were left without one of their leading strikers, and the weight of expectation fell on the broad shoulders of Gerry Hitchens, who led the attack in place of Ford for the game against Charlton. He seemed to evolve into his role as leading striker, but at the other end the City defence leaked more goals.

After a few goalless games for Gerry, he soon found the back of the net again with four goals against Arsenal and Burnley, but his goals could not stop disastrous defeats leading up to the Christmas period. Things did not get any better after Christmas and into the new year of 1957 as City continued a terrible run of six defeats in seven games.

The first games of 1957, however, saw back-to-back wins against Chelsea and Bolton, with Gerry returning to the score sheet in both games to improve his side's lowly League position. He overshadowed the classy Nat Lofthouse in the encounter against Bolton; indeed, to such an extent that the press agreed with Stan Cullis and started to talk up his chances of a first full England cap.

The 1–0 win against Aston Villa on 3 April 1957 gave City fans hope that their club could stay up in the top division for another season. Relegation blues were replaced with spirit, determination and guts as Hitchens and his teammates outmatched a Wembley-bound Villa side, who only had two shots on target.

That display against Villa at the start of April was the last time a City player scored in the next five matches, and two goalless draws and three straight defeats in a disastrous run up to the end of the season saw City win only one of the next 14 games. Their final League game of the season in front of 17,000 fans saw them face 'Busby Babes', the FA Cup finalists, Manchester United. Hitchens scored two goals to put City 2–1 ahead but, yet again the defence caved in and United came away with a 3–2 victory on the very last kick of the game (nothing changes there). Despite the defeat, Hitchens gave another outstanding performance of power, skill and strength, even though it was against an under-strength United side, who were resting key players in readiness for the impending FA Cup Final. Events finally caught up with the club and the Bluebirds were relegated after managing only 10 wins from 42 starts.

In a season which saw relegation, controversy and lots of goals (at the wrong end), Gerry had started all but one game and had finished the club's top scorer with an impressive 21 goals. He became the first Cardiff City player to score over 20 goals in a League season for over 30 years. Together with four goals in two Welsh Cup games, that was 25 for the season for Gerry in only his second term as a full-time professional.

It was at this time that the engagement of Gerry and Meriel was announced on the 19 April 1957, Meriel's 19th birthday. Gerry had bought Meriel a beautiful, five-diamond engagement ring from a jeweller in Cardiff costing £40 (which was a fair bit of money then). Meriel was training to be a physiotherapist at a Cardiff hospital at the time, and Gerry was waiting to be enlisted into the army for his two-year national service stint. Gerry was so shy that he did not actually propose to Meriel as it was taken for granted she would say 'yes' and they would spend the rest of their lives together, such was the depth of feeling they had for each other.

During the summer of 1957, 22-year-old Gerry was finally enlisted and reported for duty for the first time at Cardiff's Maindy Barracks to start two years of National Service. Gerry enlisted because he had chosen to be a full-time footballer rather than a part-time miner and footballer. His options were another four years down the mines or two years in the army: not much of a choice. He had swapped his supple football boots for a pair of stiff, heavy black army boots from the quartermaster's store. Gerry explained at the time, 'I am settling in ok. I am just going to make the best of it. I chose the army because down the mines I had little opportunity to train. I felt that I could not give my best to the public.' The question all the City fans were asking was would Gerry still play for City while he was in the army? 'Well, if they want me to, I certainly shall, and for the army team if they want me.'

Gerry spent 10 weeks on basic training at Maindy Barracks, rising to the position of Lance-Corporal Instructor. The army were obviously concerned about him playing at the weekends for Cardiff but reluctantly allowed him to do so. The army football team was managed by a very high ranking officer, Lt General Sir James Wilson, and the team included the likes of Gerry, Bobby Charlton, Alex Parker and Cliff Jones. Lt General Wilson was, however, subsequently better known as 'Jim Wilson', a football writer for *The Sunday Times* for more than 30 years from the late 1950s.

During this time Gerry was becoming extremely popular and more recognised as a future England talent. After his success on the South African tour with the England representative team, Gerry was the subject of a question on the BBC TV programme *Up for the Cup*. The question was: 'Who scored the most goals for Cardiff City last season?' Of course, the answer was Gerry Hitchens.

Pre-season saw Cardiff City prepare for life in Division Two and, being a striker short, they quickly went into the transfer market to buy West Bromwich Albion player Johnny Nicholls, who had been a prolific scorer for The Baggies.

They also drafted in Colin Hudson from Newport, while Johnny McSeveney and Neil O'Halloran were sold on.

The season started with a Welsh derby against Swansea Town (now Swansea City), a side full of Welsh internationals. It ended in a goalless draw in front of a crowd of 45,000. Early season form was poor, and to make matters worse Johnny Nicholls was transferred to Exeter City after only a few months as he had failed to strike any sort of form since his transfer.

Behind the scenes, Aston Villa were reopening negotiations with Cardiff for Gerry. Villa had already made a bid for Sunderland player Charlie Fleming, but the Wearside club seemed to be holding out for more than the £11,000 Villa and Sheffield United (then managed by Joe Mercer) were prepared to pay for the 30-year-old. Villa manager Eric Houghton was only prepared to wait for a few days, at which point he changed his plans and made a play for his number one target. Houghton knew that Hitchens would cost more money than Fleming, but his dashing, goal-bursting style was just what Houghton wanted at Villa, and he was only 22 years old. Birmingham City were also said to be interested in signing Hitchens.

Cardiff were adamant that Gerry was going nowhere. He had a long chat with City boss Trevor Morris amid speculation that they had had tentative enquiries from several clubs, but Morris told the press, 'He hasn't asked for a transfer – but I believe he is keen to get back into Division One football.' Morris added, 'Hitchens has never been available for transfer.' Although Morris refused to let Gerry leave at that time, however, when asked if he was part of the future at Cardiff or if he would be allowed to leave he replied, 'Not at the moment anyway,' and added that it was impossible to see too far ahead in football.

Cardiff were aiming to rebuild after being relegated, and they already had a young squad, with an average age of 23. They definitely did not want to release any of their youngsters; however, their financial situation was not looking good.

It took Hitchens 12 games to score his first goal of the 1957–58 season when he netted in a 3–2 victory against Derby County, and this was followed by two more against Bristol Rovers, a game which also renewed Birmingham City's interest in the striker. A Birmingham official commented before seeing Gerry face Bristol Rovers, 'Although Hitchens has scored only one goal for Cardiff so far this season, he could become a record-breaker in the right company.'

Late November saw a flurry of transfer talk about Gerry, 'If it rests with me, Gerry Hitchens will never leave Cardiff.' That was the view of Trevor Morris, but they were just words at the end of the day, as it appeared Gerry had his heart set on moving back into the top flight, and City would not be able to prevent him leaving. While all the transfer speculation went on behind the scenes, he carried on as 'normal' but did not score again for the Bluebirds after that Bristol Rovers game. Early in December 1957, Gerry was reported to have asked for a transfer when he went to see Trevor Morris to discuss his future at he club. While all this was going on, he was continuing to turn out for the army team and scored goals in their 5–2 win over Hearts. He was quoted as saying, 'There's something wrong with the atmosphere here [Cardiff]. I get goals with the army side, but when I play for Cardiff I am too tense.' To add to the speculation, he had lost his number-nine shirt to new recruit Joe Bonson, who was signed from Wolves. The unrest at the club was made worse by the news that three other players sought moves away from Ninian Park. Utility man Ron Davies, outside-left Ken Tucker and wing-half Johnny Williams were all reported to be seeking transfers. In addition to them, centre-half Danny Malloy wanted to return to Scotland. It was chaos at Ninian Park, but by mid-December 1957 it had emerged that there was a three-way battle for Gerry's signature. Aston Villa, Birmingham City and Wolves were all poised with bids, in anticipation for the announcement that 'Gerry Hitchens is available.' At this stage, Birmingham were seen as favourites by the press and were believed to have first refusal. It was thought that Cardiff were now more willing to let the Shropshire lad leave. Birmingham had first enquired about him 18 months before, and it was said that a 'promise' had been made to Birmingham manager, Arthur Turner. The three local rivals remained tight-lipped about their possible advances for Hitchens and would not reveal how or if any negotiations were taking place. Morris said, 'We think a great deal of him. He's a grand club man, and the player is very happy at Cardiff.' It was all getting to be rather 'cloak-and-dagger'. Cardiff were firmly in the driving seat: with three clubs fighting for the striker's signature the money had to be right, given their financial situation at the time. While the speculation continued, modest Gerry was more concerned with his weight than transfer requests as he had put on a stone while he had been in the army, saying he had found the army diet 'mighty heavy'.

It finally came to a head shortly after the Fulham game when City chiefs accepted a £22,500 (or £16,000 as some papers reported at the time) bid from Aston Villa. There was a late scramble for his signature, with Sheffield United manager Joe Mercer making a last-minute bid of £20,000, which was rejected by Cardiff. Other interested parties were Birmingham City, Wolves, Blackburn Rovers, Blackpool, Grimsby and Fulham, however, the fee had been agreed with Aston Villa, and Gerry was subsequently transferred on 20 December 1957, amid outcries of anger from the City faithful but sounds of glee from the City financiers, who had just made a £20,000-plus profit on one of their prized assets.

All the newspaper speculation turned out to be correct, and Gerry had played his last game for Cardiff City.

Gerry had finished his Cardiff City career on a 'low', scoring only three goals in the half season before his transfer to Villa. After a record-breaking season previously, his overall scoring record was excellent, with 57 goals in 108 League and Cup games – a ratio of a goal every two games – which is what every good striker should aim for every season.

The fee received by Cardiff was a club record. The previous record had been the £20,000 Arsenal paid for Gordon Nutt and Mike Tiddy. Villa were the FA Cup holders at the time and traditionally one of the biggest clubs in the English game, but they were actually a team in decline when Gerry joined them; however, it was Division One football that he wanted and another step up the career ladder.

Into the Lions' Den

'I am pleased with the move and looking forward to joining the crowd at Villa Park.'

Aston Villa FC
December 1957–June 1961

In the late 1950s, the sight of Villa Park situated among back-to-back terraced houses, with its floodlight pylons pointing dramatically out of the smog-laden haze, was an impressive sight. It was not hard to recognise the old ground as you turned into Trinity Road and were faced with the impressive red-brick Victorian stand, with its wide stone stairway and leaded glass windows. In contrast, behind the Trinity Road Stand was a bank of green parkland where fans often sat to catch a glimpse of their claret-and-blue heroes from afar, and then they would make a dash into the ground to see the last 20 minutes of the game just when the exit gates were opened. It certainly lived up to its billing as one of the showplaces of English football. A then capacity crowd of 75,000 and a venue for FA Cup semi-finals and the occasional international, Villa Park was the place to be for Gerry Hitchens.

It was December 1957, the same year that Aston Villa famously won their seventh FA Cup title at Wembley against the great Manchester United team known as the 'Busby Babes'; however, this Villa side was not in the same class as United and were the underdogs for the Cup. It looked like relegation for the proud club who had only known Division Two football once in 80 years. It was not until the last day of the 1955–56 season that they escaped relegation by a decimal point margin.

Yet, very nearly, that same side were at Wembley in 1957 to face the 'Mighty Reds'. The team that found its defensive feet a little late in the 1955–56 season and gave fate a chance to help them was kept together, more or less, for the next season.

On 20 December 1957 Hitchens completed his transfer from Cardiff for a reported £22,500. He had endeared himself to the Cardiff crowd in the two and half seasons he had spent at Ninian Park, and in his last full season (1956–57) for The Bluebirds he had scored 25 goals in 46 games. It was a dream move for Gerry, as Villa were always believed to be his favourite club, right from childhood.

Incidentally, it was the Villa manager Eric Houghton who had decided not to sign him back in 1954 while he was playing for Kidderminster Harriers and had decided against paying the £1,500 for the then raw 19-year-old striker. Houghton realised that the competition for Gerry's signature was fierce, and he had travelled secretly to Cardiff to have lunch with Trevor Morris to try and complete the arrangements of the deal and agree the transfer fee.

This time around, in a Cardiff hotel Houghton was trying to sweet-talk Gerry's fiancée, Meriel, into allowing him to move 100 miles away from the Valleys to the smoky and grimy Midlands city. Meriel had just begun to fall in love with football, although she did not know all the players names, but adored watching her beloved 'Geg' play, no matter what colours he was playing in. This time he would be playing in the famous claret-and-blue shirt of Aston Villa; however, Gerry wanted the weekend to think about it and to convince Meriel that this was the right move. But Houghton said, 'If you leave it you will not be eligible for the Cup tie at Stoke and I want you for the game with Birmingham at Villa Park tomorrow.' Soon after the four hours of negotiation and further talks with Meriel, Gerry signed the paperwork and Houghton had got his man. The couple were planning to marry within the next 18 months, once Meriel had completed her training and after Gerry had left the army. Gerry commented after the signing, 'I'm delighted, but gosh, I've forgotten to tell dad. I am pleased with the move and looking forward to joining the crowd at Villa Park.'

'We have fancied Hitchens for a long time. We liked him when he was with Kidderminster, but Cardiff stepped in smartly', Houghton commented at the time of signing his man. According to Houghton, 'We had won the FA Cup the season before, but I believed we needed a strong, young centre-forward, and my chief scout, Sidney Dickinson, was insistent that Gerry Hitchens was the man. Sidney had followed him everywhere, and he was so good at his job that I had to listen.' Houghton continued, 'The board of directors refused to give me the £25,000 Cardiff wanted but said they could raise half of it, so I went ahead and sold Derek Pace to Sheffield United. I was sorry to see "Doc" leave. He was a grand lad and a good player whom I had left out of the Cup Final team, but I raised £12,500 from United and went back to Cardiff and offered £20,000. In the end we split the difference, and Hitchens came for £22,500.'

It had taken a lot of negotiation to deliver his Christmas present to the Villa fans but, finally, they beat off a number of clubs, including local rivals Birmingham City and Wolverhampton Wanderers, for his signature. Gerry was 23 years old when he joined Villa and was at the time still serving in the Welch Regiment during his national service duty as a regimental policeman. During his time at Cardiff he had developed into one of the best centre-forwards in the country. At 5ft 10in tall and weighing 12st, Hitchens was ideally built for a striker and was in his prime of his career. No wonder Villa paid such a big fee for him. He also filled a long-standing need for a fully established centre-forward, ironically, absent since the loss of Trevor Ford to Sunderland back in 1950.

Shortly after signing for Villa, who had finished 10th in Division One in the previous season and had won the FA Cup, Gerry said, 'I know most of the lads because I played against them for the army recently and they are a great club. I have always been at the bottom in my professional football career – with Kidderminster and Cardiff but let's hope I can help to alter that with Villa. I hope I can help them to climb up the table.'

His debut came just 24 hours after he had signed against Birmingham City. What a baptism of fire to start his Villa career. The Villa–Birmingham derby has always been a fearsome and full-blooded affair, and he would have to encounter many more of these games in the coming seasons. Unfortunately, his debut was not the best start he could have hoped for as Villa lost to their local rivals 2–0 at Villa Park in front of a crowd of 40,000.

It took less than a week to open his Villa account. On Boxing Day 1957, over 40,000 once again watched him score his first of many goals for Villa in a 3–0 win over Arsenal at Villa Park. He handed Villa fans the best present they would have that Christmas as he notched up probably the easiest goal he would ever score four minutes from time; Arsenal 'keeper Jack Kelsey parried away a Sewell shot, and it fell into the path of Hitchens to score. 'I was beginning to worry about that big fee, but now I feel much better,' Gerry said after the game. The Villa fans were beginning to see why their club had shelled out all that money for Gerry as he raced and chased all through the Arsenal match. One Villa fan commented, 'They'll run this centre-forward into the ground in two years at the rate they're going.'

In the two matches he had played in since the transfer from Cardiff, Gerry had to do all the up-front bustling and chasing and he picked up short passes well inside his own half. It was obvious that Houghton was making Gerry play hard and work for his money, but was it a waste of his goalscoring talent? The view was that he needed stronger inside support. The Crowther–Dixon and Sewell–Hazelden pairings had been tried without real success prior to the arrival of Hitchens.

There was no doubt, however, that Hitchens could deliver consistent success, playing up front on his own or with a strike partner. In the next game against Everton at Goodison Park, Gerry scored two opportunist goals which enabled Villa to return with both points. Peter McParland provided the opportunity for the first goal after 11 minutes, with Hitchens tapping in a short-range effort. For the second goal, he took the ball down the middle from the goal-kick after Jones had slipped. Three goals in three matches was the return of a top-class striker. Although the defence held out at the end, the attack was once again lost, and Gerry found himself trying to make up ground on his own. McParland was the next best forward at the club, but as a forward line partnership they were not yet gelling; however, it was two more points and more goals for 'Hot-Shot Hitchens'.

When Villa played Sheffield Wednesday towards the end of the season, over 25,000 fans turned up hoping to see Stan Lynn equal the goalscoring record for a full-back but it was not to be, although the game ended with Villa securing another two points and Hitchens netting another two goals. It was the game which almost made sure that Wednesday were certainties for the drop. In a dour game, the only wake-up call came when Gerry scored a shock goal right out of the blue after a defensive error by England's number-one goalkeeper, Ron Springett. Ten minutes from time, with the crowd just about awake, a hefty goal-kick from Sims was headed to Hitchens by McParland, and he struck a fierce shot into the net.

In the first half-season at his new club the striker had scored 11 goals in 22 League and Cup appearances and brought Villa a top-half finish. Gerry was named as joint second top scorer for Villa behind Peter McParland, who totalled 17 goals. It was not a bad scoring ratio for Gerry and the prospect of a promising partnership with the prolific goalscoring winger, McParland, was now beginning to form. All in all, a fairly unspectacular season for the club as they only finished 14th in the League, just a season after they had won the FA Cup; however, in their final seven games they were unbeaten, with four wins and Gerry scoring four goals.

The next season, his first full year with Villa, there was considerable confidence at Villa Park that the 1958–59 season would bring much improvement from 14th position in Division One. In reality, however, the goals would dry up somewhat and the whole team would diminish. This was epitomised by the 4–0 defeat at Wolves on 17 September 1958. Wolves were League Champions in 1957–58, and they showed Villa why they were the best side in the country in a one-sided match at Molineux. Hitchens was feeling the effects of playing with the army team in Glasgow the previous night and had travelled to Wolverhampton to play the great Wolves side, led by Billy Wright. The strain showed as he was not the driving force he had been in previous matches. By October 1958 Villa were languishing in the bottom three of Division One, and wins were hard to come by with goals being leaked by the defence. Heavy away defeats in early season to the likes of West Ham (7–2), Portsmouth (5–2) and Leicester City (6–3) showed everyone that the defence needed some bolstering.

Although Villa had hit rock bottom in the League, things off the pitch were a lot happier for Gerry. After nearly three years together, the highlight of the year came on Monday 27 October 1958 when Gerry and Meriel were married at St Catherine's, a 200-year-old church in Pontypridd, South Wales. The church was special to Meriel's family as not only was it their 'local' church but Meriel had also been christened there. The service was a private affair for around 100 close friends and family, although it seemed that everyone in the town had turned out to greet the happy couple as the local police were there to keep the crowds at bay. It certainly was a big occasion in Pontypridd.

The wedding was at midday followed by the reception at a restaurant in Treforest, a village to the south-east of Pontypridd, which went on well into the evening (this was not the trend in those days as receptions usually ended after the meal). The happy couple left early, in their car decorated with the traditional 'Just Married' signs and tin cans tied to the bumpers and confetti all over the interior. They had believed the car to be well hidden in the car park, but it was obvious that it had been 'tampered' with.

The couple then travelled to Cheltenham in thick fog for their first night as a married couple. They stayed at a wonderful old hotel and were very late getting there. When they did finally get there they found that, although the room was fantastically equipped, there were two huge single beds. Meriel pleaded with Gerry to complain to reception but Gerry, being shy at the time, would not go down to the front desk to ask to swap rooms, and so they spent their first night as Mr and Mrs Hitchens sleeping in separate beds.

In the morning, Gerry took the car to the nearest garage to get it cleaned as it was covered in confetti and of all things, lipstick, before they could leave and drive to Brighton for their honeymoon. There was even confetti in the luggage and the dreadful stuff was found for days afterwards in their clothes and even flew out of an umbrella when it was opened.

The wedding had been planned to allow for the longest amount of time between matches as Hitchens had just played a home game at Bolton on the Saturday before the wedding and the next game was not scheduled until the following Saturday, an away game against Luton Town. The couple were allowed to spend the week alone in Brighton for their honeymoon, before he had to return for the match on the Saturday. There was no let-up in Gerry's training regime, as he was out training with the Brighton squad every morning so he would be match fit for Saturday's trip to Luton.

The honeymoon couple liked the town so much that they returned to Brighton and stayed at The Grand for the remainder of the weekend after the Luton match, before travelling back to their flat in Cardiff in his MG convertible sports car as Gerry was still based at Maindy Barracks in Cardiff during the week as part of his national service. While he was serving in the army he was 'living out', which meant he was living at his own house as the barracks were just down the road. Gerry had celebrated this special period in his life by scoring against Luton, but the goal failed to prevent another defeat for Villa.

The FA Cup win was now a distant memory, and Villa struggled on under the leadership of Eric Houghton until he was sacked (after he refused to resign) after 25 years at the club (20 years as a player) on 19 November 1958. Villa were left without a manager for several weeks until Joe Mercer was persuaded to leave Sheffield United after three years in charge at Bramall Lane and take over at Villa Park in December 1958. He signed on a five-year contract at a time when Villa were at the foot of Division One, and they continued to struggle throughout the rest of the season. Mercer commented on the change of leadership, 'I refuse to indulge in any mud-slinging – I think too much of Villa for that.' He said, 'I have come with a completely open mind. I don't like guessing, and you can only judge football as you see it.' By mid-March 1959, it seemed that the Mercer magic was working, and his approachable manner and tactical skill would rescue his new club from another spell in the second tier of the Football League. Mercer took the players away to Hoylake Golf Course in Cheshire for some fitness training in the hope of taking the pressure off the players before the big FA Cup semi-final against Nottingham Forest at Hillsborough. No matter how hard it was in the League, the FA Cup again proved to have the opposite effect on Villa, although it was of secondary importance to a team languishing at the wrong end of the table. A succession of good results in the Cup resulted in defeat to Forest and left them vanquished with a sense of anti-climax and irrecoverable morale.

The relegation threat was a little too close for comfort when Villa headed up to Burnden Park for a rearranged midweek clash against the 'Trotters'. Bolton could boast the legendary Nat Lofthouse, 'the Lion of Vienna' and England's battering ram centre-forward, but it was Villa's number nine, Gerry Hitchens, who took the honours with a hat-trick to take Villa three points clear of Leicester and Portsmouth at the bottom of the table. This win on 18 March 1959 gave Villa fans hope of a 'great escape'. It was Gerry's first League hat-trick for Villa, but, ironically, he had said before the match, 'I don't like playing on this ground (Burnden Park) because I never do well here.'

Gerry's first was a mis-hit shot after 27 minutes and was followed by a second six minutes later that owed much to a defensive error. Lofthouse had gone close, but there was no denying him midway through the second half when Nigel Sims in the Villa goal failed to deal with a right-wing cross and Lofthouse powered in the header. That was the cue for the 'Trotters' to batter the Villa defence, with centre-half Jimmy Dugdale earning his Brownie points. With time running out, Villa had the chance to seal it when the normally deadly left-winger, Peter McParland, found himself clear with enough time to pick his spot. Sadly, the spot he picked was by the far corner flag, so it was left to Hitchens to steady the nerves when he broke clear and buried the ball for his hat-trick. The win earned Villa a double after beating Bolton at Villa Park earlier in the season. After 31 games of the campaign, Villa were second from bottom before the Bolton game, but they finished the night three points ahead of Leicester City, who had been beaten by Birmingham City that same night, to send them below Villa in the table.

Another win at home to Luton (3–1) in the next game and two more goals for 'Hotshot Hitchens' almost blew away the relegation cobwebs. Hitchens led the line, and Villa were superior in every way. He showed in this match why he had been at the top of Eric Houghton's wish list, although his form had been patchy since signing. Now, in the space of four days, he had hit five goals.

After a winning spell of three games in March, however, during which time Gerry had scored six goals, Villa subsided. Funnily enough, the average League attendance for the season was 5,000 more than the previous campaign, but it was their away form which was too much of a burden. Out of 21 away games there were 16 defeats and only 11 wins all season. This was not the form of a team who would be able to survive the drop, and relegation was looming large for the boys in claret and blue.

In the final game of the season, Villa needed to beat local rivals West Bromwich Albion at The Hawthorns to stay up. This was a repeat situation of the 1955–56 season, but this time there would be no fairy-tale ending. Hitchens struck first for Villa in the 65th minute, and after 88 minutes Villa were still leading 1–0 until Ronnie Allen equalised for the home side with a speculative 30-yard shot and a goal which would shatter Villa's season. The game ended in a 1–1 draw and because Manchester City, who were third from bottom going into the match, won their final game, Villa were relegated to Division Two.

Villa legend, Stan Lynn, nicknamed 'Stan the Wham', remembered the crucial final game as 'the most shattering experience' of his long career. 'We knew we had to win to stay up, and when Hitchens gave us the lead on a wet and slippery night we had high hopes. Then Ronnie Allen equalised with a soft goal, hitting the ball with his shin. We were sick! An end of season "do" had been arranged for us in Edgbaston, but it felt like a funeral.' Mercer was a man of principle and said after the defeat, 'Relegation will not mean any change in our policy. Football teams are not built overnight, but as a result of day in, day out effort and procedure.'

It seemed inconceivable that a team (who were later to be known as 'The Mercer Minors') which consisted of the likes of Hitchens, Lynn, Dugdale, Crowe,

McParland and Wylie could only amass 30 points (there were two points for a win in those days), score 58 goals but let in 77.

One player that had a big impact on Gerry in that season was Ron Wylie, who had only joined the club in November 1958 but played a crucial part in polishing the 'rough edges' off Gerry. Wylie provides one good reason why: 'Players on national service were always affected, whatever they say. It was difficult for them to fall into a routine, no matter how well they thought they trained away from their club.' He continued, 'I'll go further and add that it is not until 18 months to two years after a player has left the services that he fulfils his real potential.'

With the season over, Gerry was due to finish his service in the army in the summer. During the time he had spent there he had continued to play for his clubs (both Cardiff and later Villa). There was one bizarre occasion when Gerry was put on a charge by the army for being AWOL while he went away to play for Villa. The army demoted him from Corporal to Lance Corporal for this serious act; however, a few days later this demotion was overturned after the army found out that it was the club's fault as they had not asked for permission to take Gerry out of the barracks to play football for them.

Two weeks after the final game of the season at The Hawthorns, Gerry and Meriel's first child, Marcus, was born in Pontypridd on 14 May 1959. During that long, hot summer Corporal Hitchens was no more and had been demobbed from the Welch Regiment after his two years of national service. Obviously, the years spent in the army and playing for Villa (and previously Cardiff) had taken its toll on Gerry, and he was reported to be a doubt for the first game of the new season (1959–60) in Division Two. 'He went at it [pre-season training] so hard that he has given his legs too much of a pounding,' said Mercer.

The season had promised to be similar to a rebirth for Villa. In the close season, Mercer signed John Neal, Bobby Thomson and Jimmy MacEwan. Villa's forward line was now looking like a fine blend of touch and toughness, with Hitchens as centre-forward and Wylie and McParland as wingers. The line up looked like being too good for Division Two.

The first game of the season away at Brighton was minus Gerry, but it was a dream start as Villa won the game 2–1. Defeat at Roker Park, four days later, was a big disappointment after Villa had failed to take their chances in front of goal. The fire power of Hitchens was missing for the first couple of games, and it showed, as Sewell and McParland failed to form a partnership. However, then came an impressive 14-game unbeaten run, which saw the return of Hitchens and the return of the goal threat for Villa. Hitchens returned to the fold in the first home game against Swansea Town where he led the attack, replacing Sewell, who received an injury in the previous game at Sunderland. During that run

Hitchens found the net on six occasions and saw Villa win nine games and draw five. At last the defence was holding strong, and the attackers were firing on all cylinders. Early on in the season, pundits were saying that this Villa team were 'in promotion form'. With Hitchens leading the attack and McParland and Thomson the other danger men, Villa seemed capable of making a fight for promotion at the first attempt.

After 12 games, Villa were flying high at the top of Division Two. They swaggered their way through the season, looking like the 'aristocracy' among the 'lower classes' of the division. Just as the saying goes 'what goes up, must come down', then the reverse is often the case, and what goes down can often bounce back higher and stronger than before. After nearly two seasons at Villa, relegation to the lower division seemed to kick-start Gerry's Villa career into another gear.

By now Gerry was getting used to training on a daily basis with his Villa teammates, rather than part-time as he was during his national service days. Serving in the forces and playing for a professional football club took its toll on players, and he soon turned from being inconsistent to a prolific scorer after he had left the army. Whatever struggles he had during the first couple of seasons were now laid to rest.

Expectations had risen within the club that Hitchens would provide the strength to complement the power of McParland, the effervescence of Thomson and the guile of Wylie. Added to that, the trickery of MacEwan, there was the makings for one of the best forward lines to have ever graced Villa Park. The change did not happen straight away, however, and Gerry struggled to adapt to the different demands of Division Two football. Fickle fans began calling for a change, and so did the local press. 'Hitchens was too unreliable', they said, 'too unorthodox a player for Villa'.

Newspaper reports suggested that he was 'homesick and unhappy with the club'. These reports were denied by Gerry as 'utter rubbish'. He added, 'I have never regretted my move from Cardiff to Villa for one moment.' Gerry was said to be 'unsettled' at one stage because of the difficulty in finding a suitable house for his wife and family, as is so often the case with players who have to relocate. At the time of these stories, he was waiting to move into a house in the Halesowen area and was described as 'perfectly content'. With the fans and the press on his back again, he and Peter McParland posed for pictures for the press with false beards, as they had promised they would not shave until they started scoring again. The best way any striker can answer his critics is by scoring goals, and Gerry did just that in abundance after this bit of light-hearted banter with the press.

On 14 November 1959, Gerry Hitchens turned in arguably the finest performance of his or any other Aston Villa player in history. The scoreline read:

Aston Villa 11   Charlton Athletic 1

The irony of it was that the Villa centre-forward was so near to being dropped by Mercer for this match, so great was the pressure from the press and the fickle fans, but Mercer had decided to give Gerry one more chance. Before the game, Mercer had called the forwards (Hitchens, McParland, Wylie and Thomson) into his office and told each of them that if they did not score more often they would be out of the team. Ron Wylie joked, 'I told him I never scored so I wasn't part of the argument.'

However, before the game, Gerry had said, 'It's no good. The goals won't come. I'm sick of trying.' He later confessed, 'Before the match, physiotherapist Jack Milner told me to try even harder for some goals. I told him, I've been trying too hard to get them. So, for a change, I don't think I'll try today.' Gerry trotted on to the Villa Park turf with those words ringing in his ears. Two minutes after the start he had scored his first goal for a month and Villa's opening goal. With the score at 5–0 and with Hitchens having scored four out of the five, he struck his fifth goal in the 60th minute of the game to make it 6–0, but in the process the Charlton 'keeper, Willie Duff, dislocated the third finger of his left hand and had to be replaced. Charlton left-back Don Townsend took over for nine minutes, after which centre-forward Stuart Leary, who was playing with a pulled hamstring muscle, took over. Peter McParland finished off Charlton by slamming in two more past Townsend, after Wylie, Thomson and McEwan also made a contribution to Charlton's biggest-ever defeat and Villa's biggest post-war victory.

Ron Wylie joked, 'When the inside-forwards had scored eight, we decided to let the wingers have a go. By the time we reached 10, I was beginning to feel a bit uncomfortable. I thought maybe we were rubbing it in a bit because by that time Charlton had their third goalkeeper wearing the jersey. But we certainly needed the goals.'

Gerry was reported as saying, 'Pat Saward [Villa captain] kept urging us to get as many goals as we could. If we could have made it 20 we would have done. I wasn't thinking about Charlton.' Mercer, who had demanded more goals from his side before the game, enjoyed watching his team serve up the second-biggest League victory in their history. Furthermore, Hitchens, who had only scored two goals in the previous two months, had carved up the Charlton defence and scored a hat-full in one game. After the game Gerry collected the match ball and got his teammates to sign it. It was probably the happiest and proudest day Gerry had had in his football career so far.

One thing for certain was that the Villa win gave the ground a peak of excitement which had not been touched since the never-to-be-forgotten Cup tie with Manchester United on 10 January 1948, when Villa lost by 6–4 in front of over 58,000 people; however, on this occasion only 21,997 witnessed the finest-ever Villa post-war performance. It was Villa's biggest win for 68 years, when on that occasion they beat Accrington 12–2 in a Division One match in the 1891–92 season.

To put the matter in its true perspective, it has been suggested that Villa actually played better at Liverpool in the previous week when they were beaten than they did against Charlton when they had won 11–1. However, Villa were in the 'right mood' on that day to tear apart a woeful Charlton defence. They were extremely determined to make the most of the match and turned it into a 'no mercy' mission, in which they chased the 11th goal with as much keenness as they did the first.

The Saturday night *Sports Argus* newspaper headlined:

WHAT PRICE THIS VILLA ATTACK NOW!

It went on:

Gerry Hitchens slammed his critics today in the best possible way - with five golden goals in this deep humiliation of Charlton.

Another paper's headline was:

VILLA 11 HITCHENS 5

The *Birmingham Mail* newspaper had carried a story which amounted to a warning notice to Gerry before the Charlton game. They noted that the 20-year-old striker Ken Price was challenging him for the number-nine shirt, in a 'Battle of the Villa Park centre-forwards'. The paper went on to say, 'It won't be for lack of trying if Hitchens isn't helping with that net-filling. But the trouble with Gerry is…he's unorthodox. At the same time the big asset of Gerry is…he's unorthodox.'

The diagnosis of Gerry Hitchens made in the *Mail* may have been correct, but the forecast was way off mark. Ken Price never wore the claret-and-blue jersey for the first team. A sceptical observer may feel that this piece of journalism was designed to motivate Gerry. That was not far from the truth in reality, it seemed.

A truly remarkable sequence of results followed that record victory which were even more astounding. The next two games saw Villa score another 10 goals. In the two weeks of 21 goals in three matches, Gerry had netted no less than 10.

The three scorelines read:

14 November – Villa 11 Charlton 1
Hitchens 5, Thomson 2, McParland 2, Wylie, MacEwan.
21 November – Bristol City 0 Villa 5
Hitchens 3, McParland, Wylie.
28 November – Villa 5 Scunthorpe 0
Hitchens 2, McParland 2, Thomson.

This was truly a remarkable period in the life of Gerry Hitchens and the history of Aston Villa. They were top of the League at the midway point of the season after this run of games. As is so often the case, they were brought down to earth this time by Championship rivals Rotherham United, who beat a weakened Villa side 2–1.

Another nice run of six unbeaten games followed that hiccup, with Hitchens scoring three. During that run of results Villa played Gerry's former club, Cardiff City, at Villa Park. A near-hysterical crowd of 54,000 crammed into Villa Park and witnessed a game that had it all: brilliant forward moves, iron resolution in defence, superlative goalkeeping, tough tackling, dynamic shooting and faultless refereeing. Hitchens himself had a number of good openings and eventually took his chance, one minute from time, to make it 2–0.

It is fair to say that some players are born to score and some have a goalscoring ability thrust upon them. In the case of Gerry, he was probably in the second category, but, indeed, the magic was at times mystifyingly slow to work its spell on him. His hard, galloping style earned him the nickname of 'Champion the Wonder Horse' from his Villa teammates because, 'he was so quick and he had a mane of blond hair,' said Peter McParland.

If Charlton, Bristol City and Scunthorpe could not catch the 'shooting star' during that three-match sequence earlier in the season, the police surely could. Gerry liked his sporting guns and took part in the occasional shoot. On 6 December 1959, Gerry transgressed with a double-barrelled shotgun on land at Great Witley, Worcestershire, and was summoned, along with three friends, for killing and taking several game birds on a Sunday, even though he had a licence (although newspaper reports suggested otherwise). He took a 'hat-trick' of pheasants the day after having an 'empty bag' at Rotherham. Police found the three pheasants in the back of a van in Great Witley. Gerry admitted shooting the birds but said he and his friends had permission from the landowner to shoot on his land. As he was unable to attend the court hearing, Gerry wrote a letter admitting the offences and apologising to the court. All four had not realised that it was an offence to shoot and take game on a Sunday. He was fined £5 two months later.

Gerry and Meriel were very content with life in Birmingham and their new house in Halesowen and Gerry was now settling into life at Villa quite nicely. Being a footballer in the late 1950s did not come with the glamour and trimmings that a modern-day footballer enjoys, and during this period in his life Gerry had to catch the bus every day from Halesowen to the Villa training ground, which was then situated across the road from the Villa Park stadium. On his way to training one day, Gerry was lucky enough to get a lift from a stranger who happened to be going in the same direction. As it turned out, he lived across the road from the couple and was a big Villa fan, so for him it was a thrill to drive the great Gerry Hitchens to training. This continued for some time, and from that day on Gerry and Meriel became great friends with Les and Betty Farrington.

When Villa were playing at home, Betty would babysit Marcus while Meriel went to watch Gerry play, driven to the ground by Les. Les and Betty had a son, Paul, who happened to be a big Villa fan like his father and also went to see his beloved team play.

At this time, Gerry was attracting the attention of the press more and more. When a reporter once asked him how he would spend £50, his reply was, 'If I had to spend it, I would buy the wife a new dress, get a babysitter and have a super night out – theatre, the lot.' At a time when the average player earned £20 a week with a £4 win bonus that was a lot of money indeed.

Throughout Christmas and well into the new year (1960), Villa remained top of the League, with closest rivals Cardiff City and Rotherham hot on their heels. During January and February another Villa player decided it was time he got on the scoring charts: Bobby Thomson had only scored six goals up to the new year match with Swansea Town, but he then went on a scoring spree of nine goals in the next seven League games. By the beginning of March Villa had been knocked off the top spot by Cardiff City, but a 1–0 win at Middlesbrough showed the confidence was back in the side and put them on the right track for promotion. Gerry grabbed the winner, and it was probably one of the easiest goals he had ever scored: Boro 'keeper Peter Taylor collided with his own centre-half and dropped the ball into the path of Hitchens to tap into the open net.

With Villa already in the FA Cup semi-final once again, the fans were getting excited at the chance of their club pulling off a Cup-promotion double. The team were prepared, as ever, for a long run in the most famous Cup competition in the world, with wins over Leeds United, Chelsea, Port Vale – all by 2–1 – made easier by the Villa strikers, Hitchens, McParland, Wylie and Thomson, who all contributed with goals. In the quarter-final against Preston North End, a crowd of 69,732 saw Villa win 2–0, with goals from Hitchens and McParland. Villa had made it through to their third FA Cup semi-final in four years.

Villa were receiving a lot of praise in the press for their style of play and team spirit. Mercer was a passionate man and had great enthusiasm for a 43-year-old, and these attributes showed in the players. 'I believe in footballers, I really do. As sure as God made little apples, Villa are going to have a great team again,' Mercer commented. He was sure that he could build a great team at Villa and bring back the good times and thought he was a very lucky man to have been appointed such a role, 'There are few clubs in the country which have the spirit of Villa. That is one reason why I came here from managing Sheffield United. When I took over the team were on the floor, but their spirit was terrific. My job has been to keep that spirit going: to build it up. We are football fanatics on the field. We play hard but fair, but I don't believe that you have to be fanatical and miserable.'

Mercer was the type of manager who mixed with his players, cracked jokes with them and had an old head on his young shoulders; however, he was a man of discipline as well, and any player who breached discipline or was disobedient was dealt with in private man-to-man talks, 'I try to treat my players as I would have expected a manager to treat me.'

The Villa players were encouraged by the practice of self-discipline in their leisure time. They were quick to realise that they did not have to go 'round the back' to have a drink (or smoke). He was cautious of the press and did not like stories appearing in the papers that he was about to sign a particular player. He liked to treat everyone as equals. He once told his players, 'Let's get it straight, I am always looking for new players. But I can promise you this – nobody will come here and get special treatment or privileges from me that the rest of you don't enjoy.' He did not treat the players like children when they stayed in hotels during away games and the players reciprocated and did not abuse their privileges. Mercer gave his players plenty of responsibility on the field, as well as off it, 'We have a number of basic plans concerned with simple things, such as throw-ins and so on, but we don't wrap it up in analysis, diagrams and over-elaboration. You must be able to play "off the cuff", adapting your tactics to suit conditions and opponents. But if anyone ignores anything that we have previously agreed to do, then I must step in.'

The result was a forceful fluidity in Villa's play, which spread from goalkeeper Nigel Sims up to Hitchens in attack. Before the Chelsea FA Cup tie, Mercer told his men, 'Don't worry about what they are going to do – get control from the start and let them worry about us!' Ironically, Villa were two goals clear after 30 minutes of that game.

In the semi-final at The Hawthorns, Villa met an outstanding Wolves side. In training, Mercer had used his methodical tactics and had the reserve team 'copy' the Wolves style of play so that the first team would not be overawed by the fast flowing style of play of their near neighbours. 'Any little thing helps in planning for such a big occasion and against such a first-class team…' said Mercer. 'The reserves have done extremely well to copy the Wolves so well. It gives us some idea of what we will be up against on Saturday – and some chance to plan counter-tactics in a practical way.'

A crowd of nearly 56,000 saw Wolves beat Villa 1–0 at The Hawthorns in the all-Midlands semi-final. It was the second taste of semi-final defeat in two seasons, and they had also been relegated on the same ground 12 months earlier. Even the 'lucky heather' which was presented by Villa captain Pat Saward to each of the Villa players before the game by did not help. 'I'm afraid they didn't do us much good,' said a rueful Jimmy Dugdale.

For the second year in a row, the conquerors of Villa in the semi-final went on to hoist the Cup in front of the royal box at Wembley and in front of millions watching at home. With the semi-final defeat out of the way, Villa's main aim was to win promotion. By April, they were back on top of the League and above main rivals Cardiff City. In the closing stages of the season, however, Gerry did not score again in the final six games.

However, he had done his job throughout the rest of the season as he netted 25 times in League and Cup games in just 41 appearances as Villa were crowned Division Two champions and gained promotion back to the top flight at the first attempt. Added to that, Peter McParland also scored 25 and Bobby Thomson contributed with 20. So far in his Villa career, Hitchens had clocked up 54 goals in 104 League and Cup games, covering two and half seasons, which, for any striker, is a pretty good strike rate. With his emergence as a top-class striker, scoring goals just for fun, the Villa fans flocked back to see their new hero play week after week, and the attendances at Villa Park rose to an average of over 34,000.

During the summer break he spent hours with Villa manager Joe Mercer and assistant manager Dick Taylor tightening his control. Many players would have sneered at such hard labour on basic skills, but Gerry always looked at ways to better himself and to polish his skills to make him a more successful player. That was Gerry all over.

Much was said about this Villa team of the late 1950s and early 1960s. It was a mixture of wise old heads, like Vic Crowe and Peter McParland, and ex-schoolboy internationals like Norman Ashe and Alan Baker, who were the future of the club, thrown in with newcomers like Nigel Sims, Jimmy MacEwan and Bobby Thomson, but all wanted to play a part in their history and the recovery from the lower division. They were all friendly men and made Villa Park a happy place to be.

It had been a difficult period for Villa fans when they went down to Division Two in 1959. Unlike their local rivals, Birmingham City and West Bromwich Albion, most Villa fans 'expect' their team to be winning every game, a bit like every England fan 'expects' their country to win every international fixture. Villa have always been considered the aristocracy of Midlands football, and their fans have always thought as much. So much expectation stems from having such a long and successful history, unlike their local rivals.

The early 1960s were, in hindsight, the 'last sunset of English football'. A decade with no hooliganism (as there was in the 1970s and 1980s), the national team were soon to become World Champions and money would not be the 'root of all evil' (or envy), well, almost. During these heady days the name of Gerry Hitchens was, at last, on everyone's lips, and he was again being touted for a possible England call-up for the 1962 World Cup in Chile. So the question for the first season of the new decade was, would Gerry keep the standard up back in the big League? Villa made the best possible start by winning their first game against Chelsea, with Hitchens scoring the second of three. Against West Ham in the next match, he scored, but Villa were brought back to earth as they were thumped 5–2 at Upton Park; however, there were eight goals in the first seven games of the new Division One season as Villa's canter back in the top flight began in earnest.

One day around this time, Gerry was playing golf at Halesowen Golf Course in the late August sunshine when he hit a shot at the second tee, and his ball landed in the rough. When he found the ball it was embedded in a wasps nest, and when he tried to move it he was surrounded by angry wasps, which left Gerry tearing up the fairway back to the clubhouse without finishing his round. Unfortunately, Gerry got stung by one wasp on his arm, which left a swelling and made him doubtful for the next match against Blackpool. Luckily, the swelling cleared up in time and Gerry scored two goals, but could not prevent a crushing 5–3 defeat.

Goals were not hard to come by for the Villa strikers going into October as they had notched up 22 goals, with Hitchens scoring nine. However, whatever the feelings were about the defence, 28 goals had gone against them in those first 10 games. His popularity among the fans and his teammates was at an all-time high. They liked his never-give-up galloping style and his willingness to improve. He was playing better than ever and was becoming something of a 'cult' hero. All those extra hours spent with Mercer and Taylor in pre-season were beginning to pay off. He was a more assured and polished performer and a valuable asset to Villa in a period of changes and challenges. From jeers to cheers, Gerry Hitchens had turned around the questions the fans were asking about him earlier in his Villa career and had made the press eat their unkind and unjust words.

The Football League Cup was introduced in the 1960–61 season specifically as a mid-week floodlit tournament. On 12 October 1960 Aston Villa played Huddersfield Town in their first match of the new competition at Villa Park. Villa won the tie 4–1, and Hitchens became the first Villa player to score in the competition.

By mid-October 1960, Villa sat in mid-table, and Hitchens hit top form to go on another memorable scoring run. A local derby with Birmingham City saw Villa cruise to an historic 6–2 victory at Villa Park, with the ex-Highley miner netting another hat-trick. Alan O'Neill was signed from Sunderland in the previous week, and he got his debut goal after only 25 seconds. It was quite a game and went down as one of the best local derbies ever played between the two teams. The game was played in front of 45,000 rain-soaked spectators at Villa Park, and the home fans went home the happier in a match that would have been remembered for many weeks (if not years) to come. The game had everything: apart from the eight goals, there were several near misses and a saved penalty.

A week later, in a game which had been built up by the media as a 'grudge match' or 'blood match' and even a 'vendetta match' that had to be settled between two local rivals, Hitchens scored his 13th League goal against local rivals West Bromwich Albion at The Hawthorns in front of a crowd of 41,903 in a 2–0 win. It was Villa's first away win of the season after some dreadful results on their travels. Just over 12 months previously, Villa had been relegated on the same ground by a Ronnie Allen goal, five minutes from time. This game was full of blood, guts and fierce tackling, and the standard of football suffered. The game itself lived up to the hype in the press.

A week after the Albion game, Gerry wrote in his column in the Birmingham sports newspaper, *The Sports Argus*:

THE PRESS HAVE BLOOD ON THEIR HANDS

'Most of the talk this week has been of our so-called blood match with West Bromwich Albion, at The Hawthorns, last Saturday. Some blamed the teams, others the referee. I reckon some sections of the press did as much harm as anyone.

'During the week before the match some newspapers shouted the revenge theme as loudly as they could. They made it look as though this was a vendetta that had to be settled once and for all.

'I'm not trying to sidestep the issue. We at Villa Park expected a tough match – after all there's rarely any love lost in these clashes between neighbouring sides. And we wanted very much to win.

'All of us who played in that match at The Hawthorns a couple of seasons ago remember the way the crowd jeered us into Division Two. It was something we could hardly forget.'

THAT WAS THE REASON WE WANTED TO DO WELL ON SATURDAY - JUST TO SHOW THE SPECTATORS THAT WE ARE BACK IN DIVISION ONE AND A FORCE TO BE RECKONED WITH.

'And I want to say here and now that regardless of what the press said about the match – some called it the "Battle of the Hawthorns" – it wasn't as tough as it was made out to be. There were numerous petty fouls, true – but nothing really vicious. I have seen and played in far tougher matches.

'What really spoiled the game, I thought, was that neither side played anything like as well as they can.

'By the way, I liked the way Bobby Thomson shaped in his first outing at left half. His tackling and covering were good, and he proved useful in the air.

'He has the energy needed for the job too, and it was good to see the way he came through to support the attack when needed.'

Two more goals at home to League Champions Burnley in front a big crowd at Villa Park capped off another memorable fortnight for the tall, blond striker. It would have been another hat-trick for Gerry if Burnley goalkeeper Adam Blacklaw had not stopped the ball going over the line with his hand from a Jimmy MacEwan shot, just as Hitchens slammed it into the net. The referee disallowed the goal and denied him his hat-trick. The referee, Mr Howley, explained after the game, 'Blacklaw had his hand on top of the ball when Hitchens kicked it. To kick the ball out of the goalkeeper's possession is an offence.'

The name Gerry Hitchens was now being talked about among Villa fans and the press in the same breath as former Villa legends of the past, like Harry Hampton, 'Pongo' Waring and Gerry's former Cardiff strike partner, Trevor Ford. Fifteen goals in 16 games was a first-class strike rate at any level, and

Gerry had now proved it both in Division One and Division Two. Not surprisingly, the boy from sleepy Highley was becoming the number-one idol at Villa Park. Not only was the call for Gerry to be capped by England building momentum on a national scale, but it was also being said that he was a real threat to the (then) current Tottenham and England striker, Bobby Smith – Jimmy Greaves's seemingly favoured strike partner. The press were also saying that the position of centre-forward was not adequately covered, unlike the rest of the positions in the England set-up, and that Hitchens was a ready-made replacement for Smith and he would not impair the efficiency of the England forward line. All Gerry had to do now was to convince the England selectors.

By mid-November, Villa were creeping up the Division One table and still in the hunt for the League Cup. A third-round tie against Preston ended in a draw and went to a replay at Villa Park. It was the third time the two teams had met within the space of nine days. The replay saw Villa beat Preston 3–1, with Gerry scoring the first goal to book the Midlanders into the fourth round.

Back in the League, a rousing victory over Manchester City 5–1 and two goals for 'Hot-shot Hitchens' was raising the tempo. The great City goalkeeper, Bert Trautmann, famous for the serious injury sustained after diving at the feet of Birmingham City's Peter Murphy in the 1956 FA Cup Final, described Hitchens as, '…great, simply great. What a player he has become. I remember him in his Cardiff days, and what a change there has been since then!'

Gerry's goal tally had now reached 18, level with Bobby Smith and just behind the great Jimmy Greaves. Trautmann remained convinced that Hitchens was the best centre-forward in England. Not only that, Trautmann tipped Villa for the Cup and said that 'they played with progressive force and were formidable in defence and attack alike.'

In the League Cup, Villa were drawn against Plymouth in the fourth round but it took two replays to see The Pilgrims off. Gerry grabbed another hat-trick in the second replay as Villa ran out 5–3 winners.

By the halfway point in the League, Villa were sixth but way off the pace shown by Spurs, who were top and scoring goals for fun, with Bobby Smith leading their attack. Over the busy Christmas and new year period Hitchens was still on fire, even if Villa were unable to win games, which was due in the main to a lot of injuries. He scored six goals in three games, bringing his tally in all competitions to 28, which equalled Johnny Dixon's post-war record for the club.

The start of the new year saw the birth of Nicola, Gerry and Meriel's second child, which was announced on the 3 January 1961, the day after Villa had drawn

1–1 against Manchester United at Old Trafford. The year had started on a high for Villa, and they continued it with a tie against Division Two club Bristol Rovers, beating them 4–0 after another replay with Hitchens grabbing another two. In round four they met Peterborough and beat them after yet another replay. Two games in a week against Tottenham, one in the League and one in the FA Cup, both ended in defeat for Villa. It seemed that if Villa were to win something that year they were going to do it the hard way.

In the League Cup, another two from Hitchens and one from Thomson saw off Wrexham in round five at the first attempt, but it took three games to beat a tough Burnley side in the semi-final, Villa eventually winning 2–1, with Gerry contributing a goal in each game to make sure of their place in their first-ever Final. He particularly liked this newly formed competition, scoring no fewer than 11 goals in 10 appearances.

Manager Joe Mercer had begun to tamper with his side during the mid-season period from Christmas to March, with the introduction of some young professionals like Charlie Aitken, Johnny Sleeuwenhoek, Harry Burrows and Alan Deakin. The good start to the season did not continue due to injuries and bad defensive errors, but at least Hitchens kept banging in the goals.

By the end of March 1961 Villa were seventh in the division but still a long way off the leaders Tottenham. From mid-March to the end of the season, Hitchens would only score another four goals in the League. When Bolton were the visitors to Villa Park, a week after being well beaten by the Trotters, Villa had not won a home game in four months. Ironically, the smallest crowd of the season watched Villa sweep aside the Trotters 4–0.

Gerry's scoring consistency throughout the season and his maturity seemed to be taking a long time to grow, but his build-up play had marked him out as a future international striker for some time. He was being widely tipped to be picked by Lancaster Gate selectors for the home international match against Scotland at Wembley on 15 April 1961, but after all the hype the FA decided to stick with Greaves and Smith. However, in the end it paid dividends for England as they beat the Auld Enemy 9–3, with Greaves scoring a hat-trick and Smith notching up two goals in front of a crowd of 93,000.

The season ended on a bright note with a 4–1 victory against Sheffield Wednesday and Hitchens finishing just as he had started the season, by scoring a brace. It was a success for both Villa and Gerry. Finishing ninth on their return to the top flight was an achievement, although the form had been patchy. The first-ever Football League Cup had been held, and Villa went all the way to the Final, where they would meet Rotherham United, who had only just escaped relegation from Division Two. There was public apathy over the new competition, and the size of the attendances for the 10 games leading up to the Final demonstrated that the fans cared little for the League Cup. Some things never change.

Local football fans were nominating their *Birmingham Mail* – Midlands Footballer of the Year, which aimed to find the player who commanded unqualified respect for skill, effort, loyalty, good conduct and sportsmanship. Readers of the *Mail* were asked to name the player who, in their opinion, deserved the title most. Gerry was up against top local players like Don Howe, Jimmy Dugdale, Vic Crowe, Ron Flowers and Bobby Robson. Gerry won the public vote, hands down. In reality, there was no other candidate.

The Final of the League Cup had to be rearranged from the first week of May to the end of August (for the first leg) and the first week of September (for the second leg). This was because Villa had a pre-arranged tour of Russia starting on 8 May 1961. Gerry had made himself unavailable for the tour as there were important internationals coming up, and the Villa striker was keen to impress the England manager Walter Winterbottom in case he got called-up. This was May 1961, only months before the Cuban Missile Crisis, which was a confrontation between the United States, the Soviet Union and Cuba during the Cold War. It was no time to go to Russia to play football.

Gerry had netted 42 goals in just 56 League and Cup appearances in the 1960–61 season, which was a remarkable achievement at any level. Added to the Midlands Footballer of the Year Award, he was also presented with the Aston Villa Supporters' Club Player of the Year Award, for which he received a gold watch from the club.

Don Howe, who played for local rivals West Bromwich Albion, was outspoken in a local newspaper after the announcement that Gerry had picked up the Midlands award and that former Villa player (then with Tottenham) Danny Blanchflower had been voted the National Footballer of the Year, proclaiming that his vote would have gone to his teammate Bobby Robson for both the awards. He did, however, concede that Gerry deserved an England call-up and went on to say that Robson was the best link-up man in the country and that, if Jimmy Greaves was not to play, then his loss would be less than if Robson did not play for England.

This was, undoubtedly, the best season so far for Gerry, who had by now a following at Villa of rock 'n' roll star proportions. He was also soon to become popular with Italian football scouts and agents.

There was also great popular demand for Gerry to be picked for England, and this was answered by his inclusion for the English FA match with the Scottish FA.

He now wanted to fulfil his dream of playing in a full international for England and was one step closer. That call came on 9 May 1961 as Gerry was duly called-up by Walter Winterbottom, the England manager, to play Mexico at Wembley in a friendly that very next day while his Villa teammates were on a tour of Russia. Shortly after his international debut, Gerry had heard of Italian interest for his signature. Former player and Aston Villa chairman Chris Buckley said about the transfer speculation, 'Gerry Hitchens will not be sold at any price, under any circumstances.'

With most Villa officials in Russia, it was all happening much too quickly for Villa, and at the wrong time; however, it could not happen quickly enough for the Italians. The prospective purchasers, Internazionale Milano (Inter Milan), were on tenterhooks, waiting for the internationals to finish and for Villa officials to return from Russia.

Before Gerry went away with the England party, he received a telephone call from Fred Archer, the Villa secretary, asking him and Meriel to call in at Villa Park and see Chris Buckley. It was Chris Buckley who broke the news to Gerry when he said, 'How would you like to play in Italian football?' He explained that Internazionale had been watching him for some time and had made an approach for a possible transfer. The news came as a shock to Gerry, but it was a nice shock all the same. The news also came at a time when he was feeling rather good about himself as he had been selected by England for their forthcoming tour of Europe. 'Seeing Gerry as a top footballer and playing for his country has made us very proud of him – they have been the happiest days of our lives.' Gerry's mother Violet once said.

Gerry was asked to consider the offer, which was not in any way finalised, very carefully over the following few days. Due to his particiaption in the England tour, Gerry asked if his decision could be delayed until after he returned with England. There was plenty to discuss with Meriel. Apparently, Gerry said on hearing the interest from Internazionale, 'I first heard it from an Aston Villa official. Then they [Internazionale] made a firm offer, and it was up to me.' While Gerry was away with England, he was selected for two of the three matches in Europe and scored two goals in the game against Italy. It was that match which brought the name of Gerry Hitchens to everyone's attention, especially the officials at Internazionale Milano. England won 3–2 in an historic game in Rome and the Italians became frantic. A few days later, Gerry made his third full appearance for the national team in Vienna against Austria.

Gerry and Meriel's first thoughts were for the children: Marcus was two and Nicola was only four months old. There were so many considerations – language, food, moving house, friends and family; in short, a complete cultural overhaul. A family conference was called as soon as Gerry returned from the England set-up. Meriel's parents travelled from Cardiff, and Gerry's parents made the short trip from Highley to their home in Halesowen, near Birmingham. Every angle of the move was considered. He had no reason to move from Villa, who were a wonderful club, and with Gerry scoring 42 goals in the previous season he was on top form and the 'man of the moment' and an idol to the fans. There was no real desire to leave England, but the more the couple thought about it the more interested they became.

Advice was also taken from Les and Betty Farrington, who encouraged the couple to go for it as it was only a few years out of their lives and would be a great experience. Italy was perceived as having far more opportunities in terms of football and the prospect of playing with some of the world's greatest players was becoming a major temptation for Gerry. Italy offered something new and much more in the way of financial rewards. Meriel was very keen for Gerry to sign – if the terms were right, of course.

There appeared to be a few 'red herrings' thrown across the Channel in the direction of Villa Park by the Milan club. 'We are not planning to sign 'itchens, whom we know to be an excellent forward, mainly because we have different plans', the Inter club secretary Signor Allodi explained.

Gerry was convinced at this stage that he was going to sign for Internazionale. Aston Villa chairman Chris Buckley said 'It's up to Gerry, now. The terms are not quite finalised and will not be until he makes up his mind.' It was clear from the Villa side and from Gerry that the deal was on, but the Italians were being coy. Obviously, Gerry was not going to travel 600 miles to Milan to find out he would not be required, so it was a case of waiting for confirmation. When the statement from Signor Allodi was read, Gerry and Meriel were making plans to fly to Milan. 'All I know is that we are definitely going to Milan tomorrow', Meriel said.

This brought back shades of the Jimmy Greaves 'Will he? Won't he?' transfer saga only a few weeks previously, where 21-year-old Jimmy tried to pull out of the deal with Italian football agent Gigi Peronace and AC Milan, even though the money on offer was even more than Internazionale were offering Gerry. When Gerry was called back to Villa Park on 15 June 1961, however, he met with Internazionale representative Signor Poggia Pantaleune and agreed to sign for a fee of £85,000 on a three-year contract (subject to a medical in Italy). Gerry said, 'I'm quite happy about the move. No signing-on figure has been mentioned yet. We will talk about that out there.'

The deal that was widely reported in the press was for Villa to receive £85,000 and for Gerry to be handed a £10,000 signing-on fee. As far as 1960s transfer fees were concerned, this was very good money indeed, for both Villa and for Gerry. If the Villa team, management and directors had not been away in Russia, where Villa were playing as part of their end of season tour, perhaps Joe Mercer would have persuaded him to stay at Villa.

Whether or not a signing on fee was paid, the couple saw it as only three years out of their life and the money was good, although it was not everything. Three days later, Gerry and Meriel were on the plane to Milan, alone, with the children staying at Meriel's parents until things were finalised.

Meanwhile, back in Britain, Villa defeated Rotherham 3–2 over the two legs of the League Cup Final. Although Gerry played in every match and scored 11 of the 26 goals on the way to the Final, including goals in every round, he would not feature in the Final due to his transfer to Internazionale. The club did not offer Gerry a Cup-winners' medal, something that he was very upset about.

Gerry Hitchens joined Villa in December 1957 and had amassed 96 League and Cup goals in 160 appearances. His goal ratio still remains the best for a post-war Villa player. He was almost irreplaceable. For Villa manager Joe Mercer it left a major headache – to replace a player who scored 42 goals in the season just finished. And quickly.

Mercer could not let history repeat itself by allowing the transfer of their star player affect the coming season. When Leeds United sold John Charles to Juventus for £65,000, they were relegated the very next season. Likewise, when Huddersfield Town allowed their star player, Denis Law, to move to Manchester City they then narrowly missed out on relegation to Division Three.

It is always difficult to replace someone who has the 'knack' of scoring goals, and lots of them, with a player of similar capabilities. But it was 'arrivederci' to Gerry and 'hello' to Derek Dougan in the summer of 1961. 'The Doog' was signed as a straight replacement for Gerry. He came from Blackburn Rovers for a reported £20,000 after a stint of two and a half years at Ewood Park, where he scored 26 goals in 59 appearances. He had pedigree, but he was no Gerry Hitchens.

Ciao Italia

'I wanted to see different places and play against different teams.'

Internazionale Milano (Inter Milan)
June 1961 to November 1962

When professional footballers go to ply their trade in a foreign country they should make an effort to become familiar with the ethos of that nation's footballing background, the way football is played there and the culture, not only of the club but also of the country. Unfortunately, not all foreign players in the past did their homework before they arrived to play the game they loved and to pick up the money as well.

The ethos in Italy is basic: football **IS** Italy and Italy **IS** football. It is like a religion, a passion and something which is born into most Italians. Inevitably, a narrative about the game cannot help but be a narrative about the country as a whole – its dynamics, its preoccupations, its outlook and its problems. There is one fundamental fact about the Italian people, and that is no one agrees on anything when it comes to football.

It is fitting for a nation, especially a modern European nation that has given the world the Renaissance, opera, fashion and the best food in the world, that the history of Italian football reveals a beguiling mixture of the artistic, the extravagant and the underhand tactics and schemes. Unlike football played in Spain, Germany or France, Italian football possesses a uniquely seductive quality. This is a nation where the largest selling daily newspaper is dedicated almost entirely to football, plus there are three or four daily sports newspapers, and where politics and politicians get involved in the running of the nation's football clubs. Historically, football reporters have always been more like war correspondents, and most are biased towards their own team.

Statistics, records, results and League tables exist, but this is only half the story when it comes to Italian football. Italy is a country where debate is ruled by *dietrologia* – an enduring speculation about the reality behind appearance, the 'true' events that lie behind events. As valid for politics, the workings of the Mafia or any given football game, *dietrologia* dominates footballing discourse and shapes the world view of its aficionados. Controversies from as far back as 1925 continue to rage about 'stolen' matches, fixed Championships and the alleged corruption of officials, chairmen and players. In fact, each club, as part of its mythology, has at least one element of what is termed *arbitraggio* – a particularly controversial decision that has robbed them of a trophy or an important game.

Italy is a country where nothing is taken at face value and where those stolid virtues that supposedly underpin the game the English invented – respect for officials, a sense of fair play, losing with honour – are regarded at best with bemusement, at worst as frankly moronic by Italians, both past and present; however, in the decade labelled the 'Swinging Sixties', British football emerged from the shadows of post-war restrictions and decay – and the humiliating defeats inflicted on England by the great Hungary side of the 1950s were erased from memory. Britain and British football was on the up, but so was Italian football.

After the domination of Europe by the great Real Madrid side of the late 1950s, Italian football clubs were determined to do anything to become as great as them. Although the football was sometimes poor and the entertainment was dour, the money that was thrown at players in Italy was immense in the early 1960s, and it seemed that foreigners from all over the world wanted a piece of the action, including some of the best footballers from Britain who saw teams like AC Milan, Internazionale and Juventus as the pinnacle of their profession – and the money was not too bad either.

A famous English footballer in the early 1960s once told his friend, 'I'm giving our manager the treatment. I shout out "ciao" when I enter the dressing room every morning. When the team goes into a restaurant for a meal I always order spaghetti. And I've swapped my Ford for a Fiat.' The story had most other footballers falling about in laughter at the time, but few managers and even fewer chairmen could manage more than a hollow laugh at the sentiments. For the 'Italian Affair' was then in its height, a hectic, almost hysterical episode that had no funny side for British football clubs or officials. Unfortunately, these episodes have continued in football ever since.

It was brought to light during the 1960–61 season, when footballers were increasingly restive as the Professional Footballers' Association (PFA), led by Jimmy Hill, fought to improve their wages. They felt that they should be paid for what they were worth like their Italian counterparts, rather than what the club chairman thought they could spare. British players were restricted to earning a maximum of £20 per week, and this was not good enough to compete with the endless lira the Italian clubs were offering. Because of this, top Italian clubs considered English players as prime targets. The Italian FA rules had just been changed to permit the import of foreign stars (each team could field a maximum of three foreign players), which sent the scouts and agents of the industry-sponsored Italian clubs scouring Britain and the world for new talent.

The episode ended as suddenly as it began, however, partly through yet another unpredictable swing in the Italian FA thinking and partly because history was about to be made which would change the face of British football forever.

Jimmy Hill had a four-year reign as union chairman, and it was a stormy yet very significant one. Within a couple of months of taking office in 1957, several Sunderland players refused to answer questions relating to 'under-the-counter' payments, and the FA suspended them permanently from football. It was the incident that was brought to light by allegations in Trevor Ford's serialised book in 1957 while the player was at Cardiff. The players challenged the FA head-on. They demanded an enquiry and started a petition among professionals, calling on all players who had received illegal monies to sign. They thought that so many people would own up that the FA would be forced to drop their charges against the Sunderland players. It proved to be a gamble that paid off. The Sunderland men were fined and allowed to play again, but later their fines were quashed. Furthermore, Trevor Ford later had his suspension lifted in 1960.

This scandal only made the union more determined than ever to smash the earning potential and the contracts that professional players were then subjected to. In 1961, backed by a 100 per cent strike ballot, Hill threatened to bring the game to a complete halt. Under intense pressure, the Football League conceded that, for the first time since the 19th century, players were free to earn whatever their clubs were prepared to pay them.

England captain Johnny Haynes, considered by some to be one of the finest players of his era, was of constant interest to other football clubs, which contributed to the pressure that led to the demise of the £20 per week maximum wage. Fulham chairman and comedian Tommy Trinder had boasted that Haynes was worth £100 a week, not expecting that the £20 pay cap would be abolished. Trinder's words backfired on him when the pay cap was removed. Trinder paid up without complaint to make Haynes the first footballer to earn £100 per week. Fulham famously turned down an offer of £80,000 from AC Milan for the player Pelé described as 'The Maestro' that would have been over double the record for a transfer at the time and would have made Haynes the best paid player in the world.

While it lasted, the Italian episode made lurid headlines, and a few of Britain's best players were tempted by the 'lure of the lira' and decided to fly to Italy to ply their trade. The episode left ill-feeling on both sides. English League clubs felt the

Italian promises of instant wealth had given players a deadly weapon in their fight for freedom of wage, while the Italians pointed out that some English players reneged on promises to play in Italy. 'The English players are bandits – all they think of is money', exclaimed one outraged Milan club owner. This seemed rich, since Italian players at that time had a reputation for greed.

Into this mix walked Gerry Hitchens, who was creating waves in Italy, especially after scoring 42 goals for Aston Villa and destroying the Italians on home soil in a friendly in Rome in May 1961. It was impossible for Gerry to resist the offer from such a prestigious Italian club like Internazionale and entry into the world of *calcio*. He had no ambitions whatsoever to move abroad before this episode in his life unfolded, and it happened so fast that there was hardly time to think about the 'what if's' or what the implications of going would be, but it was seen as an opportunity too good to turn down and one which may never have materialised again. He was not readily looking for fame or a luxury lifestyle – all he wanted was for his family to be comfortable and to play football. Financial security was vital to a 26-year-old man with a young family, but it was never the most important motivation for Gerry. Greed never played a part. He just was not that sort of person. He always believed it was a matter of personal choice, given the option to play in Italy. To him it was worth leaving a settled, familiar, ordinary English life to plunge himself and his family into a chaotic, Italian lifestyle in which he would earn amounts of money most ordinary people in Britain in the early 1960s could only dream of.

'My wife, Meriel, and I considered the whole thing very carefully, particularly from the family point of view, and the biggest decision we made was not so much to go there but to stick it and work hard to make it a success whatever happened. It is not the sort of life to suit everyone – the publicity, for example, is far worse than in England – and everyone must make up his own mind about it.'

'I wanted to see different places and play against different teams. A footballer's life is short. My ability had taken me a long way from the pits at Highley. I want to see just how far it will take me,' he said.

Internazionale wanted to make Gerry one of the costliest footballers in the world and were said to be offering a reported signing-on fee of around £10,000 (some newspapers stated that it was £12,500 or even £25,000), enough to buy an average player outright at that time and a three-year contract. The average wage on offer to Gerry was more than five times what Villa were willing to pay – and more than the Prime Minister earned.

All this for a quietly-spoken man, who had a reputation (from the press) of being little more than a centre-forward of the 'hustle-bustle' type. Who would have imagined that? Money was no object for a club like Internazionale, and they could afford to pay huge transfer fees, signing-on fees and even bigger salaries; however, Gerry was cautious about saying too much about the exact figures involved. 'A player negotiates his own contract and his earnings should be secret. It can cause bad feeling among the other members of the team if the figure is known.'

Gerry was brought in as a replacement for one of Inter's most outstanding goalscorers of the post-war era, the Argentinean, Antonio Valentín Angelillo, nicknamed 'the angel with the dirty face', who from 1957 to 1961 played 127 games with Internazionale, scoring on 77 occasions. Internazionale coach Helenio Herrera sold Angelillo to Roma for a reported 270 million lira, which was an enormous amount of money in 1961. Internazionale president Angelo Morratti could not resist the huge sums, although he did not want to sell Angelillo, but he was overpowered by Herrera.

There was one man who was behind most of the Anglo–Italian transfers at that time, and that was 'Gigi' Peronace. This shrewd and skilful tubby Italian was beginning to make a name for himself as the single biggest power in world football. With suitcases full of lira he would 'raid' British clubs on behalf of clubs such as Torino, Milan and Juventus and offer astronomical sums to snatch the top players away. A combined sum of nearly £200,000 prised away Joe Baker and Denis Law in the most fabulous transfer scoop of the decade. Others followed, like Toni Marchi from Tottenham and Jimmy Greaves from Chelsea. However, although Gerry knew Peronace, he was not behind his transfer to Internazionale. The biggest question was who would last the pace in Italy?

In 1960 Jimmy Greaves became the youngest ever player to score 100 League goals in English football at the age of 20. Just before the demise of the minimum wage fiasco in England in 1961, he was signed by European giants AC Milan from Chelsea, after reportedly turning down a huge offer from Newcastle United. This signing contributed to the demise of the minimum wage structure in the English League. The obvious reason why Jimmy went to Italy was the money. He was a huge star in England and was attracting the attention of the big clubs in Italy. It was said that Jimmy was offered a £15,000 signing-on fee and £130 a week plus bonuses and a 'free' flat. His club in England, Chelsea, were hard-up and needed the deal to survive; however, it appeared that Jimmy did not do his 'homework' before he agreed the contract.

When Greaves was signed by AC Milan and Inter had finally signed Hitchens, the red half of Milan boasted that their team had signed the better player. Greaves would have better supporting players at AC Milan in José Altafini, called the 'Brazilian Mazzola', who was said to be one of the world's most powerful and intelligent centre-forwards and the legendary playmaker and '*the Golden Boy*' of

Italian football, Gianni Rivera. But Greaves could not settle in Milan, and nor could his wife. She complained that she was being molested in the streets, and he was outraged about the club discipline, which even extended to regulating its married players' sex lives. Although his form was good, his relations with the club and the manager, Nereo Rocco, grew steadily worse. He was also a victim of a scurrilous campaign in the Italian media and was persecuted by journalists who dogged every step of this 'reluctant guest', as the paparazzi described him.

When Meriel and Gerry arrived at Milan airport for his medical they were treated to a VIP welcome. Senior club officials were there to greet the couple, with luxury cars waiting for them at the airport to pick them up and whisk them off to a temporary luxury hotel. On 20 June 1961 Gerry travelled with Meriel to Inter's training camp at San Pellegrino, where he was given a thorough check – heart, lungs, bones, muscles, reflections, eyesight, hearing – everything was checked. It was a bizarre day as none of the Inter staff spoke English. Only the doctor's wife spoke English, but she was sick and had to leave shortly after arriving. Meriel made herself understood by speaking in French to the club doctor, while the professor spoke to the doctor in Italian and the doctor replied to Meriel in French. As Meriel had an understanding of French and had been practising a little Italian before they arrived in Milan, she ended up translating as much as she could understand for Gerry, as he could not speak French or Italian. Gerry passed the medical, and the deal was completed on the same day. Gerry Hitchens was officially an Internazionale player. The signing-on fee was banked, and Gerry had no regrets.

Soon after he arrived in Milan with Meriel he was joined by their two children, Marcus, who was two, and Nicola, who was six months old. The club quickly found them an apartment in the exclusive Hotel Rosa (now called Starhotels Rosa), which was an elegant and refined hotel set in a privileged location in the heart of Old Milan, overlooking Piazza Fontana near the famous Duomo, while the surroundings were filled with some of the most celebrated attractions in Milan. The Rosa was the most expensive hotel in the city, where steaks cost £1.10 and bed and breakfast was £5 per night. 'Fortunately, the club are paying,' said Gerry. His first impressions of Italy were good. 'Things are better that I expected. The food is wonderful, and we live like lords – what more could a man want? I wanted the best possible standard of living for my wife and children'.

Marcus quickly became the darling of the hotel staff during their short stay at the hotel as they found themselves a more permanent home in downtown Milan. At a rough estimate, Gerry thought it was costing the club around £10 a day to keep them at the hotel – almost a week's wages of an English footballer at the time. 'We shall move into a suitable five-room flat in downtown Viale Romagna within a few weeks,' said an expectant Meriel. 'Viale Romagna is just one of the largest avenues in town. It is lined with big trees. We are looking forward to living there.'

He knew by moving to Italy that his chances of improving on his (then) three England caps might be in jeopardy as the England selectors had never chosen a player who played football on foreign soil before. At the time there were two schools of thought: there were those who thought that Hitchens was the best man for the job and then there were those who wanted to stick to the home-based players who had been utilised before. With many of the top footballers joining the 'foreign legion' during this period, including Jimmy Greaves and Joe Baker, the selectors needed to change their policy and move with the times. 'I knew that I might be ruining my chances of ever playing again for England, but as long as my wife was willing to go I felt it was too good a chance to turn down. I don't know why I shouldn't be considered for the England team. Just because I have come out here I hope they don't forget me. I would think Continental experience is an asset to any England player,' said Gerry. Little did he know that nearly two years later this would become a major issue.

Even though he had only been in Milan a matter of days, people were already asking Gerry about his future, whether he could see himself and the family settle in Italy or elsewhere. 'I may decide to stay in Italy, or I may decide to return to England or possibly go elsewhere. One thing is certain. I have no regrets about coming here. It was the most sensible decision I have ever made,' he said.

Gerry quickly became well known to the Milanese public, and every time he stepped out of the hotel he was recognised (probably because of his blond hair and his dressed-to-kill designer suits), ' 'Ullo 'itchens' or 'Meester Itching' or simply 'Jerree' they shouted excitedly to their hero as they thrust paper and pen into his hands for an autograph. One fan once shouted, ' 'itchens, sei il piu simpatico!' ('Hitchens, you're the nicest!'). Even taking the children for a walk in a local park proved intrusive, as photographers normally begged Gerry to pose with them for pictures, but Gerry being a pleasant and good-natured person always obliged. The fans not only knew his footballing background but also knew the names of his wife and children; however, he loved being a hero, even though he could not go anywhere in private. To Gerry it seemed that everybody in Milan was a football fan. They either supported AC Milan or Internazionale, and nobody supported any other Italian teams. He was receiving the adulation normally reserved for popstars, and his fans were men, women and children of all ages. Often, crowds would surround the family, some would talk, while others would just stare. Gerry and Meriel found it embarrassing at first, but it was something else to get used to that was different to how things were back home, 'Everywhere I go in Milan I'm given this film star treatment. It's amazing how many people recognise me. I suppose it's because of my fair hair? Of course it means you're in the spotlight all the time.' He had only just got used to being an 'idol' at Aston Villa but to a much lesser extent. Welcome to football Italian style!

Long before the WAGs appeared on the football scene, Meriel enjoyed watching her famous husband play the game he loved every week, sitting in the stands in rain, cold, snow or blistering heat. It could be said that Meriel and Gerry were a predecessor to 'Posh and Becks', but without the circus cavalcade, tattoos and the limitless amounts of money. They were a glamorous couple in the eyes of the Italian media – Gerry with his rugged good looks, blond hair and designer suits and Meriel, the beautiful, dark-haired lady with the Jackie Onassis looks, by his side. There is a saying which goes, 'Behind every great man, there is a great woman', and with Gerry and Meriel this was definitely the case. Even though Gerry was a success on the pitch, Meriel was the influence behind their success as a couple, and it was a great partnership in every way. Not only a beautiful lady and a strong person, she was a mother of two lovely children at the time they moved to Milan and had plans for more. They always had plans for a big family and now, with the riches that came with Gerry's career, it was no longer a dream. It was clear that a lot of thought had gone into making their decision, but it was made jointly and it had the blessing of both families. They were determined to make good and take the opportunity with both hands and enjoy themselves in the process.

After living in the Rosa for several weeks, they moved to a luxury apartment in downtown Milan. Gerry commented, 'I have a luxury flat on Milan's Via Romagna, a not too big, fully automatic American car [a white 1961 Chevrolet Corvair Monza which cost £1,500] and a stack of clothes.' Living in Milan meant living in the city, which solved one problem for Meriel, and that was that it made shopping easier. There was a supermarket quite near to their flat that sold everything that the family required.

Gerry liked his clothes and his cars. When he was searching for a new car in Milan, he was asked by one dealer if he would be photographed at the side of a car in exchange for up to 50 per cent discount. Gerry accepted being photographed but did not buy the car. He liked to drive pretty fast – like most Italian drivers do – so he felt quite at home in busy downtown Milan, where every journey was a breathtaking experience of near misses.

A typical daily routine was beginning to develop for the family: Meriel employed a girl to help with the cleaning, but she was not used to having staff and still did her own shopping. Their apartment was on the seventh floor, and on the ground floor was a butcher's, which was very convenient and sold beautifully lean and delicious red meat, which was so cheap that Meriel had been buying it in bulk for some time. Little did Meriel know, until her cleaner told her several weeks later, it was horsemeat. After discovering that she never went to that butchers again.

Gerry would normally meet Meriel for lunch after training, and they would initially go to different restaurants and try to get to know the different areas of Milan. On one occasion they went to the best fish restaurant in Milan, which used to have tanks full of fish – something that Meriel was not used to – so that customers could choose their own fish to eat. One day they went there and Meriel chose mussels, but when she got home she had food poisoning and was extremely ill. Not surprisingly, they never went back to that restaurant either.

There were constant reports back home that the Hitchens family were already 'homesick', even though they had only been in Milan for a matter of weeks. Meriel, the tall and graceful girl from the valleys, whose name alone had charmed the Italians, denied the reports, 'Homesick? No!' There were also suggestions that foreign players were 'unwelcome', but Gerry saw no evidence of that, in fact quite the opposite. After all, there were English, Scottish, Welsh, Argentinean and Danish players in Serie A at the time. For Meriel, it was another new experience as she had never been abroad with Gerry before, although she had spent holidays in France, Switzerland and Italy with her parents. She said, 'I was looking forward to living in Italy. There is only one thing I miss here – those nice back gardens where my children could play. Marcus used to play there,' referring to their house in Birmingham.

Gerry missed his former Villa teammates, particularly close friends like Nigel Sims and Jimmy Dugdale, and kept in touch with them by letter for a while. Meriel herself enjoyed the Italian lifestyle. 'Life is faster here. Everybody is in a hurry. Traffic gives you the impression that every driver wants to beat a world speed record' she said.

An obvious pleasure to anyone visiting or living in Italy has to the food – the olive oil, fresh vegetables, basil, cheeses, fresh breads and of course the coffee are all symbols of *Cucina Italiana,* 'Italian foods are excellent. The way they cook meats is first-class. I go shopping sometimes, and I find that textiles and fashions are just a little more expensive than in England, but the quality of Italian products is really good.'

When someone moves to another country where the language is different then there will be an obvious problem, but Gerry and Meriel made every effort to learn Italian by using the language records bought back in England and picking up odd words and phrases here and there. Whereas Denis Law thought that the Italians should learn how to speak English (or Scottish), Gerry was going about it the right way and integrating into Milanese society, and the locals appreciated his enthusiasm to learn. 'Probably Gerry will have more time to study it. I have two children, and I would hardly find any time to attend a school, but if I can have a chance, I will do it,' said Meriel. Both Gerry and Meriel loved watching films, and it was a surprise to them that one Milan cinema showed films in their original language, which meant that most films shown were in English. At first, there were pangs of loneliness that come about in a country where you cannot read the menu or simply nip down the road for a pint with your mates; however, it was not long before both Gerry and Meriel were proficient in Italian, learning new words daily, and on the whole the language barrier did not present much of a problem after a good few months. It is said that the most effective way to improve your speaking skills is to travel to the country where your new language is spoken and stay there for as long as you can. If nobody around you speaks your own tongue, you can improve very fast and get a first-hand experience of what and how people really speak in their everyday lives. 'Now I find I can understand most of what is said to me. It's talking to other people that's not so easy. Already, I can get the gist of what they are talking about, and I reckon that with a couple of month's constant use, I shall become fairly fluent,' Gerry said. He admitted that it was mainly trying to pronounce his teammates' names that was the problem and knowing the Italian for such terms as 'hold it' or 'pass it'.

Meriel quickly noticed that when she was out in Milan with Gerry men would stare at her incessantly. 'There is nothing wrong or impolite in their behaviour, at least as far as the Milanese are concerned.' At first, Meriel had only one friend in Milan, a British lady of the same age with whom she talked to now and then. 'When I pick up the language, I would like to meet a number of Italian ladies and I am also looking forward to meeting some members of the British colony in Milan,' she said. They later joined the British American Club, a kind of expats club, and were soon becoming friendly with several American couples and often went out into the country for barbecues and went out to dinner together.

Only a few years before Gerry had signed, Internazionale had won back-to-back Italian Championships (*scudetto*) in 1953 and 1954, but the club and its fans were desperate for a repeat of that success and had high hopes for the 1960–61 season. The great Argentinean coach, the flamboyant, autocratic and egocentric manager, Helenio Herrera, was brought in from Spanish giants FC Barcelona in 1960, where he had managed a team who won back-to-back Spanish League titles in 1959 and 1960 to become the best-paid manager in world football. Herrera had encountered several problems at Barcelona, including disagreements between him and star player Ladislao Kubala, a Hungarian–Slovak striker with an incredible goalscoring record. He had a major argument with Herrera and compelled his coach to leave the club. And so he did.

Herrera had a relatively modest career as a player, spending most of it playing for small French sides. By the time he had arrived in Milan he was 51 years old and had already managed nine clubs within a space of 15 years in France and Spain, including the likes of Athètico Madrid, Deportivo de la Coruña, Sevilla and, of course, Barcelona. With a pedigree like that he was destined to become not only one of the most successful but also one of the most influential managers in the history of the game. Herrera had definite pedigree and was nicknamed '*il Mago*' (the Wizard) or 'H.H.' (from the initials of his name) by Italian sports journalists, who recognised him as one of the finest coaches around. He was known as 'The Wizard' because of his uncanny habit of predicting the results of Sunday's games.

Herrera had an unorthodox management style and some would say a bizarre personality, but he was strong and successful and that was all that mattered to the billionaire (lira) oil tycoon and club president, Angelo Moratti. Herrera knew how to play the media, which was an important trait if you wanted to be a successful coach in Italy in the 1960s. He was famed for his pep-talk phrases, which are still quoted today. Statements such as, 'who doesn't give it all, gives nothing' or 'with 10 our team plays better than with 11' (after his team had to face the second half of a game with only 10 players on the field). Psychology was the key for Herrera's strategy. He would order his players with his relentless voice exhorting them early on a Monday morning after an away game, 'Think of next Sunday, think of the game!' when all the players wanted to do was to see their family. He said that his team would, 'win without getting on the bus.' He was known to write slogans on the dressing room walls like:

Classe + Preparazione
Atletica + Intelligenza
= SCUDETTO

In English: *Class + training + intelligence = the Championship*. This was mocked or dismissed by some players, but for Herrera it worked and brought the results. He also enforced a strict discipline code, forbidding players to drink or smoke, and he also controlled their diet. On one occasion he suspended a player after telling the press 'we came to play in Rome' instead of 'we came to win in Rome'. He was also one of the first coaches to call the support of the '12th player' – the spectators.

Moratti and Herrera together revolutionised *calcio* in many ways. They institutionalised rigid, militaristic training regimes and brought in a style of play, while defensive in nature, that was a take on the '*catenaccio*' system but slightly different to that practised by other Italian teams and the original '*verrou*', as he often used the full-backs as wing-backs (defensively supported by the '*libero*') to launch faster counter-attacks, a staple of Italian tactics. However, he never denied that the heart of his team relied on the defence. It has been said that Herrera claimed to have devised the '*catenaccio*' system, calling it, 'a tactical system which I invented.'

He was also the first coach to collect credit for his teams' performances. Up to that time coaches were the more marginal figures of a team. All teams were known for their headline-grabbing individual players, epiomised by such a star like 'Di Stéfano's Real Madrid', whereas Internazionale during the 60s were still referred to as 'Herrera's Inter'.

This 1961–62 Inter team boasted top-class footballers like Luis Suárez Miramontes, football legend, captain of Spain and at £175,000, the world's costliest footballer and regarded by some as Spain's greatest-ever player. Known for his perceptive passing and explosive shot, Suárez was voted European Footballer of the Year in 1960 and when he joined Internazionale he was at the top of his game. The Spanish genius had shortly followed Herrera from Barcelona to become his first major signing of the campaign.

Inter were building for the future and the side that Gerry was joining also included such up-and-coming names as the statuesque defender, Giacinto Facchetti, who was a truly great attacking full-back, and Mario Corso (nicknamed 'Mariolino' or 'God's left foot'), the midfielder who spent much of the game motionless, but sprang into life at the right moment and was famed for his beautiful left-footed free-kicks and crosses.

The first real issue that the Hitchens couple had to face was to be away from each other for several weeks while Gerry and his new Inter teammates held their pre-season training camp in the spa town of San Pellegrino, where the famous San Pellegrino brand of mineral water is produced and bottled at San Pellegrino Terme, in the Province of Bergamo, Lombardy, Northern Italy, about 90 minutes away from Milan. The club enforced a strict 'no wives' rule until the camp had finished in mid-August so Meriel flew back to Britain and to her family in South Wales.

Not quite used to the strict regime Herrera was running at Internazionale, Gerry soon found himself in trouble and was fined by the club when they were on a pre-season training camp because he missed the bus to take the players back to their camp, 'Someone blew a whistle and we had to trot back to the coach waiting to take us back to our training camp. I was with [Luis] Suárez and one or two others, about 200 yards behind the main group. The first lot reached the bus, jumped inside; the door was slammed, and off the coach went. We were left stranded and had to thumb a lift back. No one said a word about the incident. We had a little note in our pay packets, explaining why they were £3 light. I am not complaining. I shall not be missing the bus again.'

Just before a pre-season friendly game against Real Madrid, the Inter players went out for the night to a bull ring in Madrid and decided to send the 'new boy' out to try his luck as a matador in what became a famous incident. There he was, one of the costliest footballers in Italy, dressed in a designer suit trying to tame a young black bull in the middle of a bull ring. Gerry seemed to enjoy it, although the bull was a bit confused. There were minders all round him making sure he did not get injured as he fought with the bull, and fortunately, no harm was done to Gerry or the bull.

'The whole thing started as a joke, but someone prodded the young bull, and it charged madly towards me. Now I know why big-time matadors are so highly paid. I've known a few centre-halves who treated me worse,' he said. The incident made the news in the papers the following day.

Gerry played his part in the match as he scored a goal in a 2–2 draw at the Estadio Chamartín (the Estadio Santiago Bernabéu) against an all-star Real Madrid side, which contained the legendary Ferenc Puskás and Alfredo di Stéfano Laulhé. Soon after Herrera had signed Hitchens from Villa, he used him as a lethal striking weapon. In his first month at Inter he scored eight goals in six friendly matches during the pre-season and two Serie A matches. Although Gerry did not speak Italian (or Spanish for that matter) and his teammates did not speak English, they all communicated on the field in the international language of football, 'We get along tremendously, and the crowds. I've never know anything like it.'

What fortuneteller could have thought that Gerry Archibald Hitchens, a former miner from a small village in Shropshire, would one day grace the football fields of Italy, live a privileged lifestyle in the fashion capital of Europe and would quickly become an Italian football star? Gerry could hardly believe it himself. At last, it seemed that Internazionale had a new hero. It is fair to say he was far from the best player '*i Neroazzurri*' have ever had (or ever will have).

The start of the new Serie A 1961–62 season got off to a flying start and who could have imagined such a scoreline:

Internazionale 6   Atalanta 0

It was Gerry's debut in Serie A and for Internazionale, but it was like he had been part of the team for years. Twenty-eight minutes into the game, with the score at 1–0 to Inter through Mario Corso, Hitchens scored his first-ever League goal for his new club. He also scored the fourth just before half-time. Two more goals through striker Lorenzo Bettini made the victory even sweeter and crowned a superb debut. He was an instant hero. Two goals in his very first Serie A game at home in the San Siro. Who could have written a script like that?

If that was not enough to whet the Inter fans' appetite, then the next game was also a thriller. Inter were at Roma, and Hitchens again found the net to open the scoring for Inter after only 13 minutes. Pestrin equalised for Roma after the break, only for Luis Suárez to put Inter back into the lead. Roma again equalised shortly after, only for Bettini to win the game 3–2 for Inter with 20 minutes to go.

A succession of draws was followed by another high-scoring game against an up-and-coming Fiorentina side, who had won the Coppa Italia by beating Lazio in the Final and the European Cup-Winners' Cup (against Rangers) in the previous season. Mario Corso opened the scoring for Inter, with Luis Suárez making it 2–0 on the half hour. It was then that Gerry entered the Inter fans' hearts by grabbing two goals within three minutes to make it 4–0 at half-time. Picchi grabbed a late consolation for Fiorentina, but it was another great day for Inter and for Gerry.

With five goals in the first five games in Italian football the Milanese public quickly took to Gerry and described him as '*il cannone*' (the cannon). It must have been the staying power he got from working down the mine. The headline in *Gazzetta dello Sport* read:

HITCHENS è un CANNONE

A Milanese newspaper described Hitchens as the 'Prince of football', with the headline:

IL PRINCIPE del GIOCO del CALCIO

When he first moved to Inter, Gerry used to sit through Signor Herrera's tactical talks without understanding a word. Fortunately, H.H. spoke some English, and he was able to explain what he wanted him to do. It must have worked – five goals in five games. What must it be like in modern football teams, where there may be half a dozen different languages spoken by the players, let alone the coach?

As a centre-forward, Gerry was used to scoring many goals at his previous clubs as he was one of two strikers, but in Italy the centre-forward is usually the lone man up-field when the rest of the team are defending. It called for patience on Gerry's part, but it was clearly working as Inter were top of the League after five games with eight points.

Another victory came against Padova, with Mario Corso grabbing two goals. Then came the big derby game with AC Milan, the 'derby della Madonnina'. This game was a fairly historical occasion as it brought together not only two friends playing on opposing sides but also two of England's most lethal strikers in Jimmy Greaves and Gerry Hitchens. Both players had notched up five goals each for their respective clubs since being transferred in the summer, so the derby was built up as a battle of the two great English strikers.

In stark contrast to Gerry, who had settled into life in Milan with ease, Jimmy Greaves had reportedly asked AC Milan chief Andrea Rizzoli to be released from his contract less than 48 hours before the 'derby della Madonnina' on 1 October 1961, the biggest fixture in the Italian football calendar. He complained that if he stayed he would be washed out and finished before the season was out. 'They do not play my kind of football in Italy,' Jimmy said. He also remarked that he was not a physical player like John Charles or Gerry Hitchens. Jimmy did play in the game, however, and scored the second of three for AC Milan in a 3–1 victory over their bitterest of rivals. It was a score that Inter just did not need if they were to make a serious challenge for the scudetto.

The next two games saw victories for Inter against Spal and against Udinese, in which Hitchens scored what ended up being the winner in the fourth minute. In the game against champions Juventus, Hitchens came up against another British import in the great John Charles. Italian football was in love with British players in the early 1960s, and John Charles was the 'King' of them all, the gentleman of British footballers. He was the famous Welsh striker who had never been cautioned or sent off during his entire career, due to his philosophy of never kicking or intentionally hurting opposing players. Standing at 6ft 2in, he was nicknamed 'il Gigante Buono' (The Good Giant). The Juventus team, including Charles, had won three scudetti in four seasons and had just won their 12th in the club's history during the 1960–61 season. He formed part of a lethal partnership with Omar Sivori and Giampiero Boniperti.

In the match at the Stadio Olimpico in Turin it must have been written in the stars that Gerry Hitchens was to open the scoring, with John Charles equalising shortly after in the 20th minute. With the game all-square at half-time, Luis Suárez put Inter ahead, only to be cancelled out by a strike from Nicolè. Lorrenzo Bettini scored two late goals to seal a 4–2 away victory for the Milan side.

Gerry's next goal came several weeks later against Vicenza in a 2–1 win at the San Siro, which secured Inter's top spot in Serie A with more than a third of the season gone.

Off the pitch, Gerry was continuing to settle into life in Italy pretty well. After several months of trying to understand Helenio Herrera's team-talks, he was beginning to work out what was being said and went on to the field knowing exactly what was expected of him. You would not have thought he could not speak the language when he was on the pitch in those first 14 games, as he had scored eight goals. He also had to get used to the irritating shirt pulling, body-checking and obstruction which was associated with the Italian game. Gerry was fined the equivalent of £5 early into his Inter career for apparently swearing at a referee when in fact he was trying to complain about being jostled by the opposition.

Although Gerry was happy with his life under Herrera, he became disheartened by the 'ritiro', the system whereby Italian clubs whisk their players away to a country retreat on the Friday before a game and keep them there until the Sunday evening, or even the Monday morning. It was designed to condition the players mentally, as well as physically, in order to prepare for the match ahead. The bombastic Helenio Herrera was keen to isolate his players in this way. Given that most Italian League matches were played on a Sunday, weekends proved to be very long indeed.

There was another former British player at Inter at the same time as Gerry: Eddie Firmani was signed by Sampdoria in 1955 from Charlton Athletic for £35,000, which at the time was a record transfer fee involving a British club. This began an eight-year spell in Italy, where he gained three caps for the Italian national team (even though he was born in South Africa), qualifying for the national team as his grandfather was Italian (hence the Italian surname). He was then transferred to Internazionale in 1958 and like Gerry, Firmani, who had the malevolent nickname 'tacchino freddo' (the cold turkey), did not share Herrera's partiality for the eternal 'ritiro' system and clashed with him while playing for Inter.

The training camps were tough, and the fans never got to see this side of the player's preparation as it was usually staged away from the public arena. It was like being back in the army, but to former Corporal Hitchens this was a breeze. However, life as a footballer in Italy was no holiday, and there were strict rules given to the players like:

Bed every night (except Monday) by 10pm.

Sleep every afternoon from 2pm to 3.30pm.

Drink no alcohol other than the watered wine or occasional weak beer provided by the club at mealtimes.

Smoke no more than two cigarettes a day.

A player will be fined if he arrives a minute late for training (10am).

Frank instructions are given to married men.

Although the monetary rewards were great and life was like a pot of gold, full of glamour and gleaming new cars, it was also a life of drudgery, self-denial and iron discipline. There was a phrase that rang true for all footballers who tasted Italian football and stuck at it:

Comply – play well…and Italian soccer will line your pockets for life.

Defy – play up … and the honey-tongued men who hired you will fire you without so much as a handshake at the end of your contract.

The club did not believe in hours and hours of training, and normal sessions rarely lasted longer than an hour and a half. Concentration was the key, and slacking was not tolerated.

In a period when it was not frowned upon for footballers to smoke and drink, it was Herrera's challenge to change the 'whiskey and grappa' culture that existed in Italian football. A lot of players had a problem with the discipline code and did not like the '*ritiro*', but contrary to the general feelings among players Gerry was very philosophical about the preparation methods, although it was still alien to him: 'We play on Sundays and I train every morning with the team. After that my time is my own. As far as I am concerned, the reports that clubs are over-strict are a lot of rubbish. Obviously, there must be some restrictions, and the night before the match we stay in another hotel and go to bed early. But I don't think that is over-strict. After all, we are paid good money to be in tip-top condition.'

Gerry continued, 'It's not all that bad, and you can't grumble much when you consider the cash that's pouring into your bank account. Before the start of the season we are all whipped away for several weeks' special training away in the mountains near the Yugoslav border. But the players could take their families, and the only reason my wife missed the trip was to see that our furniture had arrived safely. True, we have to leave our families on the Friday before Sunday's game, and spend a couple of days together in the hotel, but it's just one of those things that you have to accept. After all, there are plenty of jobs which involve going away for months.'

Meriel described Herrera as 'nice enough', but it took time for her to get used to Gerry being away for long periods, especially for away games. The wives and girlfriends were allowed to spend mealtimes with their partners, but at 10pm the coach would order the wives and girlfriends away, 'Mrs 'Itchens, 'ome, 'ome,' as he pointed towards the exit. Meriel took no notice the first time he would 'order' her away, but he would come round again pointing, 'Mrs 'Itchens, 'ome, 'ome.' Not being told what to do, Meriel would again let him have his say and take no notice of the great man. After a few weeks, he understood he was never going to win this 'battle' with Mrs Hitchens and 'allowed' Meriel to stay longer, but always gave her 'the look'. Herrera was a soft touch after all!

Reflecting on life in Italian football, Gerry told a Birmingham newspaper, 'The thing I miss most about English football is scoring so many goals. Last season I cracked home 42 for Villa, but I'll be lucky indeed if I get half that many in the Italian League. A lot of the football out here is defensive stuff. It's not the 4–2–4 line ups that worry us, it's the 10–1 system. Yes, you often find 10 men playing defensive roles, leaving just one isolated forward up-field. Goals are like gold.' He was sometimes puzzled by certain aspects of Italian football, like the relegation rules for example. In those days, when one club got relegated to Serie B, they went down with a handicap, 'One club who dropped down last season began this campaign minus 10 points.' Gerry also suggested that the Italian League was not as good as the top English League, but was more difficult to score in. At the time, Internazionale were top of Serie A and Gerry was top scorer with eight goals. The top League scorer had only 10.

On 1 November 1961, after only a few months in Italy, Gerry was chosen to play an Inter-League friendly match for the Italian League against the Scottish League at Hampden Park, which ended in a 1–1 draw in front of a crowd of 67,996, and Hitchens scored the opening goal for the Italian League. He was not the only Briton in the starting line up for the Italian League All-Stars as he teamed up with Denis Law and John Charles. A week later, Gerry again teamed up with his British counterparts, including Law, Baker and Firmani, to play for the Italian League against the English League at Old Trafford, Manchester. The game ended with the Italian team winning 2–0.

Gerry's trusted friend Jimmy Greaves was continuing to feel the strain at AC Milan. Under Nereo Rocco, Jimmy felt like a little boy lost. He thought the Italian game was 'spiteful and vicious' and detested every second of his 14-game, nine-goal career and later blamed the experience for turning him into an alcoholic. He obviously was not 'advised' before his transfer that players were expected to go to the pre-game '*ritiro*', where wives were forbidden and attendance was mandatory, or that he would be unable to go out at night, drinking, or be seen in the city's nightclubs. Although Jimmy was only 21 years old at the time, he did not realise that life at an Italian club was no 'party' and that players were often spat at, poked and provoked, on and off the pitch.

He also complained at always being in the Italian press and spent the whole time 'on the run'. Years later he described the dictatorial Rocco as being 'like Mario Puzo's Godfather' and claimed, 'the Italian press murdered me. They could not have done a better assassination job had they been given a contract by the Mafia.' Jimmy was paid a fortune, but lost a lot of his money to fines as Rocco vainly attempted to get him to observe the strict Italian codes of sporting behaviour – no booze, no sex before matches, tough training camps and obedience to the coach at all times. Greaves refused to be, as he saw it, 'just another sheep in his flock of highly paid but unhappy footballers'. Rocco despaired of Greaves's late-night carousing, one night apparently nailing his hotel door shut with planks of wood. It failed to work as Jimmy repeatedly climbed out of his window three storeys up and crept along a narrow ledge while his coach waited downstairs watching the main exit.

One comfort for Jimmy was that he met up with his mate Gerry in secret at Milan's railway station for a beer on several occasions. It seemed the most unlikely of places to meet, but the railway station had a room at the back of the buffet bar that was safe from the prying eyes of the media, the public and most of all, their clubs. It was not the done thing for players of opposing city clubs to be socialising with each other, and the consumption of alcohol was definitely frowned upon by AC Milan officials. Gerry was never as relaxed as Jimmy about having a drink, but both players enjoyed their rendezvous, and it was a chance for them to talk about Jimmy's sorrows of living and playing in Milan.

On one occasion the pair must have been spotted by the paparazzi, and Gerry said, 'before I left with the Italian League team for England a few weeks ago I had a quiet drink with Jimmy Greaves. We had only a couple of drinks – yet the next morning it was plastered right across one newspaper. But by and large, it's only one paper that goes in for this sort of story.'

With their cover blown and after a few of their 'cloak and dagger' meetings, Gerry told Jimmy that he would not be able to meet him again for fear of the consequences if they were ever caught by club officials. It was not the news that Jimmy wanted to hear, as he enjoyed their chats over a pint or two, but he understood the reason.

The situation at AC Milan finally came to a head when Greaves received a letter from the club refusing him permission to play for England as a disciplinary measure, even though the club had promised him he could take part in internationals when he signed for them. Greaves was so adamant that he wanted to leave *il Rossoneri* that the club backed down and allowed him to play for his country. Although Jimmy played well for AC Milan and had a good scoring record of nine goals in his 12 matches, he was eventually transferred to Bill Nicholson's Tottenham Hotspur for an unusual fee of £99,999, on 19 November 1961. The sum was decided upon because Spurs did not want him labelled as Britain's first £100,000 player. Typical of Jimmy, he scored a hat-trick for Tottenham on his debut at White Hart Lane. AC Milan had no idea what they were missing.

Gerry himself was surprised by the unhappiness Jimmy experienced during his sad and sorry four-month spell in Milan. He was so content in his own life, on and off the pitch, that he was upset for his friend and puzzled why such a great player had had these bad experiences.

Italian football supporters have always been on the verge of fanatical. Often several thousand turn up for practice games and cheer wildly when a goal is scored by one their heroes. When teams arrived back from (victorious) away trips there were sometimes a few hundred fans waiting to welcome them home, even in the early hours of the morning. Gerry remarked, 'when I scored three goals in the friendly with Dynamo Kiev [from Russia], the Internazionale fans went mad with delight. Several hundred of them were waiting for me outside the ground. I was lifted into the air and chaired around like some conquering hero.' His playing style and goalscoring were catching the eyes of those soccer-mad Italians, and one commentator went as far as saying that Gerry was 'one of the best players ever seen on an Italian football field.'

The run-in towards the Christmas period would prove crucial for Inter's chances of securing their first *scudetto* for eight seasons. In the home game against Bologna, Inter went one down after only nine minutes, but Hitchens equalised a quarter of an hour later. The scoring continued in a 10-goal thriller, with Hitchens grabbing his second to equalise in the second half to make it 4–4. Egidio Morbello, the Internazionale striker, made sure of victory by scoring two late goals to secure two points in a 6–4 win to keep Inter top of the League. By mid-January 1962, Inter were still top with 31 points, despite a few defeats and draws, but Gerry was having a dry spell in terms of goals and had not scored for six weeks since the 6–4 win against Bologna. He soon hit form again in the home game against Mantova and scored the opening goal in a 2–0 win.

In February 1962, Gerry, accompanied by Meriel and other British players including Eddie Firmani, was invited to a high-class function by the British Chamber of Commerce in Milan. Among the other guests was the legendary car designer Sergio Pininfarina, who Meriel was lucky enough to have met on several occasions. The Honorary Vice President at the time was Sir James Henderson, a British businessman who started as a 15-year-old apprentice at J & P Coats in 1897 (now the world's largest sewing thread and needlecraft supplies manufacturer, processor and distributor) and was transferred to start up Coats in Italy after World War One. He also founded the British Chamber of Commerce and the first Rotary Club in Italy. Sir James was very well respected in Milan, and he gave a speech on the evening of the function which included a piece about football and footballers. He described the British contingent in Italy as 'ambassadors of Britain', rather than merely 'British football players playing in Italy' or 'exports'. Gerry and Meriel were subsequently invited to several other functions held by Sir James during their stay in Milan.

Incidentally, a few years later, in 1969, the Sir James Henderson British School of Milan was founded by British parents who wanted to provide a British education for their children (as fate would have it, the children of Gerry's eldest daughter, Nicola, have all attended the school in Milan).

On the field Inter were brought down to earth with a bang, and their title credentials were severely tested by a great Fiorentina side, who Inter had already beaten 4–1 in September. This time around it was the 'Violas' who were on the goal trail as they beat Inter 4–1, with Aurelio Milani scoring a hat-trick to knock Inter off the top spot for the first time in the season and taking the Tuscan side top of Serie A.

A win against Padova saw Hitchens grab a goal after only one minute, and in the return derby game against AC Milan a week later Inter clinched victory by 2–0 against their city rivals. Two weeks later, Hitchens scored again in a 2–0 victory over Udinese, and he scored his 14th goal of the season in the 2–2 draw against John Charles's Juventus. The draw proved critical for Inter's season as it saw them only a point behind Fiorentina.

The run-in to the end of the season proved too much for Inter, and defeat at Palermo and three consecutive draws saw Inter fall into fourth place, behind Bologna, Fiorentina and AC Milan in top spot. Gerry's contribution in the away wins at Bologna and Catania drew the attention of the England selectors, who voted unanimously to pick him for the forthcoming World Cup in Chile. He scored against Catania and had five other shots brilliantly saved. In the last game of the season Inter clinched runners'-up spot by beating Lecco 3–0, with Hitchens, remarkably, scoring in the last two minutes of the game to leave them five points behind their city rivals. After the match Gerry was mobbed by around 500 fans while he attempted to exit the stadium. Herrara said of his top scorer, 'He's the outstanding forward in the Italian League this season.' He finished the season (joint) second-highest scorer in Italian football with 16 goals, just behind AC Milan's prolific Brazilian striker José João Altafini and Fiorentina's Aurelio Milani, who finished the season as joint top scorers (*Capocannoniere*) with 22 League goals each.

Jimmy Greaves missed out on a successful campaign, even though AC Milan left it late to win their eighth *scudetto*. Those AC Milan fans who said that their team had signed the better player early on in the season were now eating their words. Even though AC Milan had won the title, it was the Inter fans who were now boasting, 'We had the better bargain, and Gerry wants to stay.'

The amount of money that was on offer was obviously a big factor in Gerry settling down quickly, but that went with the job. 'Apart from the signing-on fee which has made my future nice and secure, I am far better off financially than I could possibly be in England, even under "The New Deal". Bonus money varies according to the strength of the opposition, but the club has announced that next season the bonus for a win will be at least £100,' said Gerry.

Gerry's first season at Internazionale was a resounding success in terms of goals scored, and he led the goalscoring charts out of the British contingent in Italy. He had notched up 16 goals for *i Neroazzurri*, while Greaves had scored nine in the few months he was at AC Milan. Meanwhile, Denis Law scored 10 for Torino, Joe Baker seven for Torino and John Charles eight for Juventus. It was a great testament to Gerry, who went about his task quietly while other players were fighting and arguing with their clubs. The question about who would last the pace was finally answered after only the first hurdle.

His first season at Inter was over, and it had proved to be a steep learning curve for both Gerry and for Meriel, who had to settle their family into a new life. Being a positive person, Gerry only had good things to say about his new club. He felt at home in Italy and had settled in well. Even though life as a footballer in Italy was so different. He found the Italian fans to be extremely partisan, and their mindset was quite unlike anything back home. Weeks before Inter's games with the likes of AC Milan, Roma or Juventus, fans would work themselves into a frenzy, the rivalry was that fierce. Then on match days the atmosphere would be so tense, unlike anything in England at the time. When a player had a good game it would result in hundreds of fans waiting outside the players' exit to give the player the hero's treatment, but if they had a bad game, the fans would turn on their heroes and show their frustration and anger. Italian fans were fickle to say the least.

At the end of the season the family made a decision to return home for the summer to visit their families in Britain. It was hot in Italy in the summer, especially in Milan, where the average summer temperatures reached 30 degrees celsuis or more, together with the humidity and the stifling smog in the city. In April 1962 an international soccer doping row was boiling up and sent temperatures sky high for all the wrong reasons. Having being selected for the forthcoming World Cup in Chile, Gerry, along with other Italian League players, was being accused of having taken dope. A report was released by the Italian Football League which accused Gerry of taking a before-the-match pep drug. The report said that tests conducted on Hitchens after a League game on 4 March revealed 'small traces of dope.' On the same day, 82 other players were tested throughout Italy. Three of his Inter Milan teammates were alleged to have taken 'heavy amounts' and were fined £84 each. The drug used was said to be the powerful stimulant, psychotonic amine.

The story made front page headlines in some of the British daily papers, including the *Daily Express*, which ran the headline:

Bombshell on Easter's big day of sport

Soccer Dope Row

Accused: England star Hitchens.

Gerry was interviewed by the press when the headlines hit the papers and said, 'I'm absolutely dumbfounded. I don't know what they're on about. I am not having my name linked with this sort of thing by anybody. Someone will have to answer for this. I have never taken anything like dope in my life. Aspirin tablets for a headache, glucose tablets – the sort a child can buy in a chemist's – before a game in England, but never anything more than that. Think how you'd feel after a match if you did take dope. It's ridiculous. It must have been a Mickey

Finn.' Gerry went on, 'If a doctor says traces of drugs were found I cannot argue, but I don't know how I got it. It must have been slipped into my food or drink. I have never knowingly taken any pep drugs.'

The Inter Milan medical officer Dr Quarenghi said, 'the only stimulant Gerry Hitchens takes is sugar. I think the medical experts have mistaken the symptoms and erroneously diagnosed the after-effects of sugar.'

With the World Cup only a matter of weeks away, Gerry's place was brought into question by the media, but the story was only an allegation and it did not stop him being picked for England's game against Switzerland on 9 May, even though Gerry was receiving treatment for an ankle injury.

The Italian League disciplinary committee met a few days later, and Gerry's allegation was withdrawn. The next day, Gerry was due to appear on a BBC radio programme called *In Town Tonight*, which was presented by Eric Maschwitz. He had the well-known opening line, 'Once more we stop the mighty roar of London's traffic and, from the great crowds, and we bring you some of the interesting people who have come by land, sea and air to be In Town Tonight.' While Gerry was appearing on the show, he met the famous and interesting inventor, Sir Robert Watson-Watt, who was also being interviewed for the show. He was the original inventor of radio detection and ranging (or the radar gun). Watson-Watt recounted the story of being caught for exceeding the speed limit during a journey from Toronto to Port Hope, Ontario, Canada. Handing him a ticket, the policeman said that he had been caught in a radar trap. Mrs. Watson-Watt said, 'Good heavens! My husband invented radar.' Indulgently, the constable smiled and replied, 'That's what the man said about the guillotine when they led him to the execution block.'

As Inter had let the title slip in 1961–62 after leading the Serie A table for such a long time, only faltering at the last stretch and letting in their local rivals, AC Milan, Herrera questioned his team and his first answer was to look for a new striker. In those days, there were restrictions placed on the number of foreign players each team could field, so Herrera brought in Garrincha's understudy in the Brazil national side Jair da Costa from Associação Portuguesa de Desportos, for £150,000 during the close season. This ultimately led to reports that Hitchens was going to be replaced. It seemed that time was ticking on Gerry's Internazionale career from then on, although he did score a hat-trick in a friendly match and Inter sent Jair on loan for a while.

It was not all bad news, however, as in September 1962 the Hitchens family grew by one as baby Karen was born in Pontypridd, South Wales, completing a hat-trick in the space of a 40-month period – two girls and eldest son Marcus. After several months in the seventh-floor apartment that they had stayed in since moving from the Rosa, the couple moved again into a more suitable apartment just after the start of the new season. The couple had spent a few months renovating their new home, and a lot of money was spent on it.

Inter began the 1962–63 season in bad shape. Things were not going right for Herrera in terms of results, and his team lacked the ability to score goals. Eight games into the new season, Inter were in fourth place, but Hitchens had only started five times and had only scored once in a draw against Palermo. He had lost his place to Jair, and his Internazionale career was effectively over. His last game for Inter was on the 14 October 1962 when they played Napoli in the San Siro. The game ended in a 1–0 win for Inter, with Humberto Maschio scoring the winner after 80 minutes. Soon afterwards Gerry was sold to Torino for a knock-down fee of £50,000.

An alliance was being built around Internazionale president Angelo Moratti and Helenio Herrera, the coach who wanted to turn a good side into one of the best-ever clubs in the world. The side went from strength to strength, despite the departure of Hitchens, and the Italian Championship was won in 1962–63 by Internazionale, Herrera's first *scudetto*.

Like his good friend Jimmy Greaves a year earlier, Gerry missed out on winning the title with a Milan club. Little did he know that the club were about to embark on their most successful period in their history, which was affectionately known as '*La Grande Inter*'. This was the 'Great Inter', a team blessed by the hand of God, a God called Herrera. But Gerry was not part of it.

Despite this, playing for Inter and living in Milan for those 18 months had made Gerry a more rounded player, and he found that some things were not tolerated in the Italian game as they were in the English League. The late tackle from behind was something that was frowned upon in Italy, although the shirt pulling was new to him. 'While you have to put up with a lot of shirt pulling and petty obstruction, you don't have to worry about what is going to hit you from behind. You can concentrate on playing forward and beating only the people who are in front of you,' he said. His experiences had forced him to think more about the game, and this in turn had made him a more mature and sophisticated player than the one who was playing for Aston Villa a couple of years previously. Gerry thoroughly enjoyed his time at Internazionale, even though the training regime was totally alien to him and the '*ritiro*' and the style of football took some getting used to. He also admired Herrera, even though he was a strict disciplinarian and had some bizarre methods. Furthermore, he had a new language to master, but that proved easier than it first appeared, and he eventually picked up all the different dialects. It was amazing how he settled in during the 18 months in Italy.

There were high hopes for Torino after finishing a respectable seventh in the 1961–62 season, but the passionate fans were desperate for a regular goalscorer after suffering the loss of two British imports, Denis Law and Joe Baker. What kind of club was Gerry moving to, and what kind of city was Turin?

Gerry was about to find out.

Entering the Battlefields of Turin

'It was like coming out of the bloody army!'

AC Torino
November 1962 to June 1965

In the late 1940s, AC Torino (now called Torino FC) had a side who won four successive scudetti. '*Il Grande Torino*' (the Great Torino) is the name by which the legendary Torino team is popularly known in Italy. '*Il Grande Torino*' set many important records of Italian football, all of which still stand today. They played with the 4–4–2 playing system, 10 years before the great Brazil 1958 World Cup team used the same system, and some of their game tactics pre-dated by 35 years the Dutch 'Total Football' that revolutionised the game in the 1970s.

Tragedy struck on 4 May 1949, however, as a plane crash in Superga, near Turin, killed the entire playing squad, which included 10 Italian internationals. The all-star starting line up of '*il Grande Torino*' that died at Superga was the most famous in Italian football history. The city gave a hero's funeral to the 17 players who died. The streets were lined with people paying homage to '*Il Grande Torino*'.

Throughout the 1950s and into the 1960s, AC Torino fans had little to shout about as their club were in a downward spiral. The only glimmer of light was in the 1959–60 season when they won the Serie B Championship. In 1961, however, AC Torino bought the great Scottish striker Denis Law for £110,000 from Manchester City, setting a new record fee for a transfer between an English and an Italian club. Although he played well in Italy, scoring 10 times in 27 appearances for Torino, he found it difficult to settle there and famously signed for Manchester United in 1962, setting another British record transfer fee of £115,000. The English striker Joe Baker was also transferred to Torino for £75,000, after the Hibernian board refused to give him a £5 wage increase from his existing wage of £12 a week. Despite scoring a winning goal in a derby match against Juventus, his time at the Italian club was short and almost ended in tragedy: Baker was involved in a serious car crash in which he hit a lamppost in Turin, and he needed life-saving surgery and spent over a month on a drip feed. It was a generally unhappy spell for him and Law, as neither player liked the constant press intrusion, which meant that both spent much of their time locked away in their Turin apartment.

Even if Law did not settle in Turin he had his admirers. One elderly Torino fan gave him the ultimate accolade, when he said that he was greater than Valentino Mazzola, the inside-left and captain of *'il Grande Torino'* who won five consecutive *scudetti*. Mazzola was widely considered one of the best football players of all time and perhaps the first modern all-around footballer, as he was an attacking midfielder who could score, tackle and defend. A great compliment indeed.

Law said of his transfer to Manchester United in July 1962, 'In June 1961 I signed for Torino in Italy, following other British players like Jimmy Greaves at AC Milan and Gerry Hitchens at Internazionale to make money and sample the continental style of play, but I wasn't happy. What really got me down in Italy was the negative football. Nobody wanted to play. Everybody sat back grinding out results like 0–0, 1–1 and, very rarely, 2–0. It was this more than anything that made me more determined to leave. I mentioned my feelings to Matt Busby when I came to Old Trafford to play for the Italian League against the English League. Six months later nothing had improved, and Matt agreed to pay Torino £115,000 for me.' Law continued, 'They held out, threatening to sell me to Juventus instead, but I was determined. What player, if he knew Manchester United wanted to sign him, wouldn't be? Eventually, after a long contract wrangle, Torino gave in and I signed for Manchester United on 12 July 1962. I had moved three times in two years, and each time the transfer fee broke the British record. For me the money was not the important thing. What I wanted most was a football club where I could at last settle down and play good football.'

Law also said, 'The football there [in Italy] was awful, everybody played with nine men back, including us. Joe was a good pal, with a great sense of humour, which we needed over there. And if I hadn't gone, I'd always have regretted it. I came back a better player.' Baker recovered from his injuries, and he returned to the UK in July 1962, joining Billy Wright's Arsenal for a club-record fee of £70,000. The Torino fans had idolised Baker and Law as they were great strikers, even though they did not make it at the club. The fans blamed the paparazzi for hounding them out of the club and ruining their (short-lived) Italian careers.

Torino's multilingual side were being coached by another Argentinean, Beniamino Santos, who insisted in giving his teamtalks in his native Spanish. In the 1961–62 season they finished in seventh place in Serie A, and the Torino fans were clambering for a recognised goalscorer to revitalise their fading but once great club. In November 1962 Santos persuaded the club president to spend £50,000 (plus their own centre-forward) on a blond-haired Englishman who was making a name for himself at Internazionale, having scored 20 goals in his 43 League and Cup appearances for the Milan side. It was typical of the surrealism of Italian football, however, that Hitchens was signed by Torino of all clubs, having heard all about the '*brutta esperienza*' of Joe Baker and Denis Law, who left after barely a season.

There may be a Shroud in Turin, but with the arrival of Gerry Hitchens, Torino's fanatic fans had thought the real messiah had arrived at their football club. He had built up a reputation at Internazionale as a consistent goalscorer and a player who worked hard for the team, and the Torino fans liked that in a player and yearned for a new hero.

When Hitchens left Internazionale he remarked that it was 'like coming out of the bloody army.' Although he admired and respected his former Internazionale coach, it was a comment directed at Herrera and he spoke of the pressures under which he had kept the players at Inter. Having a sturdy miner's insulation, Gerry never took offence at Herrera's pre-match rants and let it all go over his head. Some players were terrified or hated the way Herrera went about his business, but Gerry accepted it. Now he was in Turin and had a new regime to contend with and new training methods to adapt to.

Turin was not a fashionable city, but Gerry was still dressed in his Italian designer clothes and looked the part. There was a beguiling, urchin quality about him with his blond hair, parted at the centre which hung over his forehead and made him stand out from the predominantly dark, Latin looks of the hardy locals.

Everything that he bought was quality. Gerry oozed quality, and that came out in his play on the field. His style fitted in with the Milanese, but would he fit in with the Torinese? Turin was a smaller and friendlier city than Milan, more 'earthy' and less cosmopolitan. Whatever Pirelli was to Milan, Fiat was to Turin. The wealth of the giant car company had run one of Italy's biggest clubs in Juventus, Torino's greatest rivals, but had created love, hate, loyalty and jealousy between the two city clubs and fans. Even though Juventus were the 'aristocrats' of the city, Torino were the '*squadra del cuore*' – the team that everyone loved. Fiat tended to look after their workers because they were the fans of Juventus (or Torino). Those who were lucky enough to work for Fiat were provided with modern flats and offered all sorts of incentives, like passes to holiday camps and numerous leisure activities.

Italian football was very different to the British game in the 1960s and wealthy businessmen were involved in the game through the love of their team and to make some money. It created an 'if we want it, we buy it' attitude, and silly money was being talked about if a team wanted to buy a player. Their money caused transfer fees in Italy to escalate. In 1963, Orfeo Pianelli was a big Italian businessman, who replaced Angelo Filippone as president of Torino. His money eventually brought some good times back to the Turin club, which started with the £110,000 transfer of Denis Law from Manchester City and now with the transfer of Gerry Hitchens. The businessmen of the day wanted to be popular with the working majority of the city and also wanted to make a name for themselves by producing a great winning team. It was all a game, but being associated with a top club and a successful club was every Italian businessman's dream. If the team was winning the fans would pay whatever it took to watch their team, their week's wage or food money would go on buying a ticket for the game on a Sunday. But if they were losing regularly, they would protest with contempt and refuse to go to the matches.

The Torino fans were extremely partisan and passionate. Once the fans had found out that Hitchens had signed for their club, they made him an instant 'cult hero', calling him 'a Saint called Gerry' or *un giocatore serio* (a serious player). Everyone liked Gerry, but with his characteristic good humour he let it all flow over his head.

Football has always been a short career, and things change very quickly. One week you can be in the team, but a few poor performances later and you can be out of the side. Some players fall out of love with their clubs, with their manager or the culture of the city they live in. The winning system of Juventus collapsed in the 1961–62 season, following their *scudetto*-winning season the year before, and this led to John Charles's return to Leeds United in 1962. Charles never settled in Leeds, however, and his second spell at Elland Road was less successful and only lasted 11 games. He claimed he 'couldn't hack the English game any longer': he had 'become too Italian'. After spending five years in Italy he found it difficult to adjust to life back in England and returned to Italy in the same year to play for AS Roma, initially with success, scoring four goals in 10 games. While playing for Roma in 1962, Charles warned Hitchens, 'Don't ever go back to England, Gerry. It's so cold. There's nobody to meet you at the station.' He did not need Charles's advice.

Like John Charles before him, Gerry soon found that Turin was another 'hotbed' of Italian football where the game was more like a religion. In Turin, footballers were the idols and were worshipped more than film stars or singers.

The Torino club presented Gerry and his family with a new luxury flat overlooking the city. He had no complaints, 'The people themselves, the supporters, they seem to, I don't know, always want to help you. If you are stuck for words, they put them into your mouth and really help you.'

For the second time in a month, Meriel was settling into new surroundings and a new city. This was a city where every Italian football fan wanted to get the very latest news of his club. There were four daily football (sports) newspapers in Italy, including the famous *La Gazzetta dello Sport* and numerous magazines. The newspaper, published on distinctive pink paper, sold hundreds of thousands of copies daily (more on Mondays when readers want to catch up on the weekend's events). Every day, hundreds of fans watched their club in training sessions. On match days in Turin, thousands converged upon the stadium, the Stadio Olimpico, and the city died on a Sunday afternoon, an abandoned city, killed by a football match. This was not like Birmingham or Cardiff on match days, this was a city where the game of football sucked everyone off the streets like a giant vacuum and blew them out into the terraces of the Stadio Olimpico, ready to watch another battle commence.

Why was Turin so obsessed with football, morning, noon and night? Perhaps Italy's history can provide an answer. Patriotism has always been local in Italy. It was 'your' city that mattered, not 'your' nation. Similarities can be found with Liverpool, where club has always come before country for the fans (of the red half of Liverpool anyway). It is the cities that count – Milan, Turin and Florence. Not so much the country – Italy. Things have changed little if you look back in history at the battles centuries ago – Rome against Naples, Florence against Pisa – the Roman battles of yesteryear.

Football can be considered in the same light. Each football match is a battle, and each Championship is a war to the millions of football fans in Italy. Battles are now on the football field, and the cities fight each other with football teams – Internazionale versus Roma, Lazio versus Napoli, Torino versus AC Milan. Shin guards are the only armour used in football matches, and breast plates have given way to coloured shirts.

John Hawkwood was a famous English mercenary, a hero, who terrorised Italy in the 14th century and was honoured in Florence with a *fresco*. The mercenaries survive in the way of foreign forwards on a football field, rather than foreign knights on a battlefield. Six hundred years later, Gerry Hitchens was just as great a hero as Hawkwood, only the arena was different. Instead of terrorising the Italian people on a battlefield, Hitchens terrorised Italian centre-halves on a football field.

The popular, down-to-earth Shropshire lad quickly became an Italian hero in Turin, where the tools of his trade were his head and two good feet. Not only that, but he had also learned a new language and experienced a different culture while he was in Milan: Gerry had been prepared for the battle ahead. From his upbringing in a Shropshire mining village to the foothills of the Italian Alps and the luxury he had been awarded, Gerry's love and passion for football had never waned. It was his passion and his life. It did not matter to Gerry where he played – Birmingham, Milan, Turin – as long as he was playing. He had the rough, strong voice of a Shropshire miner, but there was also boyishness about him, a 'pin-up' factor about his appearance. In the penalty area where it mattered he was no boy: 'I just love it. If I wasn't playing football professionally, which I am doing now, I would be putting just as much effort into the amateur game. I think being a miner or butcher has taught me that you can't get something for nothing.'

Gerry had the staying power he inherited from working in the mines, an attribute which endeared him to the fans of Internazionale, and now he had to prove it to the Torino fans. The Italians called him '*un buon minatore*' (a good miner) because he had the stamina which lasted the full 90 minutes of the game. 'I've got a heart as big as a bucket,' he once said. It took a while for Gerry to settle at Torino, however, with the club languishing in 13th place but only seven points from leaders Bologna, but he was as determined as ever to succeed.

Although there were more gifted ball players at that time in Italy, the thing that the Torino fans liked about Gerry was that he never gave up, a very British trait – a never-say-die attitude. He had pace and strength and was a player who gave his all every time he put on the club shirt. He would sometimes turn up on the left wing and cross the ball to create an opening for his teammates. He was an unselfish player, and the fans of Torino loved him for it. One old Torino fan said of Gerry, 'We haven't had a centre-forward of his class since [Guglielmo] Gabetto, "*il Grande Torino*".' Gerry was all very cool about the plaudits aimed at him, 'I let it all flow off me.'

The game in Italy was more physical and tactical than the English game, although the standard of football may not have lived up to expectations, sometimes being negative tactically. For example, the '*catenaccio*' system of play, used in Italian football in the 1950s, employed a purely defensive sweeper who only 'roamed' around the backline. This was attributed to their elegant style of play, refined technique and ability to launch counter-attacks. Their defending styles were also considered more 'classy' compared to the modern-day centre-back. Gerry was still not used to the physical and brutal side of the Italian game. He once said, 'For a forward, it is very difficult. On arriving in the penalty area you find the place, the area, absolutely crammed with players, you know, pushing and shoving, shirt pulling. You're trying to dribble; little pushes here and pushes there. From corners, it is the same. You go up to head a ball they push you off the

Gerry aged 12 (front row, middle) with Highley Scouts football team in 1946

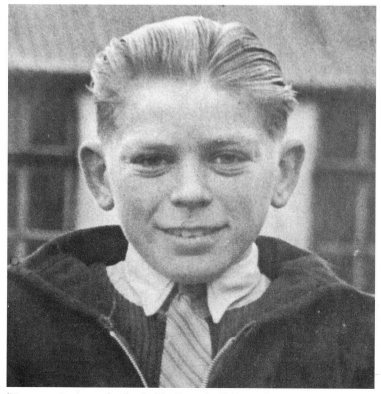

'Hurry up, I wanna play football' – Gerry in 1948, aged 14.

Highley Miners Welfare team in 1951. Gerry (front row, middle), aged 17.

Gerry with his mates on his last day at Alveley pit in 1955.

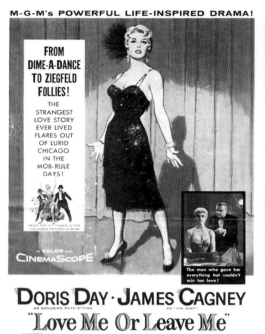

The film poster for *Love Me or Leave me* – Meriel and Gerry's first movie together in 1955.

Gerry (left) at Maindy barracks in 1956.

The Army XI football team with Gerry (bottom row, second left) and Bobby Charlton (bottom row, right) in 1956.

A 21-year-old Gerry in 1955 in his first professional season at Cardiff City.

Gerry colliding with Chelsea goalkeeper to score for Cardiff against Chelsea at Stamford Bridge.

Gerry, second from the end, licking his hands ready to meet dignitaries before a game in South Africa, c.1956.

Trevor Ford holding the Welsh Cup with Gerry looking on in 1957.

Gerry had just joined Villa in the 1957–58 season.

Gerry with Peter McParland disguised in false beards in 1959.

Gerry and Meriel on the big day,
Pontypridd, 27 October 1958.

Aston Villa Second Division Champions 1959–60.

Running off the pitch after scoring five goals in Villa's 11–1 record win, 14 November 1959.

Receiving the match ball from Nigel Sims after the Charlton 11–1 win. From left to right: Bobby Thomson, Peter McParland, Gerry Hitchens, Nigel Sims and Stan Lynn.

‘Supper's ready, Mel.’ Gerry with a pheasant
he caught while shooting in 1959.

Gerry (left), Pat Saward (middle) and Peter McParland (right) on Brighton beach in 1960.

Being presented with the Midland Player of the Year Award before his first cap for England against Mexico, May 1961.

Gerry displaying his medals, cups and first England cap.

Gerry and Marcus wearing England caps *c.*1961.

Proud parents Violet and Archie with Gerry's Midland Player of the Year Award.

While he was at Inter Milan, Gerry was an admirer of the great Helenio Herrera.

Gerry and Meriel at San Pellegrino training ground for his medical to become an Internazionale player in August 1961.

Gerry and Meriel in Milan *c.*1961.

Scoring for Internazionale in a friendly against Real Madrid at the Bernabéu, August 1961.

Internazionale Milano, 1961–62 season.

Gerry mingling with dignitaries after a Chamber of Commerce dinner in Milan.

Gerry always admired John Charles ('*il gigante buono*').

The Italian Job!

Gerry scoring his first Serie A goal for Inter against Atalanta, 27 August 1961.

Gerry fighting for the ball in a game against Roma in 1961.

'You're not in the army now, lad.' Gerry lining up with the Italian FA team at Old Trafford, Manchester, 1 November 1961.

Gerry shielding the ball from Serena while playing for Inter in 1962.

ball and so on. But I enjoy it very much.' Asked why, Gerry's response was, 'Because, I do the same thing back.'

On one occasion, Gerry did it once too often. The referee saw him push an opposing player in a game against Bologna on the 18 November, in which Torino lost 1–0. The referee sent Hitchens off for the first time in his career for unnecessarily rough play and tackling of the Bologna striker, Francesco Janich. He had only been with his new team a matter of days, and already things were not going to plan.

Just before the family had arrived in Turin and while Gerry was still with Internazionale, the BBC wrote to him to ask for permission to film a 50-minute documentary on location in Italy. Gerry eventually agreed to the filming, which would take place during November 1962. The Italian Television Service (RAI) agreed to help with the film, since he was a well-known player in Italy and such a film may well interest the Italian audience. The schedule was tight as the film would be edited a month later during December, with a view to screening it by the BBC early in 1963.

The film was to be aimed at not just football fans but a wider audience as well. In late 1962, Britain was about to make up her mind whether or not to join the Common Market (now the EU). As Italy was already part of it, the BBC thought it would make good airtime for the British public to find out what life was like in one of the most bustling and dynamic centres of the Common Market. Not only would it be a sporting and political film, but it would also be a film which would deal briefly with Gerry's early life as a miner in Shropshire and his sudden transfer to the Italian giants of Internazionale from Aston Villa. Before the film crew arrived in Italy, they filmed Gerry's family and friends in Highley and were also going to show his wife, Meriel, and his children at home in Milan and how he had adapted his life and football style in the 18 months since moving to Italy.

Agreement was obtained from the protective Herrera in a cable which stated, 'AGREED IF ALL THE FILMING IS DONE IN ITALY,' meaning that he would not allow his player to miss training by going back to Britain to do the film. Herrera had promised the film's scriptwriter and narrator Brian Glanville he would not transfer Hitchens but, as it turned out, he broke his word and he was transferred even before filming had started during the brief but customary transfer 'window' in the November of 1962.

When filming did commence the family had literally just moved into their new place in Turin within a matter of days. Meriel's sister had come over from Wales to help with the unpacking and to support her sister. They were still moving things from Milan when the film crew started their preparation for the filming.

The film crew were having a terrible time trying to set up the lighting, as all the power and the lighting were all run off one circuit and the power kept going off, so they had to keep phoning the electricity company out to reset the circuit. To make matters worse, while Meriel and her sister were unpacking, a box of saucepans and kettles was accidently knocked off a kitchen table and the noise was so loud that it could be heard in the lounge where the film crew were filming and the BBC director, Stephen Hearst, who was 'quite a character', stormed into the kitchen and Meriel and her sister felt his wrath. Meriel felt embarrassed to say the least and they never made a sound after that.

During the course of the filming Gerry had been sent off against Bologna and then faced a two-match (two-week) ban. Because of the tight schedule they had to keep, the BBC were incensed by this and telephoned the Italian FA to appeal against his sending-off. It was costing the BBC a fortune to have a big film crew in Italy, and they could little afford to be waiting around for Gerry to return to the field while he served his ban. The phone call brought a surprising reaction back home in England. The BBC launched a desperate appeal and the news of this spread throughout Turin; however, the appeal failed and the Italian FA upheld the suspension and the BBC did not film the match for the documentary. The following week Torino were due to play AS Roma on 25 November, a game which would have included a British player on each side. It would have made a nice story and would have been a piece of history in the making. John Charles had by now been transferred to AS Roma from Leeds United, following an unpleasant 11-game spell. The BBC obviously wanted to film these two British players up against each other in a Serie A match, but their plans had been dashed. The game ended in a 2–2 draw, with Manfredini for Roma and Locatelli for Torino each scoring two goals.

Because of Gerry's two-week ban from football, filming took longer than expected, with the BBC spending around three weeks in Italy. As with any documentary, there was a fee paid to the Hitchens family, but the sums were not huge. The film, narrated by Brian Glanville, was called *The European Centre Forward*, and it went on to win a Silver Bear Award in the 1963 Berlin Film Festival.

When Gerry returned from his two-match ban nothing would go right for him or Torino. The team and the board were shaken by the publicity, and this affected the players on the pitch. The directors met well into the night, deciding whom to sack.

Gerry's first goal for Torino came against AC Milan on 16 December 1962 at the San Siro in a 2–1 defeat. Torino had made a pretty poor start to the season, and the expectation of an improvement on last term was not looking good. However, just as quickly and dramatically their luck turned as Gerry's goalscoring prowess was once again in evidence against Sampdoria and his fair play and fitness returned. Once again, he proved himself to the faithful Torino fans. Torino were winning again and that was what mattered to the fans. However, by the New Year of 1963 Torino had only won five games in Serie A. In the first game of 1963, against relegation candidates Napoli, Hitchens scored twice in a 2–2 thriller.

When Torino entertained Internazionale on 13 January 1963, the score ended all-square 1–1 in front of 70,000 adoring Torino fans, with Gerry's replacement at Inter, di Giacomo, opening the scoring for the arrogant Milan side only to see Locatelli equalise from a penalty. Even though Hitchens did not score, the tribute of the fans was for the workmanship of the Englishman. In the dressing room after the game, all 23 Torino directors, including 'il Presidente' Angelo Fillipone, lined up to shake his hand and congratulate him on an excellent performance. It was as though Torino had won the European Cup. The directors were saying 'We could not sell a man like this. To suggest that is not a joke. It is a tragedy.' Gerry said in reply, 'If they sold me they would have to drag me back to England.' After the game, Gerry tried to duck a 200-strong police guard as he ran out of the back of the Stadio Communale (or Stadio Olympico as it also called) to escape the 'praise' of the crowd. Over 2,000 Torino fans waved crimson flags (Torino's club colours) and roamed outside the main gates of the stadium chanting and sounding bugles and horns in tribute to their English 'hero' who almost turned the world of Italian football upside down after the club's draw with the Serie A Champions and then leaders, Internazionale. The man they called '*l'uomo di granito*' ('the man of granite') had killed the composure of Herrera's multi-million lira team from Milan and the darlings of Italian and European football. Dozens of police vans kept the fans away from the players' exit that Gerry and his teammates were trying to escape from. Once a dozen or so fans spotted their hero clamber into his car, the fans screamed, ' 'Itchens, 'Itchens…' and hammered the roof of his car with their fists and flag poles in delight. The crowd was a little 'overexcited' to say the least. Torino fans had a reputation of getting 'excited' during their home matches, and this was no exception as they shrieked loudly all through the game as the pistol-armed police broke up fist fights between fans who clambered up advertising hoardings to drape their banners and flags.

In early 1963 Gerry was summoned to downtown Turin from his luxury home for questioning in a probe into the Italian bonus boom. There was an increase in huge (illegal) incentives payments which were rife in Italian football at the time, and Gerry had to spend a couple of hours of his day answering questions. It appeared that Internazionale, Gerry's previous club, were suspected of paying more than the regulation £16 for a draw and £32 for a win bonus to their players, who had included Gerry during the last season. 'I didn't even know there was a regulation bonus until the inquiry started,' he admitted. 'The only questions were to the point, and I simply gave my answers.' He did not face any further questioning after that.

At the same time, fellow Briton, John Charles, who was back in Italy with Roma, was also in trouble. Newspaper stories appeared in the press saying that Charles lacked drive and was 'more immobile than a statue,' and that he was 'one of the two weak links' for Roma. A few weeks later, Charles turned his back on Italian football yet again as he began to suffer from injuries and personal problems and left to join Cardiff City, where he was to finish his League career. With his Roma career short-lived and his reputation in tatters, he lasted just 10 games, and he scored four goals.

For Gerry, however, it was a different story. He loved Turin and was being praised by everyone, including the grand old man of Italian football, Vittorio Pozzo, who was most famous for leading the Italian national team to victory in the 1934 and 1938 FIFA World Cups. In his opinion, he thought that the Torino forward line had only one proper component, and 'that was Gerry Hitchens'. That was high praise indeed from such a stalwart of Italian football. Gerry always played with vigour and never moaned about anything, even the rough tackling and barging in the box, which was quite refreshing to the Italian fans as they saw some of their own players as nothing more than temperamental prima donnas. He always showed total commitment to the game, even though he was not the most skilful of players, and his schoolboy enthusiasm made up for it.

Two goals for Gerry against Palermo in a 3–0 victory was followed by a draw against Mantova, a win at Modena and a defeat at Spal. The season was beginning to feel like a roller coaster ride, with ups and downs nearly every other week; however, as the season drew to a close, the highest point came in the home game against Sampdoria. In a thrilling encounter, Hitchens scored his first hat-trick in his Italian football career in only 15 minutes of open play and the game ended 4–2. The season ended with a respectable two draws against the likes of Napoli and away to Internazionale.

In a season which saw him change clubs within the first few months of the season, be filmed for a documentary by the BBC, be sent off for the first time in his career, it was all rounded off by scoring his first hat-trick in Italian football. All in the life of Gerry Hitchens.

Torino finished the season in eighth place, which surely was not good enough to whet the appetites of those crazy fans to return for the next season, but Hitchens ended his campaign with a respectable 13 goals in all competitions. Added to that, Torino lost the Coppa Italia Final against Atalanta 3–1.

The Torino side for the 1963–64 season had some great players and some real characters. After the departure of Beniamino Santos, the great Nereo Rocco was installed as coach, who between 1961 and 1963 led AC Milan to win the *scudetto* in 1962 and the European Cup in 1963. Torino had a player known as '*la farfalla granata*' (the maroon butterfly), Luigi 'Gigi' Meroni. He could play on either wing but mainly on the right and wore the number-seven shirt. He was a very technical player who loved to dribble with the ball and was famed for wearing his socks rolled down to his ankles. However, he had anarchist ideas and was an extrovert. He apparently slept in a coffin, wore his hair like one of the Beatles, designed his own suits and took wild animals for walks. The Italian media criticised his behaviour on numerous occasions but called him '*il Sivori Italiano*' (the Italian Sivori), a reference to his dribbling skills which were likened to the Argentine player, Enrique Omar Sívori, who played for Juventus.

Gerry liked young people like Meroni and admired his attitude and style and enjoyed his company. He said, 'He's eccentric, but he doesn't harm anybody.' He loved talented young players and encouraged them to express themselves as much as they could on the field of play. Another player Gerry admired greatly was the Torino captain and midfielder, Giorgio Ferrini. He was transferred to Torino in 1959 and quickly became a legend at the club. Gerry had become great friends with Ferrini and respected him as a person and a player, and he had a big influence on Gerry's career in Turin. Ferrini was a real 'player's, player' and a fans' favourite. He thought nothing of spending half an hour signing autographs before or after games. He was also fond of Gerry's family and often spent time with them away from football. *(Incidentally, Giorgio Ferrini was one of several Torino heroes who passed away at a very young age as he died tragically due to an aneurysm in 1976 at the age of 37.)*

The new season started badly for the both the new coach, Rocco and for Gerry. He was sent off in the opening game of the season against Vicenza, only the second time in his career, but already twice in his time at Torino. Four draws and two defeats in the first six games saw the club in the bottom three. A 2–1 win at home to Genoa in the next game was a false relief for the Torino fans, who saw their side crash to three further back-to-back defeats. Respite came with a nice run of form early in the new year of 1964. Torino were in mid-table when Atalanta visited Turin and Hitchens, who had only scored two consolation goals in the season, returned to goalscoring form by netting two more to see his side win comfortably by 3–0. Two scoreless draws followed, and things came crashing down to earth when they lost 4–1 away at Bologna, with Gerry grabbing a late consolation.

February ended with another fine game at home to Mantova, and Hitchens scored an equaliser in a 5–2 win. Another three consecutive goalless draws meant that Torino were becoming hard to beat, but they were still unable to string consecutive victories together and remained in mid-table going into April.

Hitchens grabbed another two goals in a 2–2 draw at home to Roma, followed by the winner against Spal, only to see themselves crash back to earth with defeat to Fiorentina. Torino were slowly creeping up the table, but they were failing to set the world alight in the process. They finished the season unbeaten in the last five games and managed to secure seventh spot in Serie A, 19 points adrift of champions Bologna and with a reputation of being draw specialists, having drawn half their games. Gerry ended the campaign with 12 goals in all competitions. Another Coppa Italia defeat, this time against Roma, saw Hitchens finish the season again with a runners'-up medal.

It took Gerry seven games to open his account in the 1964–65 season, and it came in the game at home to Fiorentina in a 3–1 victory. The season had started unconvincingly, but a run of three straight victories, including a 4–1 win against Genoa, saw Torino in fourth place after nine games. After Christmas, the English striker opened the scoring in another convincing win against Cagliari, and Torino were in third place and hot on the heels of leaders AC Milan and Internazionale. Things were beginning to look up for the club.

Too many draws and a few defeats told the same story for Torino, however, as they teetered between fourth and sixth place for most of the season. The best result of the season came in the run-in towards the end of the season when Torino thrashed champions Bologna 5–0, with Hitchens scoring two. By this time, they could only secure third place as the two Milan clubs fought it out for the top two spots. Gerry again found the net against Roma in a 3–1 win, and in the final game a 2–2 draw secured the *scudetto* for Internazionale at the San Siro. Torino had finished third in Serie A with a respectable 44 points, 10 points behind champions Internazionale, and Hitchens had contributed a respectable eight goals in the League and 12 in all competitions.

Little did Gerry know when the season had ended on 6 June 1965 that he had played his last game for Torino in that match against Internazionale. It appeared that he was sold without his knowledge, only being told by a 21-year-old office girl, who said, 'You're going to Bergamo.' With no notice given and no explanation, Gerry was told by the secretary to go and have a medical at

Atalanta. It was apparently quite common for Italian clubs to act like this with their players, but to Gerry it was unjust and not the way to conduct business or treat a player: 'That's the way they do things here.' It certainly was not the way things happened in England. He was a bit surprised and thought that a senior official at the club could have had a word with him beforehand, but he took the news in his stride. What had he done wrong? He did not get too upset and, instead, he just got on with it and believed it came with the territory, 'The clubs here like to change players often. They like to see new faces in the team. You get used to it.' He had really settled into life in Turin. He loved the city, and the team were friendly, the coach Rocco was good, but at the age of 31 the Gerry Hitchens story was to carry on to another new club and another new city – his third in his four-year stay in Italy.

Not Just a Provisional Club

'I'm no spring chicken. I think I've got another two or three years here.'

Atalanta Bergamasca Calcio
June 1965–June 1967

It was no secret that Atalanta were no Internazionale, or Torino for that matter, but they were a proud, provincial club, sometimes called '*Regina delle provinciali*' (queen of the provincial clubs). They had very little history in Italian football, however, and were only concerned with avoiding relegation rather than winning trophies and were a club soured by feelings of discrimination (from referees favouring the 'bigger' clubs). In terms of titles the club had won, their sole silverware was the 1963 Coppa Italia. The club had never won (and still has not won to this day) the *scudetto*.

During the 1960s they had a terrible record at retaining managers, and it seemed that they did not last longer that one season in charge, which is not uncommon in Italian football anyway. The manager in charge at the time Gerry signed was Héctor Puricelli, most commonly known as Ettore Puricelli, an Italo-Uruguayan from Montevideo. He most famously played for Bologna and AC Milan, and after retiring from the playing field he became a manager at numerous clubs in Europe, including AC Milan and in 1965 became Atalanta manager, replacing Carlo Ceresoli.

Puricelli signed Gerry for around £25,000 in June 1965. It was, in a way, a downward step for Gerry, given the status of clubs he had previously played for – Aston Villa, Internazionale and Torino. At 31 years old, however, his best days as the number-one striker were behind him, but Gerry obviously wanted to extend his playing days and play regularly, rather than keeping the bench warm or playing in the reserves.

He had left Internazionale in November 1962 and had missed out on a Serie A Championship medal in that season, another *scudetto* in the following season, as well as two European Cups (in 1963–64 and 1964–65) in the period of '*la Gande Inter*'. For Gerry, the timing of his transfer to Atalanta coincided with the

Intercontinental Cup of 1965 involving Internazionale and Independiente of Argentina, for the second year running and, again, Inter won that trophy for the second successive year. But Gerry had no regrets, 'I think about it now and again. It's a pity I missed it, but I've done all right. When I started out I never expected any of the things to happen to me that did.' He was a very philosophical person.

Having relocated twice in the four years since moving to Italy, the Hitchens family had to adapt to another town in Northern Italy and carve out a new life for themselves. They found a modern flat within walking distance of the Stadio Atleti Azzurri d'Italia where Atalanta played their home games. The children were quickly introduced to their new school, a local Montessori in the pretty town of Bergamo, and Meriel and Gerry soon started making friends locally, both Italian and American.

Gerry and his family had now fully integrated themselves into Italian life, and he had fostered a passion for the opera, a very contemporary Italian pastime, 'I sit here sometimes with the opera records on and I close my eyes and listen. I just listen. There's one part in *La Bohème* when I go all goose pimples.' Meriel remembers that the first opera she took Gerry to was *Carmen* by Bizet in Turin, which is a really long opera, but Gerry did not last the pace and fell asleep halfway through. He also had a wide variety of musical tastes, including his favourite artists, Neil Diamond and Frank Sinatra.

Bergamo is a city of rare beauty, about an hour from Milan, amid an area with many fine lakes and nestles in the foothills of the Alps. Gerry and Meriel both took advantage of the time they had together, and while the children were at school they used to drive to Lake Iseo, east of Bergamo, or to Valle Brembana, near to San Pellegrino, where they went fishing for the day for perch, pike or trout. Bergamo was also said to be a very religious town and was reputedly a cold and closed place. 'Here, you're a thief until you've proved yourself honest,' a player once said.

Eldest son Marcus used to play football in the garden and on match days would watch the fans walking to the ground, shouting his father's name, 'Jay-ree! Jay-ree! Jay-ree!' With their three children already fluent in Italian, they fitted well into life in Bergamo.

Every club has their own identity and ways of doing things. Atalanta players trained twice a day, at 10am and 6.45pm. They also went into '*ritiro*' from Friday afternoon to Sunday. 'We all hate this going away,' Gerry said. Furthermore, the players could only drive cars on Mondays. This was a strict regime.

At the age of 31, Gerry knew that his best days were behind him but also believed he could still do a job in Serie A. 'I'm no spring chicken. I think I've got another two or three years here [in Italy]. I'll stay here as long as I can. Then back to Britain, and I'd like to play there too as long as I can. Division Three or Four, even non-League, I don't care. I just love the game,' he said.

Atalanta started the season poorly with two draws and three defeats in their first five games in Series A. It was not until the 10th game of the season – which was almost a third of the way through the season – that their first win came in the game away to Varese. The club had been in the bottom three most of the season and had drawn too many games already. That win saw a run of three back-to-back victories, but it was not until the 14th game that the Hitchens goalscoring machine opened fire as he scored two goals in the 3–2 win at home to Catania.

In the game against his former club, Torino, on 16 January 1966, Hitchens took a sentimental journey back to Turin where the Torino fans, who had idolised '*un buon minatore*' for the previous two seasons, saw him being presented with a gold medal in recognition of his past performances with the club he signed for in 1962. The supporters fêted him with cheers and began singing his name all through the presentation of the medal. Unfortunately, the game ended on a sour note for Gerry as Torino beat Atalanta by 2–1. The defeat failed to help their plight as they remained in the bottom four in Serie A. The next day, the Turin daily newspaper, *Gazzetta Del Popolo*, reported, 'Gerry Hitchens a "*simpatico*", smiling and cordial, brought a note of warmth and joy into the stadium's dressing rooms.'

One player that Gerry knew from his Torino days was Giancarlo 'Caje' Cella, originally a left-winger but who had grown into a midfielder. He and Gerry grew very friendly during their time spent in Turin and when Cella joined Atalanta in 1966, their friendship continued, for a season at least. In an interview for this book Giancarlo remembered Gerry with fondness, 'Towards the end of the season at Torino, we were invited to the villa of Traversa, the Torino vice-president. I didn't have a car at the time, so Gerry came to pick me up in his powerful car and drove my wife, my son Gionata and I to the party. The return journey was very eventful, but I remember his patience with us and the way he dealt with my 5-month-old son Gionata in his little Moses basket. I also remember a journey to Switzerland together to pick up a spare part for his car and also a journey to Karlo-Vivary [in the Czech Republic] with him to buy an antique wall clock.'

A few months before the World Cup in England, the striker who took part in the previous World Cup in Chile said he never thought anything about England or had any 'what ifs', 'I never think about it. I've forgotten all about it.' There were muted cries from the English press for Hitchens to be looked at as a possible surprise call-up, but at the age of 31 it was all 'pie in the sky', especially with Alf Ramsey still in charge of the national side and sticking to his policy of playing only English-based players.

During this period at his new club Gerry was now beginning to settle into life in Bergamo; however, Atalanta had been in the lower reaches of Serie A all season, but a spell of good results put the smiles back on the faces of the fans. They saw two 1–0 victories against Cagliari, with the blond striker grabbing the winner, and another 1–0 home win against a powerful Napoli side on 6 March 1966, with Hitchens again the hero when he netted again. After the Napoli victory, scenes of contorted joy overspilled on to the pitch as the fans sung, 'Jay-ree! Jay-ree! Jay-ree!' It was not because Atalanta were high in the League – on the contrary they were fifth from bottom of Serie A, even after their two great wins – it was an outburst of frustration and joy mixed together. The fans of Atalanta, even though passionate, had had little to shout about in their club's history so two straight wins was something to be joyful about.

As the players tried to escape the stadium after the game, the blond head of Gerry Hitchens disappeared among them as they kissed him and ripped his jacket off his back, ran their fingers through his thick blond hair singing, 'Eetchens, sei un dio!' ('Hitchens, you're a God!'). 'I've had more kisses from rough beards today…people slapping me on my back that haven't spoken to me all year.' The joyous behaviour of the fans and the good run of results made a change from eight games without a victory and five weeks without a single shot on goal for Gerry. Not only that, it put paid to the rude notes that had been pushed through his letterbox by angry fans complaining about his performances in recent weeks. 'I didn't get to the point where I disliked football. I'm not unhappy. I still want to stay on here, but you keep thinking, oh dear, if this is football…I get so frustrated, you know?' he said.

Gerry's parents, Archie and Violet, flew in the day before the game at home to Spal on 24 April 1966. They only planned a short trip to see Gerry and the family. Gerry insisted that his mother came to watch the match on the Sunday against Spal. Violet had never seen her son play before in Italy. 'Mom you have to come. I want to give you a present,' as Gerry implied that if he scored it would be for her.

As if he had written the script, Hitchens scored the first goal in the 49th minute, and when he turned to wave to his mother in the stand Violet was so touched that she removed her white handkerchief from her handbag, waved it in the air and then wiped away the tears from her eyes. Gerry's father put an arm around her shoulder, smiling, as if to say, 'See that. Our Gerry is still good. He can still score goals.' With the score at 1–0, Hitchens scored the second in the 79th minute for his father. What was meant to be a short trip for the couple ended up being a three-week stay as the couple enjoyed their time so much in Bergamo, and they returned to see him play in the 0–0 draw against AC Milan two weeks later.

The two goals in the game against Spal were the last in the final eight games of the season; however, the run of results included brave 0–0 draws against AC Milan and Torino. It turned out to be another poor season for the club as they finished 14th in the League and Gerry only scored six time times in the League out of a total of only 24 for Atalanta.

As with all the previous summers since they had moved to Italy, the family returned to Britain and, as always, there were the usual visits to the family and also to their friends like Les and Betty Farrington. During the five years that Gerry and Meriel had been in Italy they always looked forward to seeing the couple who had encouraged them to move to Italy from the outset. Les and Betty were excited by Gerry and Meriel's new life and had collected quite a lot of press cuttings about Gerry's games and their experiences in Italy. They became godparents to several of the children and attended christenings that were traditionally held at St Catherine's in Pontypridd during the summers the family were back in Britain.

It was 1966, and that meant the World Cup in England. During the course of the World Cup qualifiers Gerry and Meriel attended a few matches, including North Korea beating Italy 1–0 in Middlesbrough. At that match sitting next to Meriel was Torino legend and former teammate of Gerry's, 'Gigi' Meroni, who was injured at the time and could not play in the Finals. He was in tears as Italy were knocked out at the group stages, effectively by North Korea. After the game, he was saying to Meriel that he thought the fans would not let the players back into the country after that result, a result that ranks up there among the greatest shocks in World Cup history and embarrassed the whole Italian nation. North Korea – with the youngest team in the Finals – found themselves in the quarter-final stage at the expense of two-time winners, Italy.

The 'big day' was 30 July 1966, and it was a day that will always go down in history as England's finest-ever football achievement. Gerry and Meriel had been invited to stay with their old friend and BBC journalist Brian Glanville at his home in West London on the weekend of the Final. Brian was due to report on the game for the *Sunday Times,* and he kindly accompanied Gerry and Meriel to Wembley. As it was a special occasion, all the ladies got dressed up for the day, and Meriel was no exception. Meriel expected to travel to Wembley by taxi, but Brian had other ideas, so they headed to the nearest underground station.

With England World Champions and a summer of celebration over, it was back to work for Gerry and another season at Atalanta. The 1966–67 season started in the same way as the last, with a mixture of results in the first third of the season. It took Gerry until the 10th game to find the back of the net, but it was only a consolation as Atalanta were given a lesson in finishing by Torino in a 6–1 defeat. He scored again in the next game, a home defeat by Roma.

Atalanta had found mid-table safety, but goals proved hard to come by for the club and for Hitchens, who by the end of the season was no longer first choice, or even second-choice striker. Things were that bad for Gerry that his last goal of the Serie A campaign was in a 3–0 victory against Lazio in early February 1967. Although he had managed to play 26 games in League and Cups, he had only scored four times, and he was not playing regular first-team football. Even at 32 years old, this was not what Gerry expected. He wanted to play and play regular football at a high standard and did not want to get paid good money to sit on the bench or play in the reserves, week in, week out, even though he loved Italy. He did not want to drift away into obscurity.

Gerry's greatest concern, however, was not the forthcoming Serie A season or where he was playing, but for his wife, who was pregnant with their fourth child. The couple remained in Bergamo for the summer as talk of a transfer increased.

Shortly after another frustrating season for Gerry, he was asked to move on, this time to the island of Sardinia in what seemed like a dream move and one last crack at Serie A football with Cagliari. Football in the sun – what more could a man want?

During the summer, not only were Gerry and Meriel looking for somewhere to live, but they also announced the arrival of their fourth child, Jason, who was born in Bergamo in August 1967. Gerry was in 'ritiro' with Cagliari, having just joined his new teammates in pre-season training, when he had to break away as soon as he had heard that Meriel had gone into labour and arrived just in time at the hospital to be present at the birth. It had been five years since their last child Karen was born back in 1962, and during that period they had left Milan and had also lived in Turin and Bergamo. Now they were looking forward to settling down for the next couple of years in the sunshine of Sardinia.

La Dolce Vita

*'For me Bergamo or Cagliari – it makes no difference. The
importance is to play.'*

Cagliari Calcio
June 1967 – November 1969

Sardinia has a Mediterranean climate, even though it is surrounded by the
Italian Peninsula and has hot and dry summers and very mild winters.
The climate is comparable to Southern California, but it is often refreshed
by north-westerly winds and is renowned for its beautiful seaside locations.
The wines produced there are some of the best in Italy, due to this mild climate.
In the 1950s and early 1960s it was also a very poor island where people were
forced to emigrate to find work and decent money. Some parts of the island
were controlled by bandits, and kidnappings were fairly common. The
economy of Sardinia was mainly reliant upon ancient traditions of pastoral
farming.

The Sardinia that Gerry and his family were going to was beginning to change,
with the era of mass tourism. The Aga Khan had purchased huge sections of the
coastline, and hotels began to spring up around the island's edges during the
1960s. It seemed like an ideal place to play out your football career.

The Hitchens family had relocated from the changeable climate of Northern
Italy, where they had spent the best part of the previous six years, to the sunny
island of Sardinia. At the age of 32, Gerry Hitchens was transferred from Atalanta
BC to Cagliari for £5,000. The Cagliari side that Gerry joined in 1967 was
managed by Manlio Scopigno and included the (then) legendary player, Luigi
Riva, best known as 'Gigi' or by his nickname '*Rombo di Tuono*' (Thunder).

Cagliari began their meteoric rise in Italian football during the early to mid-
1960s, having spent most of the 1950s mired in Serie B. The arrival of an
unknown 19-year-old footballer called Luigi Riva in 1963 for the astronomical
sum of 37 million lira from a little-known club called Legnano galvanised the
team and was a magnet for other players to leave more fashionable clubs to
head to Sardinia. Riva was good-looking, tall and strong, and at first he was
unconvinced by Sardinia, but he grew to love the place he once described as 'the
island where they sent people in order to punish them.'

Gerry was philosophical about his move, 'For me Bergamo or Cagliari – it makes no difference. The importance is to play. I am a professional, and as such I need to adjust to the different places. The only concern was my wife at this time.' Gerry saw in Cagliari a team with real capabilities and potential, 'Cagliari can do great things. We must not forget that last year, we lost Riva for half a season. The next Championship could see Cagliari between the major teams. The defence is strong and so is the attack. We are a good all-round team.'

Just after Gerry had arrived on the island and before he had chance to settle in, Cagliari joined several other European teams in a summer 'tournament' in North America as part of a fledgling League called the United Soccer Association (USA). Meriel remained at home with new baby Jason and the rest of the family, while Gerry flew to the United States. This was a pre-season with a difference. League clubs from Europe and South America were asked to play in American and Canadian cities, with each club bearing a local name.

After a series of exhibition games, the 'USA' began on 28 May 1967 and got off to a good start. The Houston Stars attracted an opening crowd of 34,965, but subsequent attendances did not keep pace and the League finished with an average of 7,890 per game. Of the 12 teams, Los Angeles Wolves, represented by Wolverhampton Wanderers and featuring Gerry's replacement at Villa Park in 1961, Derek Dougan, Cleveland Stokers, represented by Stoke City and featuring Gordon Banks, and Washington Whips, represented by Aberdeen, emerged as the strongest sides. Gerry, who was new to the Sardinian side, also took part in several games in North America.

Roberto Boninsegna of Chicago Mustangs, represented by Cagliari, finished as the League's top scorer with 10 goals and gained 13 points for Cagliari, two behind the division (and eventually League) champions, Los Angeles Wolves. The 'USA' entered its Play-off stage in July 1967. The Western Division champions Los Angeles Wolves won the right to host the Championship game against the Eastern Division champions, Washington Whips, by the flip of a coin. The match drew a crowd of 17,824 to the Los Angeles Memorial Coliseum. Wolves won the Championship, beating the Whips 6–5 after 36 minutes of extra-time. Four goals were scored within a four-minute period midway through the second half and each team scored during extra-time. The game was decided after Whips defender Ally Shewan scored an own-goal.

The United Soccer Association, not surprisingly, survived only one season before merging with the National Professional Soccer League to form the North American Soccer League.

During his stay in North America Gerry was bizarrely caught by a policeman for 'jaywalking', a fairly serious crime in some North American states, commonly considered an infraction but in some jurisdictions a misdemeanour and required a court appearance, but more usually the penalty was a fine; however, Gerry told the 'cop' who he was and was waved away with, 'ah, that's all right then.'

Cagliari were a provincial club who, historically, had spent most of their time in mid-table mediocrity and had only ever won the Serie C1 title in 1930–31, Campionato Sardo di I Divisione in 1936–37 and became the first-ever outright champions of Serie C during the 1951–52 season – prior to that in the League the Championship was shared among more than one team. They spent the 1950s from then on in Serie B, losing a promotion Play-off in 1954. After descending to Serie C in the early 1950s, Cagliari's rise was meteoric in the 1960s and they were eventually promoted to Serie A in 1964. Up to the 1967–68 season, when Gerry was signed from Atalanta, Cagliari had never won a major domestic Cup.

Gerry was not expected to start every match, but he said he would do his best to be in the running for a place in the side every Sunday, 'It's obvious that if you deserve to play you will play, but I will wait my turn. All great teams have reserves and Cagliari is a great team.' There were high expectations for the coming season in the Cagliari ranks but the fans and players expected a harder Championship this time. 'Certainly it's going to be more difficult, but Cagliari is one of the major players.'

In the previous season, 1966–67, Cagliari had showed real signs of progress, finishing sixth in Serie A with 40 points, nine points behind champions Juventus, and even finished above the mighty AC Milan, so he was coming to a club on the up and with real potential. Riva was top goalscorer in Serie A (*Capocannoniere*) in 1966–67 with 18 goals.

Cagliari got off to the worse possible start to the 1967–68 season, with two straight away defeats to Brescia and Bologna. Their first home game of the season was against Gerry's previous club, Atalanta, and it brought their first victory, 2–1. A draw against Napoli and another defeat against Fiorentina was not a good start for his new club.

Then, in the late evening of 15 October 1967, the whole nation was mourning another tragedy. Nearly 18 years after the air crash over Superga which killed an entire Torino team, another disaster occurred which brought the whole Italian nation to their knees. Gerry's former Torino teammate Luigi 'Gigi' Meroni and his friend Fabrizio Poletti were out on the town celebrating their home victory over Sampdoria. They were in the city looking for their girlfriends when around 9pm Meroni left his new Fiat car and walked across a street with Poletti to go to a bar. Meroni was in a good mood at the time as he and his girlfriend had been talking of getting married. Before they reached the bar, the two ignored the zebra crossing and decided to take a risk and crossed the wide two-way boulevard.

Meroni suddenly stepped back to avoid a fast car approaching, but another car travelling in the opposite direction was heading at some speed directly at the two men. The car hit Poletti and injured him slightly, but Meroni was struck on the left leg and was thrown into the air and across to the other side of the road, where an onrushing moped hit him full on as he lay on the ground, dragging him along the road for over 50 metres.

The ironic thing about the tragedy was that the young man who hit Meroni and caused him to be thrown into the air was a fanatical Torino fan, whose favourite player was no other than 'Gigi' Meroni. He apparently wore his hair like his idol and had pictures of him on his bedroom wall. He had also been at the game earlier in the day. Not only that, he lived in the same street as Meroni, only 13 doors away from his idol he had just killed. He was released by police after questioning that night. In a bizarre twist of fate, the man who accidentally killed Meroni, Attilio Romero, became president of Torino in the year 2000.

Meroni's funeral was attended by 20,000 people, and it was compared to the funeral for the Superga 'heroes'. Wreaths from all over Italy were sent, including one from Meriel and Gerry, in remembrance of their friend, 'Gigi' Meroni.

While Turin and the entire nation were coming to terms with the loss of a talented young footballer, Cagliari were making good progress after a shaky start to the season. The team were developing into a force to be reckoned with, and during a good sequence of results they defeated the likes of Juventus and Roma. Gerry's first goal for his new club came in the 11th week of the campaign against Spal. A young Fabio Cappello, who had been transferred from Spal to Roma at the end of the 1966–67 season, played against Hitchens in a thrilling game, which saw five goals and a 3–2 victory for Cagliari. The game was goalless for nearly 70 minutes until 'Gigi' Riva claimed his sixth goal of the season, and Hitchens made it 2–0 a few minutes later. Small-town club Cagliari were now third in Serie A, two points behind the mighty AC Milan.

The season was full of ups and downs, with one of the highlights being a 2–0 victory against Internazionale on 14 January 1968 in Milan. This was a game which was plagued by controversy as the Cagliari player, Miguel Angelo Longo, was hit by a coin thrown by an Inter fan; however, probably the best moment of the season came in March 1968 when Cagliari took on AC Milan in the San Siro, in a game which saw Hitchens scoring the only goal and the winner within a quarter of an hour. This was followed by a 3–2 home win against Internazionale on the last day of the season and saw Cagliari finish in ninth spot in Serie A. Gerry had made 17 appearances in his first season at Cagliari and scored four Serie A goals, but his close friend 'Gigi' Riva scored a creditable 13 to become joint second top scorer in the League, behind AC Milan forward, Pierino Prati.

After their first year on the sunshine island, life could not be any better for the Hitchens family, who were making the most of the surroundings and making many friends on the island. Gerry had always enjoyed shooting, ever since his army days, and there was that well-publicised event in which Gerry was fined for shooting game on a Sunday when he was living in Birmingham. While he had been in Italy, he had bought two very special German rifles, including an automatic rifle. In Sardinia there was a species of wild boar which were bred on the island, and Gerry very often went out on the hunt for the Sardinian wild boar. This was a very rare and special occasion and attracted an invited audience. On one occasion, he was lucky enough to shoot one of these beasts, and to celebrate, the locals presented him with the famous boar's head. The family still have it, and it is still mounted on a wall in Holywell.

At this time, Gerry became friendly with the young, silky, Brazilian player, Nenè. He had no family in Italy, and Gerry and Meriel took a liking to him and looked after him. One day, Nenè was feeling ill with a cold and sore throat and so visited the club doctor. About a week later he had Sunday lunch with the Hitchens family at their home and Meriel asked him if everything was alright with the doctor. Nenè, not familiar with European medicine or medical practice, said, 'those dreadful tablets they gave me, they stuck in my throat and I couldn't swallow them.' Gerry and Meriel realised that Nenè was taking suppositories – orally! Poor Nenè could not understand why Gerry and Meriel were laughing so much. Of course, that was how they gave medicine in Italy at the time, but obviously it was not the way in Brazil!

Even though there was a 10-year age gap, Gerry and 'Gigi' Riva became close friends, and possibly 'Gigi' saw Gerry on a fatherly level. Both men had a mutual respect for each other as players and as people and enjoyed each other's company, on and off the pitch. Hitchens had no problem with the fact that Riva was such a legend at Cagliari, and he was 'the new lad' at the club. In an interview especially for this book 'Gigi' recalled his time spent with Gerry with affection, 'As travelling meant leaving the island of Sardinia, we usually had two away matches, and in between the two matches we spent, let's say, Monday and Tuesday in the hotel. We'd meet up in Gerry's room with Ferrero, Tomasini, and Gerry would ask us, "What shall we do?"'

"Let's order beers!"

'So Gerry would count how many of us there were – Ferrero, Tomasini, Gerry and me. One, two, three, four, he would lift up the phone and order 10 beers!'

Gerry's eldest son, Marcus, who was only nine or 10 at the time, was frequently allowed into the Cagliari dressing room before the matches his father played in. Marcus did not recall all of the players' names, but the name of 'Gigi'

Riva was remembered with special affection. He recalled the excitement of the team walking through the dark underground tunnel, up the steps and into the bright Sardinian sunshine to hear the cheers of the crowd.

In the late 1960s most Italian stadia did not have proper seats, and the Stadio Amsicora was no exception. Indeed, part of the ground was open and did not have a 'proper' stand. Karen and Marcus remember always having to sit on the cold concrete floor, and after a while they used to take soft cushions to sit on as it was extremely uncomfortable to sit there for 90 minutes or more.

This was a lovely period for Gerry and his family as he was not under the same pressure to be a first-team regular and the leading striker, but he still wanted to prove he could play a bit in the top League, even though he knew his playing days were probably numbered. Gerry used to carry a camera (or a cine camera) everywhere he went, even going back to the 1962 World Cup, capturing all his memories from his stay in Italy, and very often he would ask teammates or officials to take photographs of him with someone famous wherever he played. Even though Gerry was a famous face in Italian football himself, he was absolutely delighted and honoured to be on the same pitch as such players as Pelé, whose Santos team visited Cagliari for a friendly game in September 1968 in which Santos won 2–1, and Lev Yashin, the legendary Dynamo Moscow goalkeeper. They were just two of the great players to be cajoled into having their photograph taken with Gerry.

Marcus recalls his father taking him down to the training ground the morning before the evening game against Santos to meet Pelé. Gerry was more excited that his son. More than 40 years on, he gets goosebumps thinking about the memory of meeting such a great football star and having the privilege of watching him train on that morning in Cagliari in 1968.

Dining out has always been a favourite pastime for the Italians, especially with the climate that the sunny island of Sardinia offered. They were ideal conditions for *al fresco* eating and barbecuing. At the time they had a girl working for them called Nina, who taught Meriel how to cook a whole host of Italian dishes. This was a great pleasure for Meriel, who had not really had the chance to learn many culinary skills in the seven years they had been in Italy. It really was *la dolce vita* for the Hitchens family during those long, balmy days in Sardinia. Schools finished at 1pm in Sardinia, due to the heat in the afternoon, and as they lived close to the beach the family used to go to lunch a lot at one particular restaurant that they favoured, the Calamosca, a hotel located on the Bay of Calamosca, which was the perfect place to relax. The Calamosca was a family friendly restaurant and they welcomed the whole family, buggies and all. Another local family favourite was Capo Boi, a hotel they used to frequent near Cagliari. Italian restaurants were mostly family orientated and encouraged families to eat in their restaurants; unlike in Britain in the 1960s where children were rarely welcomed. Meriel remembers one year they returned to Wales for the summer and they found a pub near Whitesands beach to have lunch, armed with push chairs and carry cots and to their amazement they were turned away by the owners. They were horrified as they were not used to being treated like this back in Italy. How things have changed.

With the luxury of living by the sea there was always the opportunity to dine by the beach, but there was also plenty of beautiful countryside on Sardinia and the family made the most of its beauty and regularly went for picnics inland. Arbatax, a small town with a harbour and located in the Ogliastra region, on the east coast of Sardinia, and was a beautiful part of the island. A natural frame to this was the panorama of the surrounding mountains, the highest on the island. Very often Marcus and his father would be seen diving off high rocks and swimming in the warm sea like dolphins.

As the club was based on an island and nowhere near any other club in Serie A, they had to play two back-to-back away games on the continent (the mainland), so it was a major exercise to either ship, which meant an overnight ferry, or fly the players to their destination and then go to the next destination for the following game before returning to the island for two home games. Gerry would sometimes be away for nearly two weeks at a time, and so it was a bonus when the team played at home, but none of the players, least of all Gerry, moaned about this as living on Sardinia was such a delight.

Gerry and Meriel had been lucky enough to be invited to many functions while they had been in Italy, like the high-class functions held by Sir James Henderson for the British Chamber of Commerce in Milan during the first few years of their stay in Italy. Sardinia was a small island, but boats and ships were seen coming and going all the time, especially to and from the port of Cagliari. It seemed like some sort of ritual that when every British boat or ship arrived in the port Gerry and Meriel would be invited onboard for drinks by the British Vice Consul.

On one occasion, the (woman) Vice Consul invited the couple onboard a British minesweeper which had just docked in Cagliari. It was very unstable, even when docked, and Meriel explained to the captain that she was six months pregnant at the time. She said that she was not very good on boats anyway, to which the captain corrected her and said, 'ship, this is a ship not a boat' and advised Meriel to have a drink of 'Horses Neck', which sounded disgusting to Meriel. She found out that a 'Horse's Neck' was in fact a cocktail made with brandy (or sometimes rye whisky or bourbon) and American dry ginger ale, with a long spiral of lemon peel draped over the edge of an old-fashioned or highball glass. Meriel took the captain's advice and had the cocktail. The captain also advised Meriel not to sit down. As it turned out, the captain's advice was sound, as Meriel and Gerry were probably the only two not to be seasick that evening. The Vice Consul herself had to rush to the toilet on several occasions, and as she had been invited to dinner back on dry land she had to go home and change. Everyone else could be seen going on and off the ship every so often with the feeling of sickness.

A few days later, Gerry and Meriel invited a couple of the young midshipmen they had met on board the minesweeper out for dinner to a restaurant in Cagliari which served taster dishes. They had such a lovely evening that the two young boys wrote letters thanking Gerry and Meriel for their warm hospitality.

Gerry was asked to deliver a short speech at another Chamber of Commerce function that they attended later in his Italian career. Being quite a shy and humble person, he did not really feel comfortable giving speeches but, having been in Italy for nearly eight years and having attended so many functions and balls, he obliged on this occasion. He spoke about coming out to Italy and his time in the country. At the end of the speech he was asked what he thought when he scored and all the Italian players came over to him and hugged and kissed him (they did not do that in England at the time). Gerry replied with quick wit, 'It's all right because I insist that everyone shaves before the match.'

Although Hitchens seemed to be surplus to requirements at Cagliari, he remained a popular personality and was much-loved at the club. In late April 1969, the birth of Damian completed the family pack. They had always planned on a big family and now, with the arrival of the fifth (and last), their family was complete. After one training session, 'Gigi' Riva recalled going to visit Gerry and Meriel at the clinic, along with Giuseppe Tomasini and Giuseppe Ferrero. All the family were there, and Gerry lined them all up from the smallest, Jason, with a bunch of flowers in his hands, followed by Karen, Nicola and Marcus. The three players had brought Meriel flowers. All were bachelors at the time and thought that they were a lovely, close-knit family group.

The Sardinian club followed a ninth-place finish in 1967–68 and emerged as serious Serie A title contenders in the following season with a three-horse race involving themselves, Fiorentina and AC Milan. Fiorentina won the *scudetto* with 45 points, but little Cagliari were notable runners-up in Serie A for the very first time in their history, level on 41 points with AC Milan. Incidentally, the club Gerry had left in the summer of 1967, Atalanta, were relegated, and it was Cagliari who beat the Bergamo side in the last game of the season to send them down into Serie B.

Unfortunately, Gerry was to only play two League games for Cagliari in the 1968–69 season and did not feature in the first few months of the 1969–70 season and was reduced to the 'economy list', which meant he would only get the minimum salary allowed by the Italian FA of £166 per month. He could not live on that wage and look after his wife and children. He left the Sardinian club and made the decision to return to Britain in November 1969. For most of his last full season at Cagliari, Gerry found himself on the substitute's bench or playing for the reserve team, which he was not accustomed to, having been a major part of each team he had played for since 1953. In the eight years he had spent in Italy, Gerry had scored 73 goals in 205 Serie A games for four different clubs.

At the age of 34, Gerry realised that the adulation was coming to a gradual halt, and he was no longer the fit, young, bustling centre-forward he once was. Some professional sports people when they head towards the inevitable retirement from the sport they have played for many years have no doubts that it will become difficult to bear, although everyone is different and some accept it more gracefully than others. Even for someone of his stature and past profile, Gerry generally belonged to the latter category.

There was a tremendous battle for Gerry's signature when he finally decided to return home to Britain, thereby justifying his popularity. 'I suppose it was a compliment really,' he remarked. Cagliari were asking for a fee of around £40,000 for a 34-year-old, which seemed a bit hefty, in an attempt to keep him at the club, even though he was only warming up the bench or playing in the reserves. The club were not even offering Gerry a decent wage so that kind of money seemed ludicrous, 'my playing days were nearly over, and I felt it was time to move the family back to England, but Cagliari just didn't want to let me go.' He said at one stage he said he would pay the fee himself, but eventually he was given the green light to return home.

The Italian sports newspaper, *Corriere dello Sport*, wrote, 'he is the nicest foreign footballer in Italy. He is adored by the crowds because he is a good player and a beautiful "actor." He has the true qualities to lead men and will make an excellent coach or manager.' It was a nice thing to say, but Gerry had no intentions of becoming a coach or manager of any football team.

Following Gerry's departure, Cagliari went from strength to strength and followed up their runners'-up spot with the ultimate prize in May 1970 when they lifted the Serie A trophy for the first time ever. Riva capped the most fantastic year in the history of Cagliari by becoming *Capocannoniere* with 21 goals for the second successive season and the third time in four seasons. It was unfortunate for Gerry, as in that season his great friend 'Gigi' Riva led the Cagliari side to their very first *scudetto*, following on from the previous seasons exploits when they narrowly missed out on the Championship to Fiorentina. This time around, however, they made no mistake, and it was all based around the unique talent of one man, Luigi 'Gigi' Riva. He led the whole island into days of celebrations. Not only that, but Cagliari also qualified for the European Champions Cup for the first time in their history, and Riva became a legend among legends.

Riva later became the all-time leading scorer for the Italian national team, scoring 35 goals in only 42 international games. Even though he was not a true Sardinian, having being born in the Lombardy region, he became an eternal figurehead for Sardinia, a kind of 'mythical' player and one of the best forwards of his time. He had a fantastic scoring record for Cagliari, scoring 169 Serie A goals thanks to his great heading ability, fantastic left foot and composure in front of goal. Later in his career, Riva became president of the club in the mid-1980s, but it only lasted one season.

For Gerry and his family, after eight years of wonderful experiences and moving with the ups and downs of being a professional footballer in a soccer-mad country, it was '*arrivederci, Italia*' and a sad farewell to a country which had made them so welcome from the very beginning, right up until their final day.

Playing for Extra-time

'All I want to do now is to play football.'

It was the end of the wonderful life – *la dolce vita* was over. Now the hard work began. Finding a job back in Britain for a 34-year-old professional footballer proved easier than he thought it would. He was, after all, a household name who would be able to pull in the crowds for any lower League club. Even though it was a step down from Serie A to the English Southern Premier League, the main thing was that he would be getting first-team match practice and keeping himself fit.

During the summer Gerry was linked with many clubs in England and Wales, including Swansea, Hereford, Walsall, Merthyr and Barry. He was even spotted sitting in the stand at Aggborough, where he had started his professional career in 1953, watching a Kidderminster Harriers game. He enquired about playing for his former club, but the money they were offering was not what Gerry was hoping for; he would not be able to afford to live on the wage, and a deal did not materialise. In 1969, Kidderminster Harriers were still bringing their youngsters through the ranks and would not have broken their policy by paying big money for a 35-year-old, even though he still looked fit and his name and experience would have brought the crowds to Aggborough.

There was even a suggestion that a contract was drawn up with a South African club, but Gerry decided against this proposal. There were also serious whispers that he was wanted in the US, but that would have been a big gamble. British players going to America in the late 1960s and early 1970s was big news, and Gerry could have earned a lot of money in the process; however, with the offers coming in from abroad, the priority for Gerry and Meriel was their children's education, and that was the main reason why the family returned to Britain as the education system in Italy was not as good as it was in the UK. Meriel would have liked to have stayed in Italy and especially Sardinia for longer, but the family was their priority.

One Midlands club tried harder than anyone else to sign Gerry. Worcester City had been hot on the heels for a recognised striker for some time, and Gerry Hitchens fitted the bill. When Gerry signed the deal which saw him say *'arrivederci'* to the sunny climes of Sardinia in November 1969 and sign for

Worcester City he admitted, 'This episode of my life is over, and all I want to do now is to play football.' It was not easy to sign for Worcester, however, as the Italian FA were required to send the English FA clearance for him because he was still under contract for an Italian club.

It appeared that Gerry had visited St George's Lane several months before signing, but Cagliari placed a fee on him and refused to transfer him on a free. Worcester could not sign him in the summer break, so Gerry spent the previous four months doing little, apart from training with Cagliari to keep fit.

Marcus was 10 years old at the time and could hardly read or write in English. He was the 'blond haired kid with a sun tan' in the Italian schools he attended, having been brought up from the age of two only really knowing life in Italy and speaking Italian. When the family returned to Britain it was time for Marcus to sit the 11-plus exam, which he failed miserably, but it did him little harm in later life as he achieved an A level in English language.

It was another change of lifestyle and climate for the children. From the sunny skies of Sardinia and the warm Italian Peninsula it was back to the cooler climes of South Wales. Marcus recalls one fine, warm day going to the seaside at Porthcawl and jumping into the sea and running straight back out, terrified, asking his dad why he did not tell him how cold the sea would be.

Gerry finally received a letter from the English FA saying that they had clearance from the Italian FA, and this meant he could sign for any club under the jurisdiction of the English FA. As soon as this was received he notified Worcester City, and the transfer papers were quickly finalised.

Gerry's father-in-law had offered Gerry the chance to work for him back in South Wales on a part-time basis while filling in his time playing semi-professional football and this was a serious option to consider.

Gerry said about his latest transfer, 'I am looking forward to playing in the Southern League again. I started my career with Kidderminster Harriers in the Southern League, and I am very happy to be back in it. I am obviously not match fit, for I have not played competitively for the last four months. I have, however, kept in strict training.'

Worcester chairman, Ken Parkinson, said on Gerry's transfer, 'This is the finest thing that could have happened to us in the present circumstances. We have now secured the services of a player whom the other players can look up to. This is an investment for the club, and we hope it will show returns through the turnstiles.'

Caretaker player-manager Eddie Stuart commented, 'I am, to say the least, delighted with the signing. I think that this is just the tonic we need. I think that our need in my seasons at the Lane has always been a striker. I have gone to a lot of trouble to acquire Gerry's services, and I hope the local football followers will give us the support we need. Without this support, we cannot afford top-class players like Hitchens.'

For Gerry, the wheel had turned full circle. He said, 'this is a great little club, and I know I'm going to be happy here. I considered joining Swansea but didn't fancy their offer. They wanted me to join them for a trial period to prove myself. It made me feel as if I was begging for a job, and I would never do that.'

Gerry's family were also doing a full circle, back to Pontypridd, South Wales, where Meriel was from and where they lived when he played for Cardiff City. Playing part-time was also a new experience for Gerry as he balanced his footballing life with working at his father-in-law's ironworks firm in Pontypridd, trying to learn the trade. Meriel's father, Harold, was always greatly admired by Gerry, and Harold always saw Gerry as his own son and adored him as one. Having two daughters, he always wanted a son, having lost his own prematurely at the age of five, he really took Gerry into his heart right from when they first met back in 1955.

Gerry's first match for Worcester was on 10 November 1969 against Bath City in the Southern Premier League at St George's Lane. Average attendances at home games were around 1,800, but such was the interest in Gerry the gate for his debut was 3,037 to see the home club beat Bath City 1–0. The crowd had obviously come to see the Gerry Hitchens of old, the player who could turn defenders and ride tackles, a skill he learned during his spell in Serie A, and even at 34 years old his class and ability shone through.

The match bonuses on offer by Worcester were nothing compared to those sums thrown around in Italy, especially in his early days at Internazionale and Torino. The win bonus when he played for Inter against AC Milan was said to be £500. It was like stepping back in time, to the days when he first stepped into the limelight at Kidderminster Harriers in 1953, playing in the Southern League at Aggborough. This time he was not the 'rookie' but an experienced 34-year-old 'legend', who had just spent eight years at the very top flight of Italian football and had played for England seven times. He would be the one who the youngsters would look up to.

On 27 March 1970, Gerry came across one of his old sparring partners again, none other than Leeds United and Juventus legend, John Charles. He must have come up against Charles a number of times playing for Cardiff, Villa and in Italy, of course. Whereas Hitchens had continued with his Italian adventure two years longer than the Welshman, Charles had returned to Britain in 1963 and signed for Cardiff City before moving to Hereford United in 1966, where in fact he remarkably ended up playing more games than any of his other clubs, other than Leeds United.

The game was played at the St George's Lane ground in front of a more than healthy 3,700 fans, and it turned out to be a scrappy local derby, not helped by the performance of the referee, who appeared not to have a clue what was going on in the game. He sent off Worcester forward Robinson after a series of incidents with Bird, disallowed a good Worcester goal, denied Hereford a penalty and blew his whistle non-stop. The game ended well for Gerry as he grabbed the winner just before half-time.

City finished the season in 16th place in the League. Gerry played a total of 39 games in League and Cups and scored 19 goals, which was not a bad return for a 34-year-old. The club also won the Worcestershire Senior Cup that season.

The 1970–71 season brought a similar return – 16 League and Cup goals in 33 appearances, although he did not finish the season at Worcester. His short career with the club ended on a sour note. His last game was in mid-February 1971 after City bosses put the 35-year-old on the transfer list and informed all Southern League and Division Four clubs of his immediate availability.

It came as a shock to Gerry, just as it did when he was playing for Torino and he was told he was going to be transferred to Atalanta. After all, his scoring record, considering he was 35 years old, was impressive, and he had scored in every other game for Worcester. But obviously club bosses were not happy with Gerry. Club chairman Ken Parkinson explained, 'The reason why we have put Gerry on the list is because we feel that we are not getting the best out of him at the moment.' Team manager Wilf Grant added, 'I feel that he has got to put in extra training, and with his vast experience he could well come back and prove all his critics wrong.'

It also appeared that the demand for his services in charity matches had led to problems within the club and was a key factor in letting him go. He had actually played in three charity matches before he had made his debut.

Gerry thought that he had become a scapegoat after hearing of the club's decision, 'Well, that's up to them. I don't want to get involved in a slanging match, but it seems to me that they are trying to make me the scapegoat. When things are going wrong for the team, the directors seem to go gunning for me. It's different, of course, when things are going right.'

It was revealed that when he had signed from Cagliari in November 1969, the club had agreed for him to train in Pontypridd, along with fellow teammate Howard Madeley. Gerry, however, had decided to train with the rest of the lads at St George's Lane. Therefore, Gerry and Howard, who had become quite good friends in that short time, travelled together from Pontypridd to Worcester, sometimes several times a week, to train with the rest of the lads. 'I did not want anyone to think that Gerry Hitchens was getting special treatment. And I paid for these journeys to Worcester for the training sessions – sometimes it was twice a week – out of my own pocket,' he said.

The club had also asked Gerry about his weight, 'I didn't agree with this. I am about the same weight as I was five or six years ago. I have a contract with Worcester, and I will abide by it.'

Not only did Gerry like his food, but he had also smoked for most of his football career, probably with the exception of when he was with Internazionale, where there was a total smoking ban under the Herrera regime. At one stage in his life he must have been smoking in the region of 30 or 40 a day. Smoking is unheard of now, in modern-day professional football, but in the 1960s and 1970s it was fairly commonplace.

Gerry had been lucky all his life and was not out of work long. Almost as quickly as he was released by Worcester, Welsh club Merthyr Tydfil came in and snapped him up on a free transfer on 26 February 1971 with wages of £20 per week less tax. Merthyr were pinning their hopes of promotion to the Southern League Premier Division on the transfer of a player who was nearing retirement.

His first game was on the very next day against Rugby Town. After three games, he offered his services as a player-coach, but he was released after just eight games and one goal, although in the games he did play in his performances were 'reasonable', and he provided good support to his fellow forwards. In what proved to be his last-ever competitive game, he came on as a substitute in a match at Gravesend on 15 April 1971.

At the age of 37, Gerry's professional career as a footballer was effectively over.

Playing Until the Very End

'They have been the happiest days of our lives.'

After 18 years as a footballer (16 as a professional) and a career spanning nine clubs, it was time for Gerry to hang up his boots once and for all. Given his background, he always brought a sense of perspective to his footballing career and, while he was always a fierce competitor, he remained a modest man and a shining example of sportsmanship and good humour throughout.

In Italy, he was (and still is) affectionately remembered as '*l'uomo di granito*' (man of granite), '*Un buon minatore*' (the good miner) and '*il cannone*' (the cannon) and to this day has the longest career of an Englishman in post-war Italian football, a record which actually appears in the *Guinness Book of Records*. He had a wonderful career which took him from a miners' club team in Shropshire to Merthyr Tydfil, via Kidderminster, Cardiff, Birmingham, Milan, Turin, Bergamo, Cagliari and Worcester. He always had a reputation for being hardworking, unselfish, good in the air and rarely injured, added to the most important ingredient of all, that of scoring goals in abundance wherever he went. He had played with some of the most well-known footballers at the time – Bobby Moore, Bobby Charlton, Jimmy Greaves, Trevor Ford, Peter McParland, Luis Suárez, Giacinto Facchetti, Luigi ('Gigi') Riva to name but a few. He also played against some of the greats, including Pelé, Finney, Matthews, Lofthouse and Charles.

One of the first things that Gerry did upon leaving Merthyr was to rent a caravan big enough to fit the whole family for the whole summer of 1971. They found a suitable one in Cenarth, Cardiganshire, which was on the borders of Carmarthenshire, Pembrokeshire and Ceredigion. Cenarth was a charming and historic village nestled upon the River Teifi, within the breathtaking scenery of West Wales. For years, people have visited Cenarth to see the spectacular falls that lie at the heart of the village, and this was an ideal place for fly-fishing and complete relaxation. Just the ticket when you had served 16 years as a professional footballer. The family liked the area so much that they later bought their own fixed caravan and spent every summer for the following six years there.

Gerry loved fishing and always encouraged Marcus to participate. One summer's day, they went to the river and cast their lines just up stream from

Cenarth falls. Before too long there was a shreik from the the 12-year-old Hitchens as his rod all but disappeared into the weir pool as he hung on bravely. Gerry came to the rescue and played the 2ft salmon for 20 minutes until the fish eventually gave up and was safely in the net.

A local bailiff spotted Gerry holding the rod and congratulated him, saying 'beautiful salmon Mr Hitchens'. Gerry said excitedly that it was in fact his young son who had hooked the huge specimen, even though Marcus was too young to hold a salmon licence! After a couple of pints in the local pub the bailiff decided to turn a blind eye, and Gerry kept the fish. A few days later, however, the story made the *Pontypridd Observer*, and it led by saying Marcus was the 'fisherman of the family' as he had hooked the salmon and his father was left empty-handed from the fishing trip. The story was accompanied by a picture of Marcus with the huge fish in his hands.

As Gerry was generally well liked and good company, he was not short of invitations for charity events, golf days, gentlemen's evenings and was even known to do a bit of punditry now and again. He picked the goal of the month for the BBC TV programme *Match of the Day* in the mid-1970s and often appeared as a football pundit for BBC Wales.

Gerry never really enjoyed watching live matches when he was not playing and did not show any interest in being a coach or manager after he hung up his boots. All through his career, he wanted to participate and would become quite anxious if he was left out of the team or injured, which was not very often, and luckily he did not spend long on the sidelines during his playing days. He did enjoy watching football, especially his beloved Aston Villa, on the TV. He also loved watching boxing, ever since his younger years as a footballer, and took the opportunity to watch the big fights on TV.

One long-standing, mutual hobby that Meriel and Gerry enjoyed was dog breeding, and especially rearing Afghan Hounds. It had started when the family moved back to the UK from Italy in 1969. 'I've always loved dogs, but never thought of showing them before,' Meriel admitted. When Gerry ended his footballing career, he was able to turn his attention to breeding championship dogs. Gerry had a voluntary job as a publicity officer for the South Wales Kennel Association (Meriel was, at that time, treasurer of the same association) and helped run the annual Welsh National Dog Championships, while working full-time at his father-in-law's steel fabrication works. At that time in the early 1970s, they had six Afghan Hounds, but only Meriel had time to show them. His love of dogs replaced his interest in soccer, which had taken up most of his life it seemed, from the time he was playing with 'jumpers for goalposts' to his last professional match at Gravesend in April 1971. 'Exhibiting and breeding dogs is something the whole family can be involved in but while I was playing soccer I had to spend a lot of time away from my wife and children,' he said.

At the age of 36, Gerry temporarily became manager of his father-in-law's ironworks business in Pontypridd; however, a series of strokes forced Meriel's father, Harold, to sell the business as Gerry had not been in the business long enough to take it over completely. It was the case of 'one door closes and another one opens', as Gerry was offered the chance to manage at his brother-in-law's timber supplies and building supplies company, P.S. Williams in Gronant, near Prestatyn, North Wales. The company imported timber from all over the world and was doing well at the time. So, in 1977, the family moved again, this time to a lovely cottage in Holywell on the North Wales coast, half an hour from the Roman city of Chester.

It was his father-in-law, Harold, who introduced Gerry to the Rotary Club when they were still living in Pontypridd in the early 1970s, and he was very proud to introduce his famous son-in-law to his fellow Rotarians. However, when the family moved north to Holywell, he remained a Rotarian and joined the Holywell branch. As Gerry was working in Prestatyn and the Rotary Club held lunchtime meetings, it meant that he could not attend very often and was granted special dispensation because of his work. He could not participate as much as he wanted; nonetheless, Gerry enjoyed being part of the club. At the same time, Meriel was a member of the Inner Wheel Club, which was the ladies section of the Rotary Club. Incidentally, Meriel held office as president and treasurer for many years.

Marcus remembers his father could turn his hand to most sports, cricket, tennis, golf and was a tremendous swimmer. Gerry's cricket skills grew from his time in the army, where he used to play for the team during the summer months. He played in a cricket match in Pontypridd with his father, organised by the Rotary Club one year, and Gerry bowled out most of the opposition single-handed, then went into bat left-handed (but he was really right-handed) and managed to knock a few runs. Marcus was out for a 'duck', and his father was not impressed. Marcus also recalls playing in a football friendly with his father in Cardiff, and his team won 11–1, with Gerry scoring 10 and Marcus scoring the other.

Ifor Roberts, who used to play for Bangor and later became a great friend of Gerry's, first heard of the rumours that 'this great footballer was moving to Holywell' through local newspaper stories. It was 1977 and Ifor was asked to play in a charity match for his old side against an ex-Rhyl side, which included Gerry at Caernarfon, a match incidentally organised by Gerry's old

Cardiff teammate, Harry Kirtley. After the match, Ifor had a few pints with Gerry and a good old chat, and they later became great friends.

At that time, Ifor was a development officer for the leisure department of the local council, and he was involved in the development of laying a synthetic surface at Flint Leisure Centre. When the surface had been completed, Ifor organised a promotional event to officially open the new development. Through his contacts at Wrexham FC, he organised a Wrexham XI to play a guest XI, which included Gerry. A teenage Ian Rush, who was plying his trade at Chester at the time, was also a guest at the event, which went off splendidly and drew a sizeable crowd.

After that event, Ifor and Gerry shared many an evening playing squash, watching boxing tournaments and having the odd pint here and there, and their friendship developed. Ifor was still playing in charity matches for a solicitors XI in Mold, organised by local lawyer, Phil Lloyd-Jones. Of course, the very mention of football alerted Gerry, and he wanted a piece of the action, even though he was the best part of 44 years old now. As soon as the rest of the team knew that this great football star wanted to play with them, they were thrilled at the news, and they all wanted to be part of it.

Phil recalled the first time he met Gerry, having watched him all those years ago in the 1962 World Cup. His athleticism and build were almost identical, and he was only about half a stone over his playing weight.

Phil did not have time to introduce Gerry to his new teammates and said to him, 'Go on Gerry, just do your bit and pocket a few goals…' Nobody in the team, apart from Phil and Ifor, knew they were playing with an ex-professional, let alone someone who had played in a World Cup and in Italy for eight years. Not many of the team recognised him as most of the players were a lot younger. At half-time, one player approached Phil and said, 'that old man over there, I think he's played football before.' Phil explained that he played in the 1962 World Cup, and the player promised to keep quiet about it for the rest of the match.

The team had just beaten a Harlech TV XI by 7–0, with Gerry scoring a hat-trick, and the team were so overjoyed by their victory that they started talking about giving the team a name over a pint or three. Barry Roberts of the Harlech TV team shouted over, 'Ifor, I've got a name for your team…' There was a small pause.

'What is it then?' Ifor said.

'SAS,' he said, which prompted Ifor to think that they were thought of as a team of fit, tough guys.

'Ifor', Barry replied, 'Soft As Shit.' That became the 'unofficial' name of the team.

They also talked about other grand ideas, like a 'tour'. Gerry's 'dream' idea for a tour was Sardinia, being familiar with Italy, but in the end it was all a good-natured pipe dream, one of those we all have in the elation of victory and over a few pints. Even though the quality of the football was questionable at times, it was the camaraderie which kept the team together.

They were becoming quite well known locally and so was Ifor, who was described in one local newspaper as 'the rural Welshman whose mouth didn't stop for 90 minutes.' Ifor would say that if he 'didn't shout and bawl at his teammates they would leak goals like a sieve'. As for Gerry, he was the quiet one, and he did his talking with his feet and scored all the goals, but it did not stop Ifor shouting at him and his teammates.

On 2 March 1983 football was back on the agenda as Aston Villa were due to play Italian giants Juventus in the European Cup quarter-final at Villa Park. Villa were European champions and Juventus were Italian champions, so the billing for the match was huge – it was the battle of the heavyweights. The day before the match, Gerry was invited to play for a British Press XI against the Italian Press XI on the Villa Park pitch, organised by Ian Johnson of the *Birmingham Post* newspaper. The British Press XI won 4–0, and Gerry came up against one of his friends John Charles (the Gentle Giant). The last time the pair played against each other was 13 years ago when they were in their mid-thirties playing non-League football.

Gerry had struck up a friendship while working with his brother-in-law, and they played golf together on numerous occasions, but they flew to Portugal on a golfing holiday in the March of 1983 shortly after the match at Villa Park. At this time, Meriel had been ill since the January and was still recovering when he left for Portugal.

Being a footballer all his life, Gerry was always active, even after retirement from the game. He kept fit and was always on the go, but before he went on the golfing holiday to Portugal he injured his leg playing football in one of the charity matches.

On Wednesday 13 April 1983 he was still feeling the effects of the leg injury he had picked up from playing in a match for the 'SAS' team a few weeks before when they played on a hard 'redgra' surface, which was hated by the team as it took its toll on the muscles of the older players. Gerry decided not to go to the doctors to get it checked out and thought nothing of his injury. Karen, Gerry's youngest daughter, who was working with her mother and father at the timber merchants, warned him to be careful with his leg at work on the morning of the 13th.

Gerry had never been ill before, let alone been seriously injured in his 16 years as a professional footballer. He looked wonderfully fit and tanned from his golfing holiday, and so he decided he was fit enough to play for the 'SAS' team at the Castell Alun Sports ground in Hope, near Wrexham, North Wales, not too far from his home in Holywell. He jumped at the chance to play on a grass surface after too many matches had been played on artificial surfaces. The match was against an architect's XI from the county council.

It was a very robust and competitive game, full of bad language, flying late tackles and rubbish football, but as with any game it meant something to Gerry as he was competitive to the core. Gerry found himself, somewhat uncharacteristically, shouting and commanding and, with the game drawing to a close and the score at 3–3, Ifor Roberts produced probably the finest ball he had ever hit. He crossed the ball, and Gerry jumped majestically like a salmon and met the ball with his head, in a style reminiscent of his professional footballing days; however, the ball went skywards over the bar. Seconds later, Gerry collapsed on the ground. Unaware that Gerry was in trouble, some of his teammates shouted, 'What you doing Gerry…? How did you f*****g miss that one?' The opposition full-back stood in the penalty area waving frantically for attention. Close friend Phil Lloyd-Jones, who was in goal for the match, rushed the full length of the pitch to give Gerry mouth-to-mouth resuscitation and heart massage, but he was not getting any response, and he knew it was critical. Ifor shouted to everyone to take their shirts off to keep Gerry warm. An ambulance was immediately called and arrived sometime later, racing towards where Gerry was lying.

Once Gerry was rushed into the ambulance, Ifor immediately drove Gerry's car to locate Meriel, who at this time was unaware of the criticality of the situation. When the ambuance arrived at Wrexham General Hospital there was no hope of Gerry regaining consciousness, and he was pronounced dead on arrival.

The South Clwyd coroner was informed of the death, and an inquest was held. It was suspected that there was a thrombosis in the leg, which became an embolism blocking the main artery, which caused the heart attack.

As for Ifor, it would spell the end of a brief but wonderful friendship with a world soccer star he called his mate, and those six or seven games played with Gerry provided some great memories for him.

Holywell, and the area, were in shock for the whole week leading up to the funeral. Hundreds of well-wishing messages were received by Meriel before the service, which was held at Holywell Parish Church on Tuesday 19 April 1983. Meriel led the family, which consisted of their five children, Marcus,

Nicola, Karen, Jason and Damian. Hundreds of people lined the streets of Holywell to pay their last respects. The service was attended by over 100 guests, including Gerry's ex-Villa manager, Joe Mercer, who was one of the pall-bearers, the then Chelsea manager John Neal and former Liverpool full-back Gerry Byrne, who all escorted the coffin. Some of Gerry's footballing friends, including Jimmy Greaves, John Charles, who had played with Gerry only a few weeks before, and Bobby Charlton, were unable to attend but sent their private condolences, via lovely wreaths to the family home. Following the service, a cremation took place at Colwyn Bay.

Gerry's brother-in-law, Grahame, who owned the timber import company that Gerry managed, declared to Meriel that he 'hadn't lost a brother-in-law, but had lost a brother,' he was that close to Gerry. Later, he asked Meriel if he could 'look after' Gerry's favourite, unique, wooden-headed putter he had bought in Sweden, which she willingly obliged.

It seemed like every national newspaper in Britain and Italy ran with the story. Tributes were printed in every newspaper, including one from Joe Mercer: 'that's a shocker. Everybody thought the world of him, especially in Italy. He did a fantastic job for Villa. He was so quick and got us out of the Division Two by scoring a lot of goals. He was a hell of a man.'

While the homage was most profound in the UK, Italy was mourning the loss of probably one of the best imports to have played in Serie A. All major newspapers and sports journals in Italy were full of memories of Gerry and quotes from some of his former teammates and people who had met him. The then vice-chairman of Internazionale, Giuseppe Prisco, said of Gerry, 'I saw Hitchens play for the first time in Rome, against Italy. I was impressed by the competitive zeal. He played very well in the shirt of the English national team. I was so happy to have him at Inter. Unfortunately, in the two seasons he played with the Inter shirt, he did not have much luck but was always distinguished by the maximum commitment and professionalism he showed.'

Tarcisio Burgnich (who was coach of Como in 1983) said, 'I played a few months with Hitchens (at Inter), but I have a good memory of him, both as a player and as a man. From the technical point of view, we can say that he was generous, a fighter, always ready to fight for the ball. As a man, he was exceptional.'

Gigi Riva (who was then Cagliari manager) said of his friend, 'It is one of those news stories which leaves you stunned. Just incredible. I remember Hitchens as the prototype of physical strength and sympathy. He was a nice man who wanted all good. He came to Cagliari when his career was in a declining phase. In his first Championship he played several games because [Roberto] Boninsegna suffered a harsh disqualification. In the second season he played for Cagliari less but proved to be a true professional and never moaned about it.'

Meanwhile, Jimmy Greaves spoke of Gerry with affection, 'We were very close young lads, wandering around like lost souls, and we met when possible for a couple of pints. We were very good friends, and the death was a personal blow. I had not seen Gerry for a number of years, but you never forget old friends. I am very sorry for his wife and family.'

A few weeks later, the village of Highley in Shropshire, where Gerry spent most of his childhood playing football on the piece of waste ground called 'The Rec', turned out for a memorial service for Gerry on Sunday 8 May 1983 at St Mary's Church in Highley. Family and friends attended the private service for their hero.

Meriel and Karen were still working at the timber merchants for Grahame in the period following Gerry's death. After a few bad experiences with managers, Grahame finally sold the business, and both Meriel and Karen left Grahame's business shortly after. Meriel quickly found work through a friend and had a successful interview at Hill Samuel, which was at the time a leading British merchant bank. She was soon employed as a national investment advisor, and after taking several exams she became a senior investment advisor.

It is sometimes said that dying is about legacy and never forgetting the person whom you have just lost. The memories will always be there and, eventually, something good can come out of death and very often it does. In this case, during the autumn of 1983, the talk was of some sort of charity match in memory of Gerry being arranged.

The Mayor of Delyn at the time, Penman Griffiths, had no idea who Gerry was or any interest in football, but his main aim was to organise events for the local public. Another man who was key in the organising of the memorial match was Elfed Ellis, locally known as 'Crazy Horse'. He was an ex-council officer who later became president of the Welsh FA. It was Ellis who eventually confronted Ifor and asked him, 'What are you doing about your old mate, Gerry? Why don't you have a match?' It was Ellis who really kick-started the idea of a memorial match, and through the contacts Ellis had at the Welsh FA he pointed the way towards a joint Manchester side, who played in organised charity matches at the time. It was David Sadler, who was part of the United side in the 1960s and early 1970s, who became Ifor's first contact, but as it turned out, it was Bobby Charlton,

Gerry's former England teammate, who was the main point of contact in organising these events.

For the next few weeks, it was up to Ifor to find a side to play this joint Manchester side. Ifor knew some ex-professionals, like Dai Davies and Howard Kendall, who accepted the invitation, and the list became bigger by the day. With the match being organised by Ifor and Delyn Borough Council, along with friends and associates of Gerry, a trust fund was also set up called the Gerry Hitchens Memorial Trust Fund, for which the main aim was to raise money to support local youth sports in Flintshire. Gerry had an afinity with young people so he would have approved of the trust fund and its sentiments.

On Sunday 30 October 1983, six months after his death, the Gerry Hitchens Memorial Match was staged at Flint Town United Football Club. The two teams were a Bobby Charlton All-Star XI and a Mike England All-Star XI. Bobby Charlton, who was so helpful and gracious on the day, led the two sides out and introduced Meriel to all the players as they lined up before the match. The team sheet on the programme read like a soccer 'Who's Who', with former England internationals, including Liverpool 'hard man' Tommy Smith, Howard Kendall, Colin Bell, Mike Summerbee, Alex Stepney and David Sadler to name but a few. Others included Paddy Crerand, David Herd, Tony Dunne, Willie Morgan, and former managers Tony Book and Wilf McGuiness.

Former Cardiff City teammate of Gerry's, Harry Kirtley, also played in the match, which was attended by four of Gerry and Meriel's five children, as Nicola was unable to attend. Entrance to the match was by programme only as the law in those days did not allow an entrance fee to be paid on a Sunday (unlike today).

The match was won by the Bobby Charlton XI 4–1, but it was not the score that mattered, it was the thousands who turned out and paid by programme only to raise in excess of £2,000 for the fund. Organisers never expected such a large crowd, and Flint Town had never seen an attendance anywhere near that size before and probably never will again. There were also some famous faces in the crowd, including a young Ian Rush, a local Flint lad himself, who was now becoming a Liverpool legend.

It transpired that just before the match the local Rover dealership, Edwards of Chester, had telephoned Ifor, knowing that a host of stars and ex-stars were due to play a charity match at Flint, to see if he could ask some of the players to make an appearance at the local car dealership after the match as they had a sales promotion on and it would be good for business.

Tony Book was driving some of the players back to Manchester in a minibus and he decided this seemed like a good idea. He stopped off at the dealership and had some photographs taken to help with publicity of the garage. A lot is often said about 'greedy' footballers these days, and the same was true then, but the dealership offered the players a cheque for £50 in appreciation for making an appearance at the forecourt. David Sadler accepted the cheque and immediately sent it to Ifor to go towards the fund. It was indeed an admirable gesture on behalf of the players. All the players had given their time up free of charge to play in the match. Mr Elfed Ellis of the Welsh FA, and a trustee of the fund, said of Gerry, 'Gerry did a wonderful job for local football, and we wanted to do something to perpetuate his memory.' Ifor Roberts, who helped organise the match, said, 'I think it shows just how highly Gerry was thought of by his fellow professional soccer players.'

Shortly after the memorial match, Phil Lloyd-Jones kindly drew up the deed and made the Gerry Hitchens Memorial Fund legal and official, and Meriel was named secretary of the fund. In the years that followed, many local sports clubs benefited from the generosity of the fund, which provided football teams with kits and donated equipment to all sorts of sports clubs for children under 16 years old, including several boxing clubs. Meriel and Ifor encouraged clubs to write in and apply for a donation or help from the fund, which made it a fairer way to distribute the proceeds. It was usually through word of mouth that these clubs heard about the fund, and it kept it low key and easy to manage, but it served the purpose as a memorial and kept the name of Gerry Hitchens alive for so many years to follow.

The Rotary Club, who had been supportive of Meriel after Gerry's death, held annual youth football competitions, and the fund contributed some prizes in Gerry's memory, and these were presented to the winning teams by members of the family. These matches continued for several years after Gerry's death.

There were times when interest was low, and that was when clubs were encouraged to write in for funding. Very few were refused.

Gerry was chairman of the Rhyl Hearts Football Club at the time of his death, and the man who took over from Gerry, Kevin Matthews, presented Meriel with the Gerry Hitchens Merit Shield, which was used for future Player of the Year Awards for the club, while she also received a silver commemorative Rose Bowl for herself.

Meriel and the family had a good circle of friends around them, most notably Betty and Les Farrington. They had been friends since Gerry's time at

Villa in the late 1950s and visited the couple most summers. Even though Les was not always in the best of health, Meriel and Betty continued their friendship by phone and the odd visit to see each other. It was always meant to be a friendship that lasted forever.

With Gerry's death fresh in the minds of the family, tragedy struck in mid-July 1989 when callous thieves robbed the family home of precious, irreplaceable mementoes of their hero. Friends of Meriel rallied around and offered a four-figure reward for the recovery of the items, which included medals, key rings and precious souvenirs taken from a security cabinet, which she had planned to pass on to her five children. Gold-coloured medallions with enamelled crests and inscribed in Italian with Gerry's name and dates were among the stolen goods. The medals had been given by the Italian clubs and supporters during his career in Italy and were irreplaceable. Police came to the house and took fingerprint samples, but nothing came of the investigation and nobody was ever arrested. Unfortunately, none of the precious mementoes were ever recovered.

Over 20 years after his father's death, Marcus had a phone call one day out of the blue from his cousin, Linda, who lived near Bridgnorth, not far from Highley where Gerry grew up. She told him that there had been a collective request in the Highley area to call a wonderful fitness suite that had just been built at the Severn Centre 'The Gerry Hitchens Fitness Suite' in memory of Gerry. This was in August 2004. It was a very nice surprise to all the family.

Meriel and Marcus represented the family at the opening ceremony, and Meriel said a few words and helped in cutting the ribbon. Incidentally, two others of the five ex-professional players who were brought up in Highley at the same time as Gerry, Stan Jones and Ted Hemsley, were at the ceremony to open the rest of the sports centre on the same day.

Coincidentally, the Severn Centre stands on land, known as 'The Rec' or 'The Orchard', the very strip of wasteland that Gerry and his mates played football on every day of the week when they were youngsters back in the 1940s and early 1950s: the same strip of land which bred five professional football players of the 'jumpers for goal posts' era.

There is a popular Latin phrase *carpe diem*, which is popularly translated as 'seize the day' or, in other words, make the most of the time you have in your life and the current opportunities presented to you because life is short and time is fleeting. Gerry certainly made the most of his (sadly short) time with us. He had a solid upbringing and childhood and always played the game he loved at every opportunity. He made the most of his talent, and his dreams came true when he put on an England shirt for the first time. In Italy, he lived 'la dolce vita' during those eight years and experienced life to the full, but never to excess.

Meriel still has the many fantastic memories of those times with her husband, and his legacy will live on in this book for everyone to share forever.

Living the Dream

'I had to rub my eyes when I saw my name on the list.'

It is every schoolboy's dream that one day he could play for his country. Gerry Hitchens was no different, but his self-determination and never-give-up attitude to put himself in a position to even be considered for an England cap puts him above the average schoolboy. Every day of his school year, Gerry would practise and practise, whether it be in the street, playing with his mates on wasteland or playing for the scouts team. He was so sure that his perseverance and determination to succeed would prevail and one day his dream would come true and he would be walking up the Wembley tunnel like his idols – Nat Lofthouse, Stanley Matthews and Tom Finney.

Gerry's England career almost started with a call-up to the B squad for a match against Switzerland at The Dell, Southampton, on 21 March 1956. He was selected as a reserve but 'wasn't required'. This was a team that fielded the great Duncan Edwards; however, by that time Gerry's name was already down for a pre-season FA tour of South Africa in May 1956.

1956 FA Official Tour of South Africa

With the 1955–56 season at an end – a season which saw Gerry Hitchens named as Cardiff City's top scorer with 28 League and Cup goals – the 21-year-old striker was selected for the FA's summer tour of South Africa, a pleasant bonus for the Division One footballer who still worked at the Nantgarw pit near Pontypridd in South Wales and was playing non-League football for Kidderminster Harriers only 12 months prior.

When the squad was announced by a pressman, he thought the reporter was 'pulling his leg'. Even Cardiff City manager Trevor Morris could not believe it, 'Why?' he said, 'The lad was kicking a ball about for Kidderminster reserves only 12 months ago. This is certainly great news for him – and for Cardiff.' Gerry's strike partner, Trevor Ford, said, 'He deserves it.' Usually, the FA did not look beyond England to pick the players for their teams. To select a comparative unknown player, who played in Wales, even though he had scored a sack full of goals in Division Two, was without precedent.

The news of his selection for the tour did not really sink in with Gerry, 'I had to rub my eyes when I saw my name on the list. We were invited to put our names down and I did so without dreaming I would be chosen.' Gerry was a sensible 21-year-old youngster who did not let the news go to his head as he knew he still had a few things to learn about the crafts of forward play.

An 18-man squad was announced in March 1956 and was made up of mostly lower League club players and young squad players, who were given a chance to prove if they would be good enough to step up a grade into the Under-23 or the full squad. The hefty schedule comprised 18 matches (including four 'Test matches'), in such places as Johannesburg, Durban and Cape Town, against the amateur footballers of South Africa as at that time there was no professional soccer in the country. The party of 18 left on 6 May, one day after the 1956 FA Cup Final between Manchester City and Birmingham City. Most players selected had represented England at either Under-23 level, B level or had full caps. Only seven selected players were without representative honours, including Gerry, who was at this level for the first time as he was not selected for the B squad a couple of month prior to the tour.

There were four official matches played during June and July 1956 against a South Africa XI and Gerry played in three, scoring three goals. England notched up 12 goals in the four 'Tests' and won three out of the four, drawing the other 0–0.

Gerry tried to create a good impression on the tour as he rattled home 17 goals in 12 games (including the three in the 'Tests') and ended up being top scorer on the tour, as the FA continued to spread the gospel of football on a worldwide scale, and the football career of Gerry Hitchens was beginning to take off.

England Under-23
Denmark versus England, Copenhagen
26 September 1956

There was a big debate at the time on who would be the successor to the great Billy Wright as the next England captain. The press were talking up the chances of Johnny Haynes, the Fulham skipper and a young footballer with a man's brain who was already the Under-23 captain, and they were even going as far as betting he would be made full England captain within the next three years.

Top English managers were now beginning to wonder why they had not splashed out the £1,500 that Cardiff City did when they signed the (then) 19-year-old Hitchens in 1953 from underneath the noses of the likes of Wolves,

West Bromwich Albion, Crystal Palace and Tottenham as he had been picked for the England Under-23 match against Denmark.

The Denmark Under-23 team were basically a team of amateurs, while the England squad included such names as Jimmy Armfield, Johnny Haynes, Jimmy Bloomfield and Ron Flowers, all of whom would later go on to full international recognition.

The match ended in an England victory, and the young team triumphed in Copenhagen, watched by a capacity crowd of 15,000. This was a very inexperienced England side, and reports suggested that none of the team were ready for a full international call-up. Gerry, as always, contributed to the game with a disallowed goal for offside in the 79th minute and then struck an easy goal two minutes from time to make it 3–0.

This turned out to be his one and only appearance for the Under-23 side, probably partly due to the fact that he had been called up for his national service.

Warm-up Friendlies

Gerry was selected to play for the English FA against the Scottish FA at Ibrox on 22 March 1961. He was released by Aston Villa, who were due to play Everton in the League, in order to play for the English FA team in the friendly game.

Two months later, on 5 May 1961, Gerry was selected to play for England against Young England in an (uncapped) warm-up match at Stamford Bridge, a prelude to the up-coming tour of Europe.

First Full Cap
England 8 Mexico 0
Wembley, 10 May 1961, Friendly

It was not until nearly five years after his debut in the Under-23 team that the England selectors were prompted by the exploits of Gerry Hitchens when he scored 42 League and Cup goals for Aston Villa during the 1960–61 season. His stock was increasing, and the eyes of the world were fixed on this strong, tall, blond lad from a Shropshire mining town. The next few weeks would see his life change forever, in more ways than one.

He was informed by manager Walter Winterbottom on 9 May that he was in the squad and that he would be leading the attack against Mexico at Wembley the very next day. Gerry jumped for joy when he was told the news that he would get his first England cap, 'This is the day I have dreamed about for so long. It has been my life ambition to play for England – and now I have the chance. I am deeply grateful to my Villa colleagues, the club and the fans at Villa Park for helping me to reach my target.'

Before the match, Gerry was presented with the *Birmingham Mail* Midlands Footballer of the Year Award by the editor of the paper. Walter Winterbottom, and the England team watched the presentation take place. Gerry said, 'What a wonderful day. First the news of this England cap, and now the surprise presentation of this wonderful honour. It is a day for me to remember as long as I live.'

The news that Spurs striker Bobby Smith was injured helped Gerry's cause, but he fully deserved selection on his own merits. Smith was told by specialists to rest and to have injections for his swollen knee. Gerry was the happiest man in the England party as he was waiting for the team pictures to be taken prior to the game. Not only was one forward injured, but Jimmy Greaves was suspended by Chelsea (for refusing to go on a club tour to Israel on the eve of his move to AC Milan).

The Mexicans were reported to be on a £100 per man bonus to beat England and did not announce their side until a few minutes before the kick-off. It did not take Gerry long to make a name for himself: England seemingly did not need Smith and Greaves as the floodgates were kicked open by Hitchens and his strike partner Derek Kevan. He made a sensational start to his England career, scoring with his first shot after just 90 seconds as he fooled the goalkeeper, Mota, by shooting instead of centring from a Charlton pass.

Hitchens and Charlton struck up a good understanding together up front. On the left wing, Bobby Charlton hammered his first international hat-trick. Kevan, playing in place of Greaves, missed three gilt-edged scoring opportunities, but the performance of Hitchens caught the eye as not only did he open the scoring but he also assisted in three other goals. The question on many lips was, 'How many goals would whizz-kid Jimmy Greaves have helped himself to against the overwhelmed Mexican defence?'

Credit had to go to Walter Winterbottom, the quiet but effective manager, much criticised in the past, but on this performance he had got his tactics right. He continued to use the 4–2–4 formation he had adopted from the Brazilians. It was one of the finest England post-war performances, even though it was only Mexico who had actually beaten England 2–1 two seasons previously. Words like 'elegant', 'revenge' and massacre' were used as the opposition were swept aside with ease. Seven or eight-man moves were common all match long as England grew in confidence with each goal.

After the game, captain Johnny Haynes made the ritual round, handing out the coveted tasselled blue caps to his players. 'Well played, Gerry. I hope this will be the first of many,' he reportedly said to the blond striker.

There was talk after his first cap of many more caps to come for Gerry. Newspaper headlines read:

SUBSTITUTE HITCHENS HERE TO STAY

There was even early talk of Italian agents among the Wembley crowd watching him play.

Gerry's parents were unable to be at Wembley to watch their son get his first full cap, but they remembered watching him on television. 'We were unable to be at the match but we were watching television at home and a *Bridgnorth Journal* reporter called at the front door to ask what we thought about his selection.' Violet said.

It was a great start for Gerry and his international career. No matter how good his debut was, though, it was not enough for Walter Winterbottom to pick Gerry for his first World Cup match. The next international and the start of England's European tour was a World Cup qualifier against Portugal in Lisbon, 11 days after the Mexico friendly, and Gerry was left out of the side after only one game and one goal.

England: Springett, Armfield, McNeil, Robson, Swan, Flowers, Douglas, Kevan, Hitchens, Haynes, R. Charlton.
Mexico: Mota, Peña, Jáurgui, Cardenas, Sepúlveda, Portugal, Del Aguila, Reyes, Gonzalez, Flores, Mercado.
Attendance: 77,000

Second Full Cap
Italy 2 England 3
Rome, 24 May 1961, Friendly

Bobby Smith, the free-scoring Tottenham centre-forward, had previously scored eight goals in six internationals for England but was bitterly upset and deeply hurt to be left out of the team to play Italy in Rome for this 'friendly' match. He was training in his usual role a day before the game when he was told by Walter Winterbottom that 'we are going to give Gerry Hitchens a run tomorrow.' Smith nodded and replied, 'That's all right.' A disappointed Smith was later reported as saying, 'I was too choked to say much when I was told I was out. When I was playing centre-forward in the training session today, I thought I was in the team all right.' He stated that he had not played well in the previous game against Portugal, but he was not the only one that day; however, Smith, who was a warm-hearted player, wished Hitchens good luck for the game. Winterbottom defended the decision, 'We had intended to use the matches against Italy and Austria to try out some of the other players.'

England captain Johnny Haynes was doubtful for the match with a leg injury and had received two courses of treatment at a private clinic before the game. George Eastham was waiting in the wings, but in the end Haynes recovered to keep his place.

The match would prove to be a tough test for England. It was a hot, sunny day in Rome, in front of 90,000 explosive Italian fans in the classically-designed, Stadio Olimpico. The howl of the Italian fans can be the most frightening crowds in the world, but England were there to win the game and not to make up the numbers.

Jimmy Greaves was the man all the Italians wanted to see, and he was protected from the paparazzi, who were clamouring for his life story and his future plans. At the time of the match, Greaves, who was still playing at his beloved Chelsea, was being tracked by Italian giants, AC Milan, who had a delegation in the stands to watch the striker. He had made it clear that his future would not be decided before the game.

As for Gerry, his debut performance against Mexico proved enough to earn him a place in this match against Italy. This was the game that was destined to change his life, and the eyes of Italy (if not the world) would be focused on Gerry Hitchens and not Jimmy Greaves for once.

Italy had never beaten England and were desperate to do so in front of a typically partisan crowd. Hitchens played a key role in making sure the Italians went home frustrated after a pulsating game. The first goal of the game came off the head of Hitchens in the 39th minute (Check it out on *YouTube*). The Italians paraded the gifted and flamboyant Argentinean-born Omar Sivori (who had previously played for Argentina), with his socks wrapped around his ankles, and he was the ace in their pack, and the Juventus inside-left took control of the game after the shock of going behind to the early Hitchens goal. Sivori equalised five minutes later with a flashing shot after side-stepping a challenge, as Italy began to dominate the game.

With the score at 1–1, the Italy goalkeeper, Lorenzo Buffon, was injured as he went to save a certain goal from Johnny Haynes, whose foot accidently carried through into Buffon's face as he dived for the ball, and he had to be substituted.

The Italian domination was further rewarded with a second goal, scored by centre-forward Sergio Brighenti in the 74th minute to take his side into the lead for the first time in the game. Sivori was convinced that victory was complete, and he started playing to the crowd, but his exhibitionism proved premature. Four minutes later, Hitchens hit a fairly strong shot, which the substitute 'keeper Giuseppe Vavassori should have saved but allowed to pass through his legs to score the equaliser. With five minutes to go in the game, Haynes put through a nice pass to Jimmy Greaves, who beat the right-back Losi for speed and fired in to give England the lead again. The Italians stormed the England goal in the closing minutes but were unable to increase their score.

The victory brought England's goal tally to 44 in eight games. It was a famous victory to rank alongside the 1948 triumph in Turin; however, some post-match reports suggested it was a 'lucky' victory. It was a victory nonetheless. To prove how much it meant to the England team, captain Johnny Haynes led the England players on a lap of honour at the end as the 90,000 crowd whistled and hooted both them and their own players. Cries of '*sporchi ladri!*' ('dirty thieves!') rang in the England players' ears as they ran down the tunnel, and the Italian fans went home thinking they had been robbed of victory. It was only a 'friendly', but it meant so much to both sides.

It was only the fourth win for England in Europe in five years and Italy's first defeat for a year. Reporters suggested that it made a mockery of the Italians' skill and superiority. For Gerry, not only did he score two goals, but he was also a dangerous leader of the line. His inclusion in the side proved to be a success, not only for the England team, but also on a personal note, as he captured the imagination of the Italian scouts and fans.

Italy: Buffon, Losi, Castelletti, Bolchi, Salvadore, Trapattoni, Mora, Lojacona, Brighenti, Sivori, Corso.
England: Springett, Armfield, McNeil, Robson, Swan, Flowers, Douglas, Greaves, Hitchens, Haynes, R. Charlton.
Attendance: 90,000

Third Full Cap
Austria 3 England 1
Vienna, 27 May 1961, Friendly

The next game was held three days later in Vienna against Austria. For the second game running, Gerry kept his place in front of another 90,000 partisan fans.

England's run of eight matches without defeat ended in the Prater Stadium. The Austrians played a clever retreating defensive game and concentrated on hitting England with quick counter-attacks. Jimmy Greaves equalised an early goal, but the England defence – in which Burnley teammates John Angus and

Brian Miller were winning their first and only caps – lacked its usual understanding, and they conceded two late goals against an innovative Austrian attack. The demand of playing three games in seven days proved too much for an England team who wilted after matching the Austrians for the first hour.

Austria: Buzek, Fraydl, Hanappi, Hof, Koller, Nemec, Rafreider, Senekowitsch, Stotz, Strobl, Trubrig.
England: Springett, Armfield, Angus, Miller, Swan, Flowers, Douglas, Greaves, Hitchens, Haynes, R. Charlton.
Attendance: 90,000

With the transfer to Internazionale in June 1961, Gerry was about to embark on another frustrating international season, with England manager Walter Winterbottom constantly changing his strike force. There was no safe position in the England side, and even the goalscoring genius Jimmy Greaves was in and out of the side.

Not surprisingly, Gerry did not feature in the first few internationals of the 1961–62 season. A World Cup qualifier against Luxembourg was a breeze for England, and neither Greaves nor Hitchens featured. The home internationals against Wales (in October) and Northern Ireland (in November), together with the World Cup qualifier against Portugal at Wembley, did not feature either striker, who were, at the time, plying their trade in the Italian city of Milan for opposing clubs.

The new year of 1962 started in the same fashion. A friendly against Austria in April again did not feature Greaves or Hitchens, but the home international against Scotland earned Greaves a recall in front of 132,000 fans at Hampden Park.

The 1962 World Cup in Chile was fast approaching, and for both Greaves and Hitchens it seemed that while playing out in Milan it was a case of 'out of sight, out of mind'. It was disconcerting and unsettling for both strikers while the selectors were deciding on the World Cup squad.

Fourth Full Cap
England 3 Switzerland 1
Wembley, 9 May 1962, Friendly

After an absence of nearly a year from the international scene, the inclusion for the Switzerland friendly made Gerry the first post-war player on the books of an

Italian club to play for England, as he was by now a fully established Internazionale player, and a nice run of international matches followed. A friendly against Switzerland earned him his fourth full cap and rekindled his partnership with his friend Jimmy Greaves in front of a disappointing crowd of only 35,000 at Wembley on 9 May 1962.

Only a series of stunning saves by Ron Springett saved England from defeat after they had swept to a 3–1 lead in the first half hour with goals from Ron Flowers, Hitchens and John Connelly. Hitchens and Greaves smacked shots against the woodwork, but England became caught in the clutches of complacency, and the Swiss staged a second-half revival that brought the best out of Springett. The major concern for England – with the World Cup Finals looming – was that the 'Dynamic Duo' of Johnny Haynes and Bobby Robson had lost their powers of command. Suddenly, the shadow of the selectors' axe hung over Robson, who had given a succession of brilliant performances during the peak moments of his 20-cap career. Now a new young player was challenging for his place. His name was Robert Frederick Chelsea Moore.

England: Springett, Armfield, Wilson, Swan, Connolly, Flowers, Robson, Greaves, Hitchens, Haynes, R. Charlton.
Switzerland: Allemann, Antenen, Durr, Eschmann, Grobety, Permunian, Rosch, Schneiter, Tacchella, Vonlanthen, Weber.
Attendance: 35,000

Fifth Full Cap
Peru 0 England 4
Lima, 20 May 1962, Friendly

Nearly three weeks later, England travelled to Lima to face Peru, and once again the Greaves–Hitchens partnership was given another chance to shine.

The final warm-up match before the 1962 World Cup Finals was notable for a hat-trick from Jimmy Greaves and the cool, commanding debut performance of a 21-year-old Bobby Moore. Ron Flowers gave England the lead from the penalty spot before Greaves scored his three goals. Greaves also struck a shot against a post and Johnny Haynes hit the crossbar. Ron Springett saved a spot-kick to become the first England goalkeeper to make two penalty saves, while Tottenham centre-half Maurice Norman made his bow at the heart of the defence after Peter Swan had pulled out with tonsillitis.

There were calls from the press for Hitchens to be selected for the World Cup in Chile, as the alternatives for the centre-forward spot as Crawford, Smith and

Pointer proved in warm-up matches that they were not good enough. It was said that Hitchens should not be kept in a kind of 'solitary confinement', just because he was playing in a different country at the time and that he should be considered along with any other striker.

Peru: Bazan, de la Vega, Donayre, Fleming, Grimaldo, Guzman, Lobaton, Montalvo, Nieri, Zegarra, Zevallos.
England: Springett, Armfield, Wilson, Norman, Moore, Flowers, Douglas, Greaves, Hitchens, Haynes, R. Charlton.
Attendance: 32, 565

Sixth Full Cap
Hungary 2 England 1
Chile, 31 May 1962, World Cup

With all the pre-World Cup matches out of the way, Hitchens and Greaves had both done enough to earn themselves a place in the squad.

The 1962 World Cup was the first to really benefit from television; however, the fans back home witnessed something that came to typify most of the England campaigns before and after their success in 1966. The fear of failure was the dominant factor in some poor performances. What promised to be 'a feast of football' and the FA advertising the event as 'a World Cup to remember' resulted in some very fractious games between European and South American teams and some poor matches. The sudden loss of some key England players promised to destroy all the hype before the tournament started. Their preparations for the tournament were much criticised, along with the reliance on the captain, Johnny Haynes. However, there was a new dawn in the England set-up, with a crop of young players, like Bobby Moore, Bobby Charlton and Jimmy Greaves (who were to later form part of the most classic of England teams).

It is always best to win the opening match of any tournament, and if you do not you make sure you win the second, but England's first game proved too much, even against a Hungary side without the silky skills of Puskas. Bobby Smith was replaced by Hitchens for the opening game on 31 May 1962, but England were unable to find any rhythm.

It was a depressing start to the World Cup campaign which had promised everything. Ron Springett was deceived by the flight of a harmless-looking 15-yard shot from Tichy in the 20th minute to put Hungary into the lead, and from then on England were struggling to get into the game on a wet, slippery surface that made every step a challenge. Fifteen minutes into the second half a goal-bound Greaves shot was handled on the line, and Ron Flowers scored from the penalty spot. Flowers was reluctantly responsible for Hungary's winning goal: he slipped on the soaked turf and left Florian Albert free to race away and score with a low shot. The form England had shown 13 months earlier in the 9–3 slaughter of Scotland seemed light years away.

Walter Winterbottom changed the line up for the second game against Argentina and replaced Hitchens with Alan Peacock, a young striker from Division Two outfit Middlesbrough, for his international debut. It was a fairly youthful side, and some of the players had only a few caps each. The question was, why would you award a player with their first cap in a very important World Cup game and expect them to form an instant partnership with one of the greats (Greaves)?

For Greaves, he had to form a relationship with yet another strike partner, and quickly! Through no fault of their own, the Greaves–Hitchens partnership did not seem to work, and they failed to read one another, for whatever reason, and so were constantly dropped by Winterbottom.

However, it seemed to work and England got the 3–1 win to keep them in the World Cup. For the final group match against Bulgaria, Hitchens was again excluded in favour of Peacock in an unchanged side. The game ended in a 0–0 draw and was, in a word, forgettable; however, it was enough to take England through to the knockout phase in second place. As Jimmy Greaves put it, 'There are some good players here, playing some rubbish, and they're afraid to hold on to the ball in case they get killed.'

Hungary: Albert, Fenyvesi, Grosics, Matral, Meszoly, Rakosi, Sandor, Sarosi, Sipos, Solymosi, Tichy.
England: Springett, Armfield, Wilson, Norman, Moore, Flowers, Douglas, Greaves, Hitchens, Haynes, R. Charlton.
Attendance: 7,938

Seventh Full Cap
Brazil 3   England 1
Chile, 10 June 1962, World Cup

England had got one stage further in the 1962 World Cup than they did four years earlier in Sweden, where they were knocked out in the group stages. It at least showed an improvement on their basic skills, if not their quality. The quarter-final against Brazil saw a surprise recall for Hitchens for his seventh cap as an injury to Alan Peacock gave him one last chance to form a partnership with

Jimmy Greaves. Winterbottom probably thought that Gerry's experience in Italian football would be better suited in playing against the silky Brazilians, but the injury to Peacock made his decision easier.

England's World Cup life was eventually snuffed out by the samba sensations of the Brazilian team, who had won the World Cup in Europe four years before but were minus their talismanic player, Pelé, victim of a torn muscle from their qualifier against Czechoslovakia. They did have the magnificent Garrincha (Little Bird) at his bewildering best, while other Brazilians such as Didi and Vava had moments when they were uncontainable.

England were not devoid of confidence but went warily into the match in the coastal town of Vina del Mar. The ball-conjuring Garrincha put Brazil in the lead 13 minutes before half-time when he moved like a whippet to out-jump Norman (who was six inches taller than Garrincha) and head in a Zagallo comer which passed Springett in the England goal. England hit back with an equaliser six minutes later to level the scores, with Greaves heading a Haynes free-kick against the crossbar and Hitchens gobbling up the rebound to score his first-ever, and ultimately only, World Cup goal and his fifth international goal in seven games.

England went in level at half-time, but it was not long before the Brazilians were in the lead again. The brilliant Garrincha decided the match early in the second half with a powerful free-kick from 25 yards which was too hot to handle for Springett, and as he pushed the ball out Vava followed up to head it into the net. Then, Garrincha, the man with two left feet, sent a viciously swerving shot curling out of Springett's reach and into the roof of the net to make it 3–1 and it was game over for England. They had played with pride and passion but were simply outclassed by a team with all the talents, even without the legendary Pelé and even playing some so-called 'negative' football. England had been beaten by a weapon against which they had no protection called Manoel dos Santos Francisco or simply Garrincha, and the team, of course, went on to win the 1962 World Cup.

Brazil: Gilmar, D. Santos, Mauro (c), Zózimo, N. Santos, Zito, Garrincha, Didi, Vavá, Amarildo, Zagalo.
England: Springett, Armfield, Wilson, Moore, Norman, Flowers, Douglas, Greaves, Hitchens, Haynes, R. Charlton.
Attendance: 17,736

Life After Winterbottom

England were out of the World Cup, and the players were probably glad in one respect. The living conditions at the Braden Copper Company 'resort' in

Rancagua left a lot to be desired, and even the stadia would not pass for a training ground these days. Jimmy Greaves remembers sharing with Bobby Moore, and they would watch the rain bounce off the roof as they stared upwards in their 'camp beds'. The nearest bar was two miles away, and they ate with the workers in the canteen, and relaxation consisted of playing mini golf, walking around the mountain ranges or staring into space.

Games were held in tiny stadia holding anything between 2,000 and 15,000 people, and there were only a handful of England fans cheering the team on. The players simply could not wait to get home.

This game signalled the end of an era in more ways than one. Walter Winterbottom, England manager for 16 years, paid the ultimate price of failure in the World Cup as he surprised the FA and stepped down from the job in the autumn of 1962. This led the path clear for Alf Ramsey to step into the 'hot seat', but not until his contract had ended at Ipswich Town. In addition to this, Gerry's short England career subsequently ended with the Brazil game, and he was not picked by the new manager.

There were, however, some fond personal memories of the World Cup of 1962 for Gerry, some of which were historically captured on cine film and are still held by the Hitchens family for posterity. Gerry had bought a cine camera and decided to take it to Chile to record himself and his England teammates while they were there, with the attitude that 'this is the World Cup, it's really special and I'm going to take it all in as this may not happen again'. There are some great shots of the team arriving in Chile, roaming around the grounds of the hotel, some scenes of the team playing and what they got up to in their free time, socialising and mixing with the locals. There is even film of some England players carrying bags full of footballs – something which just would not happen these days. This film may be the only colour film of its kind, especially as it shows 'behind the scenes' images of some of England's great players at the Chile World Cup, such as a young Bobby Moore, Jimmy Greaves, Jimmy Armfield and Bobby Charlton. This was the 1966 team – a 'work in progress.'

That World Cup was known as the 'Battle of Santiago' and will be remembered as a bad-tempered affair, with over 50 players sent to hospital and four receiving fractured bones as tackles went flying in from every angle. However, there was a more light-hearted incident during England's final game against Brazil when a little dog managed to get on to the pitch. The dog proved too quick for both officials and players, who ran after the terrier. After several attempts to coerce the dog to come to them, it was left to Jimmy Greaves to grab the hound by the scruff of its neck. Though successful in catching the dog, it proceeded to urinate all over Greaves's England shirt. The Brazilian player

Garrincha thought the incident was so amusing that he apparently took the dog home as a pet. The incident was covered on worldwide TV.

The England performances were not bad on the whole, and they were only narrowly beaten by Hungary, who were in tip-top form. The performance against Argentina was encouraging, although the Bulgaria match was not worth commenting further upon.

It was noticed by the press, however, that Gerry's performances appeared to be a little slower, and he was a little less in control of the ball than before he was transferred to Internazionale. This may have been as much the effect upon him of defensive Italian football as a barely perceptible speeding up and better control acquired by his teammates in the ensuing 12 months since his transfer.

Walter Winterbottom was appointed as England's national director of coaching in 1946 and was made manager in May 1947. His first game was a 7–2 victory over Ireland in September 1946. He managed the team (and arranged travel, accommodation and meals) through four World Cup competitions, including the fateful 1962 World Cup in Chile, until he resigned in 1963. It is sometimes reported that Winterbottom had no control over team selection and that his role was mainly an administrative and training one. In fact, while a selection committee did choose the squads, it was Winterbottom who selected the starting XI.

The 1962 World Cup proved to be a disaster for the national team and inevitably for manager Walter Winterbottom, who went about trying to create a 'new' England team capable of competing with the best teams in the next World Cup which was to be held in England. For England's first game of the 1962–63 season against France, he introduced four new forwards and continued with Jimmy Greaves. That meant there was no place on the team sheet again for Gerry, and he would never be called up by Alf Ramsey, who took control of the England side early in 1963. The game ended in a draw and signalled the end of the Winterbottom years, as the press quickly turned on the man who had been in charge for 15 years.

During the 1962–63 season Ramsey had taken his Ipswich Town side, then surprise champions of England, to Italy to play AC Milan in a second-round, first-leg European Cup tie. Around this time the BBC were making a documentary about Gerry's move to Italy and the writer and narrator of the film, Brian Glanville (now a world famous journalist and author), shared a lift with Gerry to Milan to watch the game. Brian remembers the evening well. As they both approached the stadium, Gerry turned to Brian and said, 'Must say hallo to Alf. I must wish "good luck" to the lads.'

They then walked down to the dressing room corridor where Ramsey was standing and went to greet the Ipswich party. 'Hallo, Alf.' Gerry said, offering

Ramsey a warm welcome on his arrival to the stadium. Ramsey looked at him coolly. 'Oh, yes,' he said, 'you're playing in these parts.'

All through the match – which Ipswich lost badly – Gerry sat beside Brian, who was reporting on the match in the press box, fuming at Alf's aloofness towards him and muttering under his breath, 'Prat! Prat! You're playing in these parts! Prat!'

When Ramsey took over the post of full-time England manager in May 1963, he demanded complete control over squad selections, which led to him being referred to as 'England's first proper manager'. Once appointed, the England players soon found that Ramsey was a firm but fair manager. He often came across as an aloof and proud figure, who talked what was once described as 'sergeant-major posh', despite coming from the working-class area of Dagenham. He was often regarded as a complex character and a difficult person to talk to by the press. He ran a strict regime with his players and made sure that no one felt that they enjoyed special status, star player or not.

Few could call Ramsey a 'friend' because friendship did not come easily to him. But no player who turned out for England under Ramsey's management ever uttered a bad word about him or had cause to question his loyalty. He quickly made it known that only players playing in England would be considered for the national team, and Gerry was able to forget any lingering international ambitions he may have harboured. Although that did not come as much of a surprise to Gerry, it must have been demeaning for such a talented footballer to be excluded from playing for his country, just because he played in foreign climes. Just imagine how many caps he would have got if he was playing in England during the period 1963–66? Many people still believe that he may have been in with a chance of being included in the 1966 World Cup squad had Alf Ramsey not been so pedantic in picking only home-based players.

Ironically, when Gerry signed for Internazionale in the summer of 1961, he was told that he would be allowed to play for England if selected. But with Ramsey in charge that would not matter anymore. For Gerry, though, it was not so much regret that he did not play more than seven times for his country, but more of a disappointment that he was overlooked by the stubbornness and aloofness of the great Alf Ramsey. It would be fair to say that Ramsey was not on the Hitchens family Christmas card list.

Memorable Matches

Gerry Hitchens played in well over 600 professional football matches in his long career, so it was difficult to choose a small selection of matches to talk about in more detail. Here, I have picked half a dozen truly memorable games in which Gerry excelled, and they show why he was considered to be a football 'great'.

Memorable Match One

Gerry scored five goals in one match.

14 November 1959
Aston Villa 11 Charlton Athletic 1

Villa Park, Birmingham, England.

This incredible match will be long remembered as Aston Villa's highest-ever League score in the 20th century and the highlight of the 1959–60 season, which saw Villa win the Division Two Championship. Goals came almost as frequently as the raindrops and helped excite the 22,000 crowd at a cold Villa Park. Gerry Hitchens was at that time much criticised by the press, but he scored the first five of six goals to silence his critics.

Villa began well, with a goal from Hitchens within the first two minutes. It was his first goal in five appearances as a centre-forward. Charlton scored an equaliser in the 22nd minute, but Bobby Thomson hit a second Villa goal in the 26th minute, his first goal in 10 games. At this point in the match it looked like Charlton were giving Villa a game. Villa's third goal was scored by Hitchens in the 29th minute. Charlton 'keeper Duff saved from Thomson, but he could not hold the ball and Hitchens dashed in to score as the defenders stood and watched, dismayed by his opportunism. This really demoralised Charlton and was a big factor in their demise in the game.

Five minutes before half-time, Hitchens struck another blow to the Londoners when he nipped in to score his hat-trick, as the Charlton defenders stood and watched in mysterious contemplation. The score was now 4–1 to Villa.

After the break, Villa continued in the same vein, and Hitchens demonstrated to the full the inefficiencies of the Charlton defence by picking up the ball from a Villa goal-kick and running on to score without another player touching the ball. This was what Gerry Hitchens was all about.

The centre-forward hooked in his fifth goal in the 60th minute, and when Duff went off with a injured finger with Villa leading 6–1 the home team were still hungry for more goals. It is fair to say that Charlton were now handicapped by the injury to their goalkeeper; however, if Duff had stayed on the field the final score might have been much larger.

Charlton tried two deputy 'keepers, but neither had much success. In the following 10 minutes, Villa scored a further three goals through Wylie, Thomson (with his second) and MacEwan.

Peter McParland scored Villa's 10th goal in the 72nd minute, and it was not until the 86th minute that the 11th and final goal went in, again through McParland to claim his second of the game. It was a great finale to one of the biggest Villa League successes ever, secured by the individualism of Gerry Hitchens and the collective opportunism and intelligence of the Villa midfield.

Aston Villa: Sims, Lynn, Neal, Crowe, Dugdale, Saward, MacEwan, Thomson, Hitchens, Wylie, McParland.
Charlton Athletic: Duff, Sewell, Townsend, Hinton, Ufton, Klernan, Lawrie, Lucas, Leary, Edwards, Summers.
Attendance: 21,997

Memorable Match Two

Gerry scored a hat-trick in this game after he scored five goals against Charlton.

21 November 1959
Bristol City 0 Aston Villa 5

Ashton Gate, Bristol, England.

The game following Villa's historic 11–1 victory over Charlton turned out to be another emphatic win for 'The Villans'.

It would have taken a brave manager to change the Villa side that beat Charlton in the previous game. In the game at Ashton Gate, which saw their biggest crowd of the season, Bristol City fielded their new signing Ally Hill from Dundee, and he soon impressed the home fans by the way he was prepared to chase the ball and his use of both wings. City had the best of the opening 10 minutes, but an error in the City defence almost resulted in a Villa goal; however, Bobby Thomson shot wide.

After half an hour Villa almost took the lead when they carved open the City defence. Thomson was given a clear view of goal, but his shot was well to the left of the goalkeeper, who pushed the ball away. With half-time looming and after a series of attacks, City defender, Cavanagh, committed a foul on Peter McParland 10 yards outside the penalty area, but Stan Lynn pumped the free-kick over the bar.

The visitors had more luck a minute later when Hitchens rammed the ball into the back of the net following a miskick from a City defender. On the 42nd minute it was 2–0 to the visitors when a MacEwan centre was headed deftly into the net by Hitchens. Shortly after the break, Lynn nearly made it three, but the chance came to nothing. Hitchens might have made it a hat-trick when he received the ball in a good position on the edge of the penalty area, but he hurried the shot, half-hit the ball and the diving 'keeper was able to smother it.

On 56 minutes, McParland took a quick throw-in, and the ball was helped on by Hitchens into the path of Wylie, who thumped it on the volley into the net and left the 'keeper motionless.

It was one-way traffic, with the visitors determined to improve their lead, but the City defence held together for a while. There was a major let-off for City when Williams, apparently aiming to give away a corner under extreme pressure, saw the ball hammer against his own post. An amazing situation occurred when McParland tangled with Cavanagh, which resulted in the City captain being helped off the field with blood streaming down his face. The referee appeared to book the international winger, who was booed by the City fans every time he touched the ball.

Things got worse for City when Cavanagh returned to the field with a plaster across his face and Jacobs was carried off after a nasty tackle.

Villa launched a tremendous late rally and showed up the deficient City defence. In the 86th minute Hitchens was allowed to score a fine goal, while a minute later McParland scored the best goal of the game. Some City fans showed appalling taste and booed the Irish winger, but others applauded a brilliant goal. At the final whistle McParland was given a police escort off the field.

Bristol City: Cook, Collinson, Threasher, Cavanagh, Williams, Jacobs, Coggins, Atyeo, Hill, Graham, McCann.
Aston Villa: Sims, Lynn, Neal, Crowe, Dugdale, Saward, MacEwan, Thomson, Hitchens, Wylie, McParland.
Attendance: 29,738

Memorable Match Three

Gerry was the first post-war player to score a hat-trick in a second City derby.

22 October 1960
Aston Villa 6 Birmingham City 2
Villa Park, Birmingham, England.

With a goal in the first 25 seconds by Villa debutant Alan O'Neill – who scored with his first kick – and three in the last six minutes, this was a match that made 45,000 rain-soaked fans forget the weather and roar on their favourites from start to finish. What a thriller at the Villa! This was surely one of the most incident-packed derbies ever put on by these two rivals.

Birmingham were robbed of their fighting power by a blow dealt to them by Villa on the half-hour. It came in the form of a Gerry Hitchens goal and was Villa's second of the night. When the centre-forward received a pass from Wylie his path to goal was blocked by Sissons, but Hitchens twisted round the City centre-half so cleverly that suddenly the path to goal was clear, and taking it with huge strides he beat the 'keeper with a tremendous shot.

This opening up of the Birmingham defence seemed like a planned robbery – effortless and precise. Birmingham were in command for a time, and the Villa defence had a difficult time as corner after corner were conceded. In the 34th minute Birmingham had a penalty saved by Sims, but after that it was never going to be their day.

Four minutes after the break, McParland scored a simple goal which effectively killed the game, but there was more excitement to come.

Birmingham pulled a goal back in the 66th minute as Hellawell headed past Sims in the Villa goal, but a minute later O'Neill claimed his second and Villa's fourth when he volleyed the ball in from a most difficult angle after Farmer had turned away a shot from McParland.

A moment later, the Irishman headed against the post, and O'Neill missed two chances to put the game way beyond Birmingham. Hitchens, however, put the game beyond doubt with two quick goals in the 84th and 87th minutes and became the only player in a post-war Second City derby to score a hat-trick. Bobby Thomson scored in the wrong end a minute later as the game ended just as amazingly as it started.

Aston Villa: Sims, Neal, Winton, Thomson, Dugdale, Saward, MacEwan, O'Neill, Hitchens, Wylie, McParland.
Birmingham City: Schofield, Farmer, Allen, Watts, Sissons, Neal, Hellawell, Rudd, Gordon, Singer, Astall.
Attendance: 45,000

Memorable Match Four

Gerry played his last game for Aston Villa and partnered Johnny Dixon in his final game before retiring.

29 April 1961
Aston Villa 4 Sheffield Wednesday 1

Villa Park, Birmingham, England.

This was Villa's last game in the successful 1960–61 season, but little did the Villa manager or players know that it would be the last game for Gerry Hitchens in a Villa shirt. The legendary Johnny Dixon was brought back especially to partner Hitchens against a Sheffield Wednesday side who were second in the League.

Dixon, at the age of 37, was brought into the team for the first time in the season and his last of his long career, but he gave one of those displays for which he was noted, scoring the last goal and ending up with a broken nose.

An 18-year-old Charlie Aitken made his full start for the club and had a successful debut. The young Scot tackled well and always used the ball to his advantage and left Wednesday's right-winger, Alan Finney, without much change.

Not knowing that this would be his last performance for Villa, the blond striker gave another star performance in front of the home fans and gave his England teammate, Peter Swan, a worrying afternoon. He gained Villa the lead after only five minutes. Dixon neatly back-headed a Jimmy MacEwan centre to Hitchens, who gave Ron Springett no chance with a shot from close range. Dixon then brought the best out of England 'keeper, Springett, with a powerful right-footed drive which the goalkeeper could only tip over the bar for a corner.

Bobby Thomson notched up Villa's second goal after 27 minutes, after Harry Burrows swept a ball to Hitchens, who saw his shot cannon off Springett. The 'keeper chased after the ball and stopped Burrows from getting it by diving at his feet, but the ball ran loose to Thomson, who neatly lobbed it into an open net.

After the break, with Villa leading 2–0, Griffin pulled one back for the visitors, only to see Hitchens score a great goal in the 68th minute, with a powerful shot from a difficult angle. Two minutes later, Dixon scored the goal everyone in the ground had been waiting for. The veteran inside-forward chased after a Deakin pass, and he managed to side-foot it past Springett. It was as though he had written the script. It took the referee some minutes to clear the young boys who had invaded the pitch.

It was a great finale to Villa's League programme as the home side often outclassed the Championship-chasing side; however, with the legendary Johnny Dixon set to retire and the impending departure of 'Hot-shot Hitchens', where would the goals come from in the 1961–62 season?

Aston Villa: Sims, Neal, Aitken, Crowe, Dugdale, Deakin, MacEwan, Thomson, Hitchens, Dixon, Burrows.
Sheffield Wednesday: Springett, Johnson, Megson, McAnearney, Swan, Kay, Finney, Craig, Ellis, Fantham, Griffin.
Attendance: 26,034

Memorable Match Five

Gerry endeared himself to the Internazionale fans immediately as he scored two goals on his debut game in Serie A.

27 August 1961
Internazionale 6 Atalanta 0

Stadio Giuseppe Meazza (San Siro), Milan, Italy.

It was his first experience of Serie A football, and Gerry played at centre-forward for his debut game for Internazionale against Atalanta at the San Siro. He made an instant impact by scoring two goals for his new club and put in at least a dozen rasping shots that had the 55,000 crowd cheering madly.

Hitchens was acclaimed for a brilliant game. He worked splendidly with his new teammates, who kept him well supplied with passes, particularly from Luis Suárez. The Atalanta defence could not cope and were too busy watching his blond hair as they left big gaps for other forward players to take advantage of.

He always had the Atalanta defence at full stretch and scored with a header for his first in the 29th minute and sent the Milan fans wild. Then, in the 44th minute, the fans blew their bugles and chanted his name when he scored his second with a 20-yard drive.

The Inter fans had a new hero. It was 'his' match. Two goals and constant efforts on goal, upsetting the Atalanta defence with his wandering and bustling, was just what they had waited to see from the ex-Villa man.

Memorable Match Six

Gerry scored the winner for Cagliari against the 1966–67 champions, who were unbeaten at the San Siro until then.

3 March 1968
AC Milan 0 Cagliari 1

Stadio Giuseppe Meazza (San Siro), Milan, Italy.

Cagliari were showing signs of being a good side when Gerry joined them at the beginning of the 1967–68 season. They had finished sixth in the previous season and were a team in the ascendancy. Milan were the current champions and had been unbeaten in the San Siro all season until Hitchens and this Cagliari side played there in early March. Cagliari had earned a draw in Sardinia earlier in the season, with 'Gigi' Riva scoring two goals so confidence was high.

Milan dominated the play, but within a quarter of an hour Hitchens scored a rather casual goal out of the blue from a rare Cagliari move, after being tightly marked by the Milan defence. It remained 1–0 to the away side for the rest of the game, which was dominated by Milan as they could not break down a tight Cagliari defence. It was an amazing win for Cagliari, but it left Milan still five points in the lead at the top of Serie A.

As the players went off the pitch, the Milan team waved to their fans, but Gerry casually walked off the pitch having done his job. To him it was just another game; however, it was an historic victory for his progressive side.

How the Stars Remembered Gerry

Numerous ex-players have kindly contributed their memories especially for this book to their extremely popular and well-liked friend, thereby making this into a very special chapter.

A tribute from Sir Bobby Charlton, taken from the Gerry Hitchens Memorial Match programme, Sunday 30 October 1983.

Gerry Hitchens was not only a very good footballer but he was also an extremely nice person. I particularly remember playing with Gerry when he gained his first full England cap against Mexico. Of course, his excellent performance in the international against Italy in Rome was instrumental in him later moving abroad.

Gerry was a big, strong, honest footballer and British football sorely missed him when he went to Italy. Our loss was the Italians' gain and Gerry's strength of character ensured that he had a most successful footballing career in that country. Gerry was very well liked by all who had the privilege of meeting him.

The following tributes are taken from interviews carried out especially for this book.

Jimmy Armfield, OBE, played all of his club career for Blackpool and was capped 43 times for England and played several times with Gerry.

I remember Gerry very well at Cardiff and at Villa and more especially when he went with us to Chile in 1962. I recall him scoring in Italy when we won in Rome. He was a good player and off the field he was the one who smiled easily and I always liked him for that. He was a popular member of the squad, but of course he went off to Italy and I sort of lost touch.

'Gigi' Riva, best known by his nickname, Rombo di Tuono (Thunder), is a former Cagliari teammate of Gerry's. He is an Italian legend and the all-time leading scorer for the Italian national team. He was one of the best forwards of

his time and had a fantastic scoring record for Cagliari thanks to his great heading ability, fantastic left foot and composure in front of goal.

I recall when he arrived at Inter [Milan]. I was so fascinated by this centre-forward, the way he ran impressed everybody. Good-looking and blond. On the pitch he was very generous, brave, one who was never afraid to get stuck in. A 'lion' of great temperament and of determination. In '*ritiro*', seeing that we were all not Sardinians, we were very close – Ferrero, Tomasini, Gerry and I. We played cards, snooker and never felt lonely. We were inseparable.

He really connected people, created union, encouraged the team, even if he was not playing (you knew he was at the end of his career). He was fun and brought everybody together. Everybody in Sardinia has splendid memories of him, a real gentleman in every way. As a man and as a player, everybody was fond of him, without enemies, always kind. He was a great person. Great memories!

Luis Suárez was a legendary player known for his perceptive passing and explosive shot, and he was voted European Footballer of the Year in 1960. He played with Gerry during his spell with Internazionale between 1961 and 1962.

Gerry's introduction into the team was very good right from the start, and he soon established a friendly relationship with his teammates. He was very easy-going and cheerful, and everybody was very fond of him. He was a very 'generous' player on the pitch. He did not speak the language, and there were not many English players at that time. I am Spanish and our coach was too so it was easier for me in a way. The team helped him in this respect and little by little he settled in. He certainly was not used to the '*ritiro*', which he found difficult and suffered more than we did. The lifestyle he was used to was different and he was more retiring. On the other hand, he was cheerful and good-natured and did his best to settle in.

We were in San Pellegrino in '*ritiro*' one August. It was very hot and the initial training periods were tough and tiring, but we needed to be fit before the season started. Gerry trained in his shorts, with no tee shirt or clothing on his torso. At the end of one particular day, after the training had finished, Gerry continued exercising after the others had finished and I asked him, 'Gerry, aren't you ever tired?' Smiling he answered, 'tired! This is fun to me, running around in this beautiful place in the open air. I was used to crawling underground for 12 to 14 hours in a mine! This is a prize for me.'

This was the spirit of Gerry, and it rubbed off to everybody. He was always ready for sacrifice, strong but without creating ill feelings.

We all had extremely fond memories of an extraordinary person.

The Brit pack in Manchester ready for the Italian FA versus English FA match. From left to right: Eddie Firmani, Joe Baker, Gerry Hitchens, John Charles and Dennis Law.

Gerry meeting up with his friend, Jimmy Greaves, before the Italy versus England game in Rome, May 1961.

Gerry loved his Frank Sinatra LPs, c.1961 Milan.

Gerry with his beloved cine
camera filming in Venice in 1961.

Gerry and Marcus, father and son, Milan, *c*.1961.

The 1962 England World Cup squad.

Gerry fooling around with Jimmy Greaves during their rest time in Chile, *c.*1962.

Jimmy Greaves and Gerry before a Milan derby on 1 October 1961.

The apartment in Turin: Meriel holds Karen, with Gerry, Marcus and Nicola.

AC Torino team, 1962–63.

Gerry making headway through the Bologna defence in 1963.

On the stairs in the family's Turin Apartment, c.1963.

Scoring for Torino against Fiorentina in 1963.

Violet, Gerry and Meriel with Marcus and Nicola in Highley, *c.*1963.

Meriel and Gerry with Karen in a Turin restaurant, c.1964.

Gerry with Carlo Crippa (left) and Giorgio Ferrini (in white jacket).

Atalanta BC team, 1965–66.

In Atalanta kit, *c.*1965.

Singing in the rain – Gerry (kneeling) with Giancarlo Danova (standing) and Giancarlo Cella (lying down).

Scoring for Atalanta against Cagliari in 1965.

Gerry spots Meriel and Marcus in the crowd after a game for Cagliari, *c.*1968.

Gerry with one of the world's greatest-ever goalkeepers, Dynamo Moscow's and Russia's Lev Yashin, Cagliari, Sardinia, 1968–69.

Gerry and Meriel in their Sardinian house before a function in 1968.

'Good God, Geg, what on earth is she wearing?'

Mr Cool! Gerry wearing his Stetson, Catania, Sicily, c.1968.

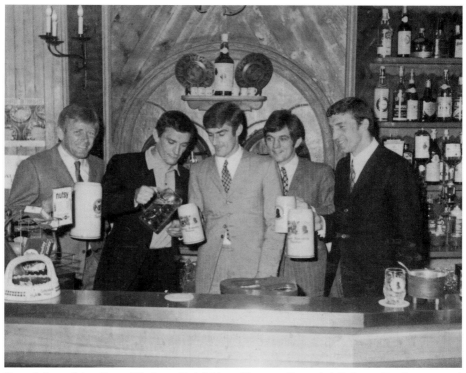

From left to right: Gerry Hitchens, Luigi Riva, Giuseppe Tomasini, Roberto Boninsegna and Giuseppe Ferrero enjoying a drink in 1968.

The Hitchens family back in Pontypridd, South Wales, after their nine-year adventure in Italy.

Gerry and Archie with pals at The Malt Shovel in Highley.

Archie (back row, left), Gerry (back row, fourth right) and Les Farrington (front row, second right) visiting old mates at the Alveley pit, *c.* 1970.

Going Full Circle – Gerry still happy playing in 1971, aged 37 with his smiling Royal Oak teammates in Pontshonnorton, near Pontypridd, South Wales.

Gerry with Simona in 1973.

John Charles (left) tugging for the number-nine shirt with Gerry before the Aston Villa versus Juventus European Cup match, March 1983.

Meriel with Elfed Ellis and Marcus, Karen, Damian and Jason looking on after the Memorial Match, *c.*1983.

Mario Corso was nicknamed 'God's Left Foot' for his beautiful free-kicks and crosses and was an important player for Internazionale during the spell Gerry played at the San Siro.

I remember Gerry very well, a wonderful man. He was a great character and an excellent player who scored many goals. We did not really socialise off the pitch as we younger boys were very much in awe of the likes of Gerry. But he always had a kind word for us.

Giancarlo 'Ceje' Cella was a midfielder who played with Gerry at Torino and Atalanta and was a very good friend of his.

Gerry was an exceptional person – selfless by nature, generous with a big heart. I was lucky enough to have been a teammate of his at both Torino and Atalanta, and we both played at Internazionale, but in different seasons.

He never had a cross word with his opponents or a criticism of a teammate. He always fought like a lion and was never afraid to get stuck in and was never a prima donna. During the 1960s he was one of the very few British players to adapt to Italian football.

I have many fond memories of my friend, Gerry. I still have vivid memories of a day spent in Bobbio (my home town) with him after a morning session with Atalanta. It was August and we decided to have a swim in the river which runs through the town, the Trebbia. It was wonderful. That evening a group of us went dancing. He was very discreet and would not join us when we bet on who could get the ugliest girl to dance.

We were away from our families during the pre-season, and we always ate together. Our families were always in our thoughts. Gerry was a gentleman. Very close to his family and only had eyes for his beautiful wife and children.

He was a gentleman and a dear friend. Ciao Gerry.

Peter McParland, MBE, Aston Villa striker, 1952–62.

I remember reading in the local papers about Gerry playing for Kidderminster Harriers in the Southern League when he was transferred to Cardiff City. Villa had missed out on a cheap deal compared with what they paid for him when we signed him from Cardiff.

He was big, strong, fast and, indeed, quite brave. He was a handful for defenders who do not like players who would make them turn and keep coming back at them. Gerry did all that. Blond hair that tossed about when he was running and sprinting, he soon obtained the name of 'Champion', called after *Champion the Wonder Horse*, with a great blond mane, it was in a TV show back then.

He developed his goalscoring touch, and we soon reaped the rewards of having him around. He scored five goals in one game, then three the week after. I would like to say I helped him develop his goalscoring touch because he always wanted to be ahead of me in scoring, and he did that by miles.

Gerry liked a smoke and decided to kick the habit with his new year's wish of 1959. I think that season we reached the FA Cup semi-final, playing Nottingham Forest at Hillsborough. We stayed at Buxton Spa, Derbyshire, before the game. On the Saturday morning of the game Gerry roomed with Jimmy Dugdale, our very experienced big-match player and he developed nerves, which was normal, but as the morning progressed Gerry did not settle at all and Jimmy's advice was to say to Gerry 'have a fag', which he did throughout the pre-match build-up. I am not sure if he continued smoking after that, but it was a nerve-settler that day, or maybe it was an excuse for a fag.

Gerry had a wild goalscoring run the next season and signed for the Italian team, Inter Milan, during that close season.

I was working abroad when I heard the shocking news of Gerry's sudden death.

Bobby Thomson, Aston Villa inside-forward, 1959–1964.

I have a lot of memories of Gerry. I was very fond of him, and I cannot say anything bad about him.

In one game, he scored five goals against Charlton, but I thumped a few shots at Duff [the goalkeeper] and Gerry tapped them in. I joked with Gerry that three of them were mine. That day, he could have scored all 11, because that was the sort of player he was.

I had two seasons with Gerry. It was a good team. I loved playing in that team, with Gerry, 'Craggy' MacEwan, Ronnie Wylie, Peter McParland, Jimmy Dugdale, etc. Most of them were the Cup Final team of 1957.

I remember MacEwan used to say he 'made me' and McParland used to say he 'made me'. So, I had to say to Gerry, I 'made him'. I am sure he would not mind me saying that. Me and Gerry used to kid each other on.

Ronnie Wylie used to take the mickey out of everyone. He used to say things like, 'Gerry the superstar Hitchens scores five' or 'hotshot Hitchens scores a hat-trick.'

Gerry was a 'raw' lad. He was still doing his national service when he joined Villa. Eric Houghton signed him I think. Gerry was a bit gangly, but that is not being disrespectful to him. We hit it off straight away, me and Gerry, on the field. I could play with anyone. We all had jobs to do in the team. He was the 'main man' as far as getting goals. I was just alongside Gerry to help him score those goals. Any scraps I had I would take them, but he was the 'main man'. He could not have been that on his own, without the team.

In those days we had to attack and defend as inside-forwards – we were up and down the field all the time. When a ball came over, we all wanted it more than anyone else. Gerry learned to do the easy things, pull it back and push it where the player was going.

We played a lot of games up front together. It was up to me and Gerry to get the goals. In Division Two (season 1959–60), Gerry scored 25 goals, I scored 20 and Peter McParland scored 25 as well. But if someone was injured, I would drop back into midfield and someone else went up front. I think the rough edges were knocked off him in that season. He was raw when he joined Villa, but then it just clicked.

He did everything simple and did not do a great deal of dribbling. I am not sure if I saw Gerry score from outside the box. Gerry did plenty of tap-ins after I did all the hard work [Bobby joked]. But he could head, and he was brave and worked hard. You could not do anything else in that team. We were a 'team' and we helped each other. I knew what Gerry would do and he knew what I would do. We relied on each other.

I remember he would just go after the ball and run. Gerry was one of these players that if you were a defender you did not know what he was going to do next. For a defender, he was the worse type of centre-forward to play against – a bit awkward to mark because he was all arms and legs.

Thinking about Gerry, he enjoyed playing, he just loved it. He loved the game. He never said a great deal. He did not need to. I am sure he would have said that his success was down to the other players. I think the team moulded Gerry into a better player. We knew Gerry was going to get us goals. Whatever goals he missed, I got. I was there to pick up the 'loose ends'. We had a team of winners, and Gerry was a winner, without a doubt.

I used to go out sometimes after the game for a pint with Gerry. He liked his pints, but nothing excessive. I think he liked a smoke as well. After one game, we were in a private club with Nigel Sims, and they had the TV on showing Gerry scoring and me tackling. We were watching and I said 'he's [Gerry] the power, I'm the glory and Nigel's the life ever after – the power, the glory and the life ever after.' That was the sort of camaraderie we had.

We had a 'television school', with Jimmy MacEwan, Vic Crowe, Stan Lynn, Paddy Saward and Ronnie Wylie, and a 'drinking school', which I tagged on to with Gerry and the rest. Mercer used to say, 'go on and enjoy yourself, but you had better do the business on Saturday. If you don't give me 90 minutes on Saturday, you are in trouble.'

When Gerry left we did not hear anything about it. It was a total surprise. We replaced him with another great player in Derek Dougan. I do not think I saw Gerry again when he left. There was a game against Inter Milan at the end of that season, which was part of the signing-on deal with Gerry, but Gerry did not play as he was away with England.

When I heard about his death I was queuing up in a shop at the time and there was a chap in front of me reading a paper on the counter, and I read the headline, 'Villa Star Dies' and I said, 'excuse me can I have a look at the paper?' I was just stumped. I just could not believe it. Even after 25 years it was still a shock, and it is still sad today.

Now, I look back and see these teams and players as 'my family', and losing Gerry was like losing a member of the family. You spent more time with them than with your respective partners.

To describe Gerry in one word, he was just great. He was just a nice bloke.

Ron Wylie, Aston Villa inside-forward, 1958–65.

Gerry was good to play with. He chased every through ball. He was quick and very strong in the air. He was a player who could turn a bad ball into a good one.

He was a gentleman, a really nice 'fella' who knew how to handle himself properly on the pitch and off it. He was always immaculately dressed. He was a quiet chap, kept himself to himself usually and was fairly serious. We always thought he was well educated. I am not saying he did not have a bit of a temper, but that can be good in a footballer. It made him a fiery player, and when he learned to control it this became a fantastic asset. As a footballer, well, he was not unlike Gary Lineker, except that he was heavier. He looked rather like an American football player in a way and had that special turn of pace to frighten high-quality defenders.

I remember he loved training and trained well and hard. He worked hard for the team. In those days we had a great team spirit and Gerry fitted in well.

I think he would fit into any modern-day team as a centre-forward.

Jimmy MacEwan, Aston Villa outside right, 1959–66.

I did not spend long with Gerry, about two seasons, but he was the ideal centre-forward to play alongside.

I remember saying, 'are you the only bugger that scores goals?' because he would always shoot at goal, rather than pass the ball. He took any opportunity to score a goal. I suppose that is what centre-forwards are all about.

Gerry was quiet and did not seem to mix much from what I can remember. He did not see himself as a 'star', just part of the team.

The author wishes to thank everyone who contributed to this chapter.

Tributes from the Terraces

Gerry Hitchens was known the world over and had many fans, especially in England and in Italy when he was playing in the 1950s and 1960s. Some touching and some funny memories have been collated here, including some from the Hitchens family and from fans from all over the world who have paid tribute to Gerry as a player and a person.

Damian Hitchens, Gerry's youngest son, shares a couple of funny stories about his memories with his father when he was younger.

I was only about 13 or 14 when dad died, and I had no idea how famous he was, probably not until the day he died. I did not really appreciate how popular he was, and the more people I spoke to the more I realised who he was.

Just after moving to Holywell in about 1978, there was a signing session with Ian St John and Jimmy Greaves, and I took some photos of dad in and put them in front of Jimmy and said, 'You obviously know who that is? I'm his son.' Jimmy replied, 'Good God! How's your mum?' I said, surprised, 'How's me mum?' Obviously, I made an impression with Jimmy.

On another occasion, when I was about nine years old, I was going to Carmel School at the time. Somehow, the school had arranged a signing session at the local monastery in Carmel. I do not know who had arranged it, but it was with Kevin Keegan and a couple of other players. I was a massive Kevin Keegan fan, and there was this 'older bloke' who I did not care about. For weeks leading up to the event, I was saying to dad, 'Kevin Keegan's coming, Kevin Keegan's coming…oh, and there's some other bloke's going to be there, apparently you'll know him.' Dad said, 'What's his name?' I said 'I don't know and I don't really care.'

So when we got there, everyone was in awe of Kevin Keegan and there was a question and answer session and afterwards we all filed in line to get the book signed. When I got to Kevin Keegan I was quaking in my boots, and he said, 'What's ya name son?' 'Damian', I replied. Kevin said, 'Second name?'

'Hitchens.' I replied. He stopped and said, 'Hitchens, Damian Hitchens? There's a famous footballer called Hitchens.'

'Yeah, it's me dad. Gerry Hitchens.' Keegan leaned forward to 'the other bloke' and said, 'Joe. Gerry Hitchens's lad.' It was Joe Mercer. I did not know who he was, never heard of the guy before. I was like, 'Who's Joe Mercer?' I was saying to Kevin, 'I don't care about him, just sign me book.'

Joe Mercer got up, and I just could not believe it, he was asking me, 'Where do you live?' I told him I lived about a mile away, and he replied, 'Is your dad in?' 'Yeah, dad's home.' So, he asked permission from the teachers to drive me home to meet dad. They agreed and he drove me home. I went to the door, and Mercer said he would hide by the porch. So I rang the bell and dad came to the door, and he asked if I had a good night, 'Yeah, great, great. You know that guy whose name I couldn't remember?' Dad said, 'Oh, aye, who was it?'

'Well, he's here.' Joe Mercer stood in front of the door and dad went white. He was speechless. It was the first time Gerry had met Joe since 1961.

One of the funniest and best memories I have is when he used the saying, 'Shanks's pony'. We used to go swimming regularly and on this particular day it was cold, and we came out of the swimming baths and had not dried our hair.

I telephoned my father and asked for a lift back home, reversing the charges as usual.

Dad declined, saying, 'No way, take Shanks's pony!' ['Shanks's pony' is an idiom meaning 'walk there']

I asked what that meant.

Dad replied, 'Well, how ya going to get home?'

Then I said I would have to walk if he would not pick me up.

Dad quickly responded, 'Well, exactly!'

Federico Perrone, Milan, Italy, Gerry's grandson.

I never met Gerry Hitchens, although he is my grandad, but I have understood that he was a great footballer and a great dad. Reading all the Italian books about him in Serie A and with Aston Villa, I would have immensely wanted to meet him and discuss about my present love of football. My grandad will always be in my heart.

Brian Glanville, the world-renowned football writer and novelist, remembers his time with Gerry and Meriel during the 1960s. Brian wrote a piece especially for this book.

I have so many memories of Gerry. One of these was the two goals he scored on a sunny May afternoon in 1961, for England against Italy, and the goal scored five years later in Bergamo to beat Napoli with Atalanta when he remarked to me, 'I've never had so many kisses from rough beards,' and significantly, not least in terms of Alf Ramsey's personality rather than his cheerful own, their meeting in the San Siro tunnel one wet evening in 1962.

It was when Steven Hearst, the highly intellectual Viennese-born director, and I the narrator and writer were making a television documentary for the BBC in Turin called *European Centre Forward*. It should have been made in Milan, where, the previous season, Gerry had been playing with such prolific success for Inter, scoring no fewer than 16 Serie A goals, a total he would never come close to again with his other three Italian clubs. But while Stephen, I and the TV crew were all poised to go, there were rumours that, despite all his goals, Inter were preparing to sell Gerry when it came to the then brief, customary transfer 'window' in November 1962. I telephoned Helenio Herrera, the flamboyant, autocratic manager of Inter, to ask him if this would happen. Typically enough, he assured me that it would not, so, of course, it did!

With Gerry moving westward to Turin and to Torino, it meant we had to radically refocus our efforts. It would be Turin now, rather than Milan. Herrera had not untypically lied to me when I phoned him in Milan to ask whether Gerry would be staying. Not that Gerry, despite the fact that his ejection seemed a poor reward for such an impressive and productive season, was much distressed.

He had made a fine start at Wembley in May 1961, leading the attack in an 8–0 thrashing of Mexico. But you might say that Gerry reached his apogee soon afterwards in Rome, when at the Stadio Olimpico he scored two of England's goals in a 3–2 win over Italy. Gerry put England ahead, then Omar Sivori whipped in a characteristic left-footer for Italy, his adopted country, and centre-forward Brighenti (who told me after the game that he was 'demoralised') scored; however, the Italian defence was not the same after, and in the 56th minute the experienced 'keeper Renzo Buffon had his nose smashed in a collision with Johnny Haynes's knee and had to give way to the far less reliable Vavassori. So Gerry scored again and Jimmy Greaves added another.

Next, Gerry left Aston Villa to join Inter. It was widely assumed that his goals against Italy had been decisive in the move, but he assured me that it had already been planned before the game.

In the summer of 1961, he was one of four British players who moved to Italy, the others being Joe Baker and Denis Law, who joined Torino, and Jimmy Greaves who went – but not for long – to Milan before coming home, you might say, for Christmas. Arguably, Gerry was the least talented of the four, but he was the only one who survived the season and carved out a career in Italian football. This I would attribute to his robust, coal miner's personality. Law, like Greaves, flourished on the field, but neither of them, like Joe Baker, could conform to the ways of Italian football. By contrast, Gerry, who had coped with the vicissitudes of the pit, had the resilience to adjust to the demands and the culture shock of the new experience.

Our documentary film proved a highly praised, perhaps over-praised novelty. Stephen Hearst, who knew his Italy as well as I knew mine, compared the rivalry between Italian clubs with the bygone wars between the big cities. I remember the ineffable David Coleman, the TV commentator, telling me at a London cocktail party that I still had a lot to learn about writing for television, which might well have been true, though in another context I had already been writing many sketches for the BBC satirical programme, *That Was the Week That Was*. Coleman's own verbal infelicities had led to the establishment in *Private Eye* magazine of the feature, 'Colemanballs', still running today, with its plethora of fatuities. As it was, the BBC entered our film for the Berlin Film Festival, where it won the top Silver Bear documentary award.

My friendship with Gerry and his delightful wife, Meriel, continued for some years to come. I saw a great deal of them early in 1966 in Bergamo, where he was playing, popular as ever, for Atalanta, and on the evening after England's triumph in the World Cup Final they both stayed as guests in my West London house.

Gerry's premature death came as an appalling shock. How cruel and how wholly unpredictable. But I am sure that Stephen Hearst, like myself, will never forget him and his unfailing exuberant resourcefulness.

Enrico Fiorio was the team doctor when Gerry played for Torino.

Gerry and some of his teammates used to call me up late in the evening to go for a beer. They would knock on the locked doors of their local bars, and the bars would immediately open and let the celebrity [Gerry] in. I have very fond memories of Gerry.

Mr John Lerwill, Aston Villa club historian and lifelong Villa fan, gives a fan's view of Gerry Hitchens.

My first view of Gerry Hitchens was not of him in a Villa shirt, but in Cardiff City colours in a match at Villa Park towards the end of Villa's FA Cup-winning season of 1957. It was one of those very rare occasions when I went to a match with both my parents, and it was [because of no floodlights at that point] played on a Wednesday afternoon. Villa won easily that day, 4–1, but my father had eyes for the opponent's centre-forward. 'Good player', my dad said afterwards, and I took his word for it, but I was more interested in what the Villa players were doing; however, it was Hitchens that had scored the Cardiff goal.

My dad knew a thing or two about fine footballers. His heyday as a young Villa supporter had been in those starry times at the end of the 1920s and early 1930s when the Villa again threatened to take the football world by storm. In those days, there were certain players like Jimmy Gibson, Billy Walker, 'Pongo' Waring and Eric Houghton to admire. He also saw Trevor Ford later on. So, dad had a fair measuring stick to go by.

And so it was that at the end of 1957, Gerry signed for the Villa. That made my dad happy. For me, I was not so sure. This Gerry Hitchens looked alright but nothing fantastic I thought. I was not sure what my dad had seen. Neither was I sure whether the fact that Gerry was on his national service had anything to do with it, after all, a footballer is a footballer, is he not? What did serving in the army have to do with things?

But, slowly, Gerry grew on me. And when it came to the decisive match against the West Bromwich Albion in April 1959 – to decide the relegation issue – Gerry scored the opening goal and, until two minutes from the end, Villa looked safe from relegation. It was not Gerry's fault that Villa did go down. He had done his part of the job – in my book at least.

It was that year that Gerry came into his own though, with the army becoming past history. By November 1959, Villa were doing alright in Division Two, but the Villa forwards were not setting the world alight with their goalscoring. Joe Mercer [Villa's manager] put pressure on his men by threatening he would play the reserves if they did not start hitting the net more often. The result was startling – 11 goals were scored against Charlton Athletic. Gerry scored five of those, the last breaking the poor 'keeper's finger as he tried to save it.

The magnificent goalscoring did not end there. Villa then scored five at Bristol City (Gerry grabbing another three), and then five more at home against Scunthorpe, Gerry getting two more, to make his tally for those three consecutive matches a lovely 10 goals. Villa gained promotion that season, and Gerry and Peter McParland finished with 25 goals apiece.

The next season (1960–61) proved to be the pinnacle year for Gerry in England. At one point he was regularly scoring two goals a week and finished with 29 League goals and 42 goals overall. Apart from his hat-trick against our cross-city neighbours, Birmingham City, my most vivid memory of him in his last season – reflecting both his determination and confidence – was in a home match against Blackpool (31 December 1960). At that time Blackpool were a club not yet on the wane, still having a player of the class of Jimmy Armfield, then England's regular right-back. It was Gerry who pursued Armfield to the byline, stole the ball off him and, after moving closer to goal, hit a stunning shot from an angle of no more than 30 degrees and a distance of 18 yards. I was virtually right behind that shot, and I saw the ball hit the back of the net off the far upright before you could blink. And that with a heavy leather ball.

The final Villa game of the 1960–61 season (and, indeed, Gerry's final game for Villa) was against League runners-up Sheffield Wednesday (29 April 1961) and England goalkeeper Ron Springett. Villa won 4–1. Villa brought back old Cup-winning legendary skipper, Johnny Dixon, for his last match, and the *Birmingham Post* headline read: 'Hitchens Finds a Foil – Too Late', clearly indicating the degree of Dixon's help to Hitchens (who scored two, the first – early in the match – from an adept Dixon assist). It was extraordinary that Villa's old skipper and Hitchens played their last match that day for the Villa. Both looked like supreme strikers, and we would have loved it if they could have continued in that partnership.

Gerry Hitchens won his first England cap while still a Villa player against Mexico, which England won 8–0. He scored the first goal in the first minute or two and played in an England team that contained the likes of Johnny Haynes, Bobby Charlton and Bobby Robson. He did not look out of place in that company.

Not long after came the news that Inter Milan had signed Gerry. It was a hammer-blow for the supporters, and even though Tony Hateley eventually came and showed his great scoring skills, it was never going to be the same without Gerry. As Villa languished in the lower reaches of the Football League some 10 years later, the rumour started that Gerry was coming back to England from Italy, and that he might re-sign for the Villa. The thought of that was akin to the news of King Richard returning from the Holy Land to return to his subjects, but, alas, it was not to be.

And, of course, the announcement of his premature death in 1983 was a great shock to me and every Villa fan.

If Gerry Hitchens was not the best centre-forward Villa have ever had, then all I can say is that he must have been very close to that standard. An unselfish player, he remains the Villa's most regular goalscorer since the war, and his cowboy-like style when he was on the scoring warpath was a sight to be seen.

Colin C. Youngjohns is the chairman of Kidderminster Harriers FC and watched Gerry as a youngster in the mid-1950s.

Normally, I cannot think of a player who compares to another, but today when I see the Liverpool striker, Fernando Torres, turn and take off and run past players, I think of Gerry. I remember Gerry had a shock of blond hair, and he was quick and used to chase people down. Gerry was a big 'lost cause' merchant, which is what teams today are still looking for. He had the attitude to make the runs nobody else would make.

Derek Morgan, New Zealand.

I played against Gerry during his army days when he played for the Welch Regiment in Cardiff – a class act and a great lad. We were lucky enough to beat them that day in an army Cup match, great days.

John White, Yatton, North Somerset, England.

I was in the same 'digs' in Cardiff with Gerry. Somewhere I have some pictures of him taken at the 'digs'. I watched him playing in all Cardiff home games at Ninian Park. He was a great footballer and personality. We were all astonished at him going to Villa but pleased for him.

Dave Yeomans, Moscow, Russia.

Born in Aston in 1939, I have always been a Villa man. I shall always remember Gerry Hitchens as my greatest and most exciting centre-forward, and remember the anticipation I felt whenever Gerry got the ball. Such talent and pace is rarely seen in a lifetime. A good man and a great footballing role model.

Mick Walker, Birmingham, England.

I remember seeing the Villa versus Chelsea game. Chelsea had just signed Bobby Evans, the Scottish international. Gerry dragged the ball back and left him for dead and went on to score. Alas, we lost 2–1. Greaves got the second in the last 10 minutes. For me, Gerry was the best number nine we ever had.

George Tustin, Pontypridd, South Wales.

I grew up in Aston in the late 1950s and early 1960s and was a home and often away Villa fan. Of course, I remember standing on the Witton End on a wettish day when Gerry played such a big part in the 11–1 match against Charlton Athletic.

Bob Harrison, Winchburgh, Scotland.

I was an avid Villa fan – still am – and Gerry was my hero. 96 goals in 160 games for the lads tells it all. Lightning pace too: I saw him give Trevor Smith of the Blues a five yards start and was in front by two yards after 10…to lash the ball into the Tilton Road net. I was devastated when he went to Italy, but still treasure the memories of him 'down the Villa'.

Richard Morris, Caernarfon, North Wales.

I remember going to Old Trafford in the late 1950s to watch the English League play the Italian League. If I remember correctly there were five or six British-born players playing for the Italian League. They were Hitchens, John Charles, Eddie Firmani, and I cannot remember the other two or three. It was great at Old Trafford standing on the 'bank'.

Warwick Maskrey, Cognac, France.

Gerry Hitchens [was] absolutely the best centre-forward at the Villa. I am 62 now and have supported the lads since 1950 and still manage to get over a few times a season. Gerry is still my hero, and I was devastated when he went to Italy.

Mart Rogers, Carmel, North Wales.

I remember delivering milk to Gerry's house in the early 1980s. The dogs used to terrify us, and we would often sit in the milk van arguing about who was going to get out and deliver the silver top. Happy days!

Brian Atwick, Bodmin, Cornwall.

I remember Gerry's five goals against Charlton. I was standing at the Holte End when he cut in from the left and curled a brilliant shot around the 'keeper. It felt like a personal honour as Gerry was picked for England. I can still remember the feeling of emptiness when hearing of his transfer to Inter Milan all those years ago. I was Villa mad as a kid and spent a lot of my school holidays watching the Villa train at their Trinity Road training ground with my mate, John Flanner. I would love a pound for every autograph that Gerry gave us. He was a great player.

Ron Carter, Wales.

Gerry was my great friend. I saw most of his matches when he played for Cardiff City, but it was not until he left Italy and took up showing and breeding Afghan Hounds that our friendship developed. He worked hard for local charities in Pontypridd, which also included playing in charity matches he had arranged. He was a great guy, a gentleman.

Greg Power, Melbourne, Australia.

I have followed the Villa since 1957 and Gerry Hitchens was my schoolboy hero. I saw the Mexico game at Wembley when Gerry scored, and those great memories of him will never be forgotten. He was my favourite forward then and always will be. A star forever.

Chris Powis, Hereford, England.

Late in his career I watched him play for Worcester City against Hereford United in the Southern League. John Charles was playing for Hereford. Can you imagine that, Charles and Hitchens on the same pitch in non-League!

Dr John Harris, Begelly, Wales.

I first watched Villa in 1958, and the best forward that I ever saw was Gerry Hitchens. He should have won more caps for England but was in competition with Bobby Smith of Spurs. He was brilliant on the floor and in the air.

Enrico, Bergamo, Italy.

Gerry Hitchens was my football hero when I was a child and used to go to watch Atalanta, the Italian Serie A team from Bergamo. Gerry played a couple of seasons in Atalanta, scoring several goals, and I believe most people of my age still remember him well. He was a talented player and a nice person.

Steve Newnham, Birmingham, England.

I was eight years old when I first saw the Villa, and from 1959 until his transfer to Inter Milan I saw most of Gerry's home games for the Villa. The five he scored against Charlton still remains the best individual performance I have ever seen from a Villa player, and he and Peter McParland were a terrific pair of strikers.

Essential Facts and Figures

Gerry Hitchens – Professional Career Record

Gerry Hitchens played in 626 senior matches and scored 282 goals during his 16-year playing career, which included 175 English Division One appearances and 92 goals, and he appeared in 205 Italian Serie A matches, scoring 73 goals in eight seasons. His professional scoring average was a goal every 2.22 games. He was awarded seven full England caps, including two World Cup matches and scored five goals. He also represented the England Under-23 team on one occasion and scored one goal and represented the English FA in an 'unofficial' tour of South Africa in 1956, scoring 17 goals in 12 games.

Professional League & Cup Record – 1953–54 – 1971

Club	Season	Played	Goals
Kidderminster Harriers	1953–54	14	6
Kidderminster Harriers	1954–55	24	14
Cardiff City	1954–55	3	1
Cardiff City	1955–56	43	28
Cardiff City	1956–57	46	25
Cardiff City	1957–58	16	3
Aston Villa	1957–58	22	11
Aston Villa	1958–59	41	18
Aston Villa	1959–60	41	25
Aston Villa	1960–61	*56	42
Internazionale	1961–62	37	18
Internazionale	1962–63	**6	2
AC Torino	1962–63	30	13
AC Torino	1963–64	40	12
AC Torino	1964–65	43	12
Atalanta Bergamo	1965–66	38	8

Atalanta Bergamo	1966–67	26	4
Cagliari Calcio	1967–68	17	4
Cagliari Calcio	1968–69	4	0
Cagliari Calcio	1969–70	0	0
Worcester City	1969–70	39	19
Worcester City	1970–71	32	16
Merthyr Tydfil	1970–71	8(1)	1

Total League and Cup Appearances   **626**
Total League and Cup Goals   **282**

* Aston Villa won the first-ever Football League Cup after Gerry had left the club, when he scored 11 goals in the competition.
**Internazionale won the scudetto (Serie A) in 1962–63 after Gerry left the club.

International Career Record (full caps) 1961–62

Date	Opponents	Venue	Competition	Result	Goals
10 May 1961	Mexico	Wembley	Friendly	8–0	1
24 May 1961	Italy	Rome	Friendly	3–2	2
27 May 1961	Austria	Vienna	Friendly	1–3	0
9 May 1962	Switzerland	Wembley	Friendly	3–1	1
20 May 1962	Peru	Lima	Friendly	4–0	0
31 May 1962	Hungary	Rancagua	World Cup	1–2	0
10 June 1962	Brazil	Vina del Mar	World Cup	1–3	1

Total England Capped Appearances   **7**
Total England Goals   **5**

Major Honours

Season	Competition	Club
1956–57	Welsh Cup winner	Cardiff City
1959–60	Division Two champions	Aston Villa
1969–70	Worcester Senior Cup	Worcester City

Fascinating Facts

⊛ Gerry was the first Cardiff City player to score 20 League goals for over 30 years during season 1956–57.

⊛ He was top League scorer with 15 goals in his first full season as a professional with Cardiff City.

⊛ He netted 12 goals in five Welsh Cup games in 1956.

⊛ Aston Villa were not prepared to pay £1,000 for Gerry in 1954 when he was a 19-year-old playing for Kidderminster Harriers. Three years later, they paid 20 times that amount.

⊛ On 14 November 1959, Gerry turned in his finest performance (and the finest post-war performance of any Aston Villa player ever) when he scored five goals in an 11–1 victory against Charlton Athletic.

⊛ Within the following 14 days, he scored another five goals in two games.

⊛ Gerry Hitchens is considered by some Villa fans to be their greatest-ever number nine and is considered an Aston Villa legend. He still has the best post-war goal ratio for Villa.

⊛ Although he scored 11 goals in the 1961 League Cup run, which was eventually won by Aston Villa, Gerry did not receive a medal as the Final took place after he left for Internazionale.

⊛ He was the first player to represent England while playing his club football on foreign soil, a record which remains in the *Guinness Book of World Records*.

⊛ He made his full England debut in 1961 and scored within two minutes.

⊛ Internazionale bought Hitchens for a staggering £85,000 in June 1961. He was (reportedly) paid a signing-on fee of £12,500 and wages of five times what he was on at Aston Villa.

⊛ Gerry played against his England strike-partner, Jimmy Greaves, in a Milan derby in 1961.

⊛ When Gerry left Internazionale halfway through the season, he left a side that would go on to win the *scudetto* (Serie A) and become champions in 1962–63, but the club sent him an honorary medal.

☻ Gerry played in the Torino side who were runners-up in the Coppa Italia two seasons in a row (1962–63 and 1963–64).

☻ He was twice leading scorer for Torino (1962–63 and 1963–64).

☻ He was sent off twice in his professional career, both times playing for Torino in Italy.

☻ Gerry is the best British post-war 'export' to Italy as he played in Serie A for eight seasons, a record which is in the *Guinness Book of Records*.

☻ His first game for Worcester City on 10 November 1969 was watched by a crowd of 3,037. The average crowd for that season was 1,852.

☻ Alf Ramsey made a point of not selecting any player who played outside of the English League system. Therefore, Gerry's international career ended after the 1962 World Cup.

☻ When he signed for Cagliari in the summer of 1967, Gerry took part in the first (and only) games of a fledgling League called the United Soccer Association.

☻ The season after he left Cagliari (1969–70), they won the *scudetto* for the very first time in their history.

Chronology

Gerald (Gerry) Archibald Hitchens

8 October 1934	Born Rawnsley, Staffordshire, England.
12 September 1953	Signed his first contract with non-League Kidderminster Harriers FC, England, at the age of 18.
25 January 1955	Turned professional and joined Cardiff City FC, Wales, for £1,500.
20 December 1957	Joined Aston Villa FC, England, for £22,500.
27 October 1958	Gerry married Meriel Jones.
14 November 1959	Scored five goals in one game for Aston Villa against Charlton Athletic.
May 1961	Awarded *Birmingham Mail* Midlands Footballer of the Year and was Aston Villa Player of the Year.
10 May 1961	Awarded first cap for England against Mexico and scored on his debut.
June 1961	Joined Internazionale, Italy, for £85,000.
31 May 1962	Made his first World Cup appearance, against Hungary.
10 June 1962	Played his last game for England, against Brazil.
November 1962	Joined Torino, Italy, for £50,000.
June 1965	Joined Atalanta, Italy, for £25,000.

June 1967   Joined Cagliari, Sardinia, Italy, for £5,000.

6 November 1969   Returned to England, aged 35 and joined Southern Premier League side Worcester City, England, on a free transfer.

26 February 1971   Joined non-League Merthyr Tydfil, Wales, on a free transfer.

May 1972   Retired from football.

13 April 1983   Died on a football field playing for a solicitors' team in a charity match.

Postscript

'Have you written a book before?' This was the question Marcus Hitchens first asked me when I said I would like to write his famous father's life story. The answer was 'no', but the more we spoke about the idea of 'The Gerry Hitchens Story' the more it became less and less of a fallible idea. Marcus knew my father and his background as a writer and his admiration of Gerry as a player, so the production of this book quickly turned into a discussion and soon became a reality. The more we spoke about Gerry and about the content of the book and the more (famous) people who thought that the idea of a book about Gerry was worth contributing to it became a total obsession for the both of us. So, when you say you are going to do something, then you should go and do it – and I did.

It was my dear mother who always told me that 'everything in life is meant to happen for a reason', and writing this book has made me believe this may be the case after all. Fate is a word that few people believe in, but I think that the events leading up to me writing this book, including the loss of my father in the autumn of 2008 and his lifelong admiration of Gerry Hitchens, have led me to write something special for the Hitchens family and for my father.

The first time I spoke with the lovely Meriel and the more conversations I had with Marcus, I knew it was the right thing to do. Opportunities like this do not come around very often in a lifetime, if at all, and I would like to thank the Hitchens family for sharing so many personal memories – some funny and some sad – and I feel so privelaged to have been given this opportunity by such a lovely and proud family.

It has been an amazing journey exploring the life and times of a soccer hero, especially one who lived through the 'heyday' of football, and reading and listening to some great stories about Gerry the footballer, the husband and the family man. Great friendships have grown from this book, and many hours have been spent talking about how we would make it happen and how to turn the bare bones of an idea into something which we hoped would be 'a bit different and a bit special.' It was a real team effort, just one of the attributes which was always associated with Gerry.

We hope this book brings as much pleasure to you as it did for us putting it together and turning it into something that Gerry and my own father would have been very proud of, watching from the 'terraces' above.

Simon Goodyear

Glossary of Italian Words and Phrases

A brief guide to the Italian words and phrases that have been used in this book.

La Grande Inter 'The Great Inter' is the name given to the Internazionale team led by Helenio Herrera that won back-to-back European Cups in 1964 and 1965. The team is also known for their dominance in Serie A during the 1960s when they won seven *scudetti*.

Scudetto (scudetti – plural) Meaning 'little shield'. The Italian League Champions are the annual winners of Serie A, Italy's premier annual football League competition.

'il Mago' 'The wizard'. The name given to Helenio Herrera.

Catenaccio This is a tactical system in football with an emphasis on defence. In Italian *catenaccio* means 'door-bolt', and it means a highly organised and effective backline defence which is intended to prevent goals.

Verrou A system of play where the centre-forward is employed to confuse the opposing defenders. The complex Swiss *verrou* system, perfected by Karl Rappan, saw players switch positions and duties depending on the game's pattern.

Libero The sweeper is a more versatile type of centre-back that 'sweeps up' the ball if the opponent manages to breach the defensive line. His position is rather more fluid than other defenders, who man-mark their designated opponents. Because of this, the position is sometimes referred to as *libero*, from the Italian word meaning 'free'.

Ritiro Meaning 'withdrawals'. It is the system whereby some Italian clubs whisk their players away to a country retreat on the Friday before a game and keep them there until the Sunday evening, or even the Monday morning.

Derby della Mole The Turin derby is the local derby played out between the city's two most successful teams, Juventus FC and Torino FC.

Derby della Madonnina The Milan derby, as it is sometimes known, is a football match between the Italian clubs AC Milan and FC Internazionale Milano (Inter). It is a hotly contested local derby and is one of the most followed derbies in the football world.

'il Grande Torino' Between 1942–43 and 1948–49, the Great Torino were widely considered the best-ever team in Italian football history, and won five straight scudetti led by captain, Valentino Mazzola.

'il gigante buono' 'The good giant'. The name given by Juventus fans to John Charles.

Fresco It is any of several related painting types, done on plaster on walls or ceilings. The word *fresco* comes from the Italian word *affresco* that derives from the adjective *fresco* (fresh), which has Latin origins. Frescos were often made during the Renaissance and other early periods.

'Un buon minatore' Meaning 'a good miner'. The name given by Torino fans to Gerry when he played for the Turin club.

'il cannone' Meaning 'the cannon'. The name given by Internazionale fans to Gerry when he played for the club.

'l'uomo di granito' A name given to Gerry by Torino fans, translated as 'the man of granite'; in other words 'the hard man'.

'un giocatore serio'	Meaning 'a serious player'. A name given by Torino fans to Gerry.
'il Rossonerri'	The nickname given to AC Milan – the 'red-blacks' – as they play in red-and-black-striped shirts.
'i Neroazzurri'	The nickname given to Internazionale – the 'blue-blacks' – as they play in blue-and-black-striped shirts.
Arrivederci	A farewell remark meaning 'goodbye'.
Ciao	The word *ciao* (pronounced 'chaow') is an informal Italian verbal salutation or greeting, meaning either 'goodbye' or 'hello'.
Calcio	Translated as meaning soccer (not football).
'La farfalla granata'	The name given to Luigi Meroni – 'the maroon butterfly'.
Simpatico	An Italian word meaning 'likeable'.
Lega Calcio Serie A	The official name given to the Premier League in Italy, otherwise known simply as Serie A.
'il Sivori Italiano'	The Italian Sivori (with reference to Enrique Omar Sivori).
Capocannoniere	The name given to the highest goalscorer in Serie A.
La dolce vita	Translated to mean 'the sweet life'.
Dietrologia	The Italian word for the science of what is behind: Italians never take things at face value.
Arbitraggio	Meaning arbitration in sports refereeing.
'Rombo di Tuono'	The name given to Luigi Riva, meaning 'thunder'.

'Brutta esperienza' Meaning bad experiences and referring to the signings of Denis Law and Joe Baker by Torino.

'Squadra del cuore' Referring to Torino as the team that the city loves.

Cucina Italiana Meaning the Italian kitchen.

'Regina delle provinciali' The name given to Atalanta BC, meaning 'the Queen of the provisional clubs'.

Media References

The following media references were used to help compile this book:

All photographs used in this publication belong to the Hitchens family.

Aston Villa – A Complete Record 1874–1992 by David W. Goodyear and Tony Matthews.

Cardiff City Football Club – The Official History of The Bluebirds by John Crooks.

Aston Villa Greats by Leon Hickman.

The Marshall Cavendish Book of Football.

The Centenary History of Kidderminster Harriers Football Club by Colin C. Youngjohns.

Illustrated History of Aston Villa – 1874–1998 by Graham McColl.

Calcio. A History of Italian Football by John Foot.

www.rsssf.com

European Centre Forward – The BBC video of 1963 has been used as reference, with permission from Brian Glanville.

Thanks also go to the following for providing statistical and historical information:

Mr Colin C. Youngjohns, chairman of Kidderminster Harriers FC
Mr Jon Farrelly
Mr Mike Tilt
Mr Kevan Lobb
Aston Villa FC
FC Internazionale Milano
Torino FC 1906
Atalanta Bergamasca Calcio
Cagliari Calcio
Worcester City FC
Merthyr Tydfil FC

Dedication to Gerry's Family

Gerry was very much a family man, and when he sadly passed away in April 1983 he left five children, Marcus, the eldest, Nicola, Karen, Jason and Damian. It is therefore fitting that their children, who have grown up with the legacy of their famous grandfather, whom they had heard all about but sadly did not get the opportunity to meet, are mentioned in this book.

Marcus and son Gerald and daughters Lydia and Glesni.

Nicola and son Federico and daughters Margherita and Francesca.

Karen and sons Marcus and Joe.

Jason and daughter Violet and sons Jack and Tomas.

Damian and daughters Mia and Victoria.

Index

Gerry Hitchens

1934–1983